AN
HISTORICAL INTRODUCTION
TO THE
ECONOMIC GEOGRAPHY OF GREAT BRITAIN

BELL'S ADVANCED ECONOMIC GEOGRAPHIES

General Editor

PROFESSOR R. O. BUCHANAN

M.A.(N.Z.), B.Sc.(Econ.), Ph.D.(London)
Professor Emeritus, University of London

A. Systematic Studies

AN ECONOMIC GEOGRAPHY OF OIL
Peter R. Odell, B.A., Ph.D.

PLANTATION AGRICULTURE
P. P. Courtenay, B.A., Ph.D.

NEW ENGLAND: A STUDY IN INDUSTRIAL ADJUSTMENT
R. C. Estall, B.Sc.(Econ.), Ph.D.

GREATER LONDON: AN INDUSTRIAL GEOGRAPHY
J. E. Martin, B.Sc.(Econ.), Ph.D.

GEOGRAPHY AND ECONOMICS
Michael Chisholm, M.A.

AGRICULTURAL GEOGRAPHY
Leslie Symons, B.Sc.(Econ.), Ph.D.

REGIONAL ANALYSIS AND ECONOMIC GEOGRAPHY
John N. H. Britton, M.A., Ph.D.

B. Regional Studies

AN ECONOMIC GEOGRAPHY OF EAST AFRICA
A. M. O'Connor, B.A., Ph.D.

YUGOSLAVIA: PATTERNS OF ECONOMIC ACTIVITY
F. E. Ian Hamilton, B.Sc.(Econ.), Ph.D.

In Preparation

THE GEOGRAPHY OF RURAL LAND USE
Professor J. W. Birch, B.A., Ph.D.

AN ECONOMIC GEOGRAPHY OF CARIBBEAN AMERICA
Peter R. Odell, B.A., Ph.D.

AN AGRICULTURAL GEOGRAPHY OF GREAT BRITAIN
Professor J. T. Coppock, M.A., Ph.D.

AN ECONOMIC GEOGRAPHY OF BRAZIL
J. D. Henshall, M.A., M.Sc. & R. P. Momsen, A.B., M.A., Ph.D.

WILFRED SMITH

An Historical Introduction to the Economic Geography of Great Britain

WILFRED SMITH

Late John Rankin Professor of Geography
University of Liverpool

With an Appreciation by

M. J. WISE

Professor of Geography
London School of Economics and Political Science

LONDON
G. BELL & SONS, LTD
1968

First published 1949 by
Methuen and Co. Ltd., London, as Part I of
An Economic Geography of Great Britain
Reprinted 1968 by G. Bell and Sons Ltd.

'An Appreciation' Copyright © 1968 by
G. Bell and Sons, Ltd.
York House, Portugal Street,
London, W.C.2

S.B.N. 7135 15090

Printed in Great Britain by
NEILL & CO. LTD., EDINBURGH

Preface

The reprinting of part of an established work is a new departure in this series, and perhaps deserves a word of explanation. The idea owes its inception to Professor R. W. Steel, Wilfred Smith's successor as head of the Department of Geography of the University of Liverpool. Not only did he urge the undesirability of allowing a classic of British Geography to be out of print, but he also generously placed at my disposal the cartographic resources of his Department for the redrawing of the maps. It is a pleasure to acknowledge this debt and also to thank the cartographer, Mr. A. G. Hodgkiss, for the excellence of his work.

My very sincere thanks are also due to my colleague, Professor M. J. Wise, of the London School of Economics, for his ready acceptance of the task of writing an appreciation of Wilfred Smith and his work. Professor Wise's own stature in the subject made him the obvious choice, and I am proud, as editor, to be able to include within the covers of one book contributions from two of the masters in British Economic Geography.

R.O.B.

Contents

List of Tables

Maps and Diagrams

Wilfred Smith

An Appreciation by M. J. Wise

I

Professor Wilfred Smith died on 27th September, 1955, at the age of 52. At the time of his death he was Dean of the Faculty of Arts and John Rankin Professor of Geography in the University of Liverpool, the university at which he had studied as an undergraduate and which he had served as a member of the academic staff since 1928. He had been Head of the Department of Geography since 1949. His working life had thus been devoted to the study of geography and to the interests of the University.

He was born at Halifax and educated at Blackpool Grammar School. He entered the University of Liverpool as a Bibby Scholar in 1921, graduated with first class honours in geography in 1924, gained his M.A. in 1926, and served as a Tutor until his appointment in 1928 as Assistant Lecturer. Thus most of his life was spent in or near to the industrial districts of northern England: it is likely that these realms of hill and dale, of smoke and stone, of coal, iron, weaving and spinning gained a hold on his mind and caused him to search for the antecedents of landscapes which he came to know so well.

Wilfred Smith was one of a number of gifted geographers who came under the influence of P. M. Roxby, the first professor of the subject in the University and a teacher of great ability and lasting influence. Not surprisingly in view of Roxby's interest in the study of China, Smith's first published work was on the geography of coal and iron in China.[1] Although he made some further contributions to the study of China, his main interest emerged in the 1930s as the economic geography of Great Britain with special reference to the regional patterns of the

---

[1] Wilfred Smith: *A Geographical Study of Coal and Iron in China*, The University Press of Liverpool, 1926.

north of England, and of Merseyside in particular. Many years were spent in preparation for *An Economic Geography of Great Britain*, undoubtedly his greatest work, published in 1949, of which the *Historical Introduction* forms the first part.

His services in the University were not limited to the work of his own department. He held many administrative posts, and in the words of Professor H. C. Darby brought to administrative matters 'the same methodical and penetrating insight that he brought to problems of scholarship'.[1] He taught also in the Department of Education, especially on the principles of the teaching of geography in schools. He lectured in the University's department of Civic Design and contributed a number of articles to town and country planning journals. He was President of the successful Liverpool branch of the Geographical Association, and became President of the Institute of British Geographers in 1954.

Wilfred Smith was a modest, scholarly man. Those who knew him best have written how colleagues and students never went to him for help or advice, academic or personal, without receiving it in full measure. He gave encouragement also to young economic geographers, not only of his own university, and at least one of them has cause to be grateful to him for kindly advice.

II

WILFRED SMITH'S APPROACH
TO ECONOMIC GEOGRAPHY

In his original introduction to *An Economic Geography of Great Britain* Smith took the opportunity briefly to indicate his view of the nature of economic geography, orienting his work, as it were, both within the field of geography and within the fields of activity of scholars of a number of disciplines who had concerned themselves with the problems of the spatial organisation of society. Economic geography—one facet of the whole geographical complex—had as its special task 'the analysis of the distribution forms or patterns of economic life'. Its objective was to lay bare the rationale of economic distributions. The distributions, he went on, 'display an extraordinary richness

[1] *Geography*, XL, November, 1955, p. 278.

and variety and embody the effects of the whole complex of factors—physical, economic, technical, cultural and political—which model economic activity'. What were the relevant distribution patterns and under what conditions had they come to assume those forms? In conducting his enquiries the economic geographer should not feel himself tied only to those distributions which bore an apparently obvious relationship to the physical environment. While one of the objects of the study was to elicit and evaluate such relationships, they were not themselves necessary conditions of the study: the relationships between the distribution patterns of, say, individual manufacturing industries might well be more meaningful and just as geographically relevant. Smith's attitude thus differed markedly from that of some earlier economic geographers who had viewed the subject as 'the study of the influence exerted upon the economic activities of man by his physical environment'[1] and for whom 'geographical control' had been an essential ingredient.

One of the attractive features for him of the study of economic geography arose from the dynamic nature of the raw material. Distributions were rarely static: change through time was normal. He was fascinated by the detective work involved in discovering past distributions and in revealing the nature of geographical change. How far was such change a response to technical improvement, to new methods of management, new sources of capital? To what extent did it reflect changes in the geographical value of particular locations arising from new factors either within or external to the distribution pattern itself? What was the impact of the opening of new sources of raw materials, the discovery of new markets? Nor could change in geography be understood without reference to the individuals involved and, somewhat unusually for a textbook in economic geography, the names and activities of persons appeared on his pages: Tull, Boulton, Arkwright, Bessemer—all had their place.

Within the terms of his view of economic geography as the study of the distribution forms or patterns of economic life, the tasks were clear. First it was necessary precisely to establish the facts of distribution, from the best sources, checked where possible by systematic and detailed field survey. 'General

---

[1] J. McFarlane: *Economic Geography*, London, p. 1.

distributions are not enough; the economic geographer must work with precision.' Next came the understanding and explanation of the established facts. His work rested on the assumption that distribution patterns of economic activity reflected order and reasoned decisions—'the fortuitous tends to have a low survival rate'. He went on, 'distribution patterns have been developed by trial and error, by conscious experiment and by spontaneous variation, on the part of a host of individual entrepreneurs in order to facilitate the practice of a particular economic activity.'[1]

Order was there to be discovered, given the tools. And the geographer could count himself fortunate in his special tools, those of field survey and of the map. 'There must be movement backwards and forwards between the laboratory of the field and the laboratory of the study and the drawing desk. The cartographical manipulation of data enables the isolation of single phenomena for examination and it enables one pattern of distribution to be related to another. The geographer experiments with the map and assembles on it combinations of phenomena at will.'[2]

Nor was economic geography an isolated study. The problems presented by changing distributions, centrally geographical by nature, led the student, without ever feeling that he had crossed a frontier, to the works of economic and social historians. The location problem led him into the realms of location theory and the contributions of the economists. One of the tasks was to reveal the paths followed by flows of goods and services between places and areas, and immediately the work of students of transport sprang into relevance. Provided the focus was clear and the problem defined, traditional subject boundaries were not very important. To Wilfred Smith the challenge presented by his selected problems was great and the effort of response both demanding and satisfying. The study of economic geography required 'the same prolonged intellectual effort, the same persistent inquiry, the same powers of reasoning, the same rigorous criticism, and the same ability to see the distant horizon towards which the argument moves as any

[1] Wilfred Smith: *Geography and the Location of Industry*, An inaugural lecture, University Press of Liverpool, 1952, p. 4.

[2] *Ibid.* p. 5.

subject within the compass of a University'.[1] In looking back through Smith's published work one senses his ability to maintain throughout his academic lifetime the same group of academic problems: equally impressive are the indications of his endeavour to improve his technique and to develop new tools of analysis and understanding, especially in the statistical field.

III

AN ECONOMIC GEOGRAPHY OF GREAT BRITAIN

The Historical Introduction, reprinted in this volume, stood as Part One of *An Economic Geography of Great Britain*. 'In view of the dynamic quality of economic geography,' he wrote, 'an historical introduction is essential.' While the origins of the economic geography of the country lay far back in pre-history, and though a number of relict features survived from early times, his historical introduction was concerned only with the immediate antecedents—with the geographical changes accompanying, and also influencing, the transformation of the medieval into the modern economy. The economic geography of the Agrarian and Industrial Revolutions remained to be written: it was not Smith's purpose to attempt this task. His objective was to indicate those trends and features of change in economic geography in modern times without which a knowledge of the present economic geography would be incomplete.

No attempt has been made to revise Smith's historical introduction. While the advantages of revising his work to include the results of recent studies by historical geographers and economic historians have been considered, it has been thought better to leave the work essentially as it stood—as Smith's own assessment of the origins of the modern economic geography of Great Britain.

Consideration has also been given, since Wilfred Smith's death, to the revision of Part Two of *An Economic Geography of Britain*: the task has not proved possible. Part of the difficulty no doubt lies in the personal character of Smith's own contribution into which work from another hand would not fit

---

[1] Wilfred Smith: *Geography and the Location of Industry*, An inaugural lecture, University Press of Liverpool, 1952, p. 4.

easily. A greater difficulty lies in the extent of the new material which it would be necessary to introduce to bring up to date the discussion of geographical change. Much of Smith's discussion was concerned with the distribution of economic activity up to 1939 and while, in the second edition, some of the material was revised to include data for 1950, the examination of post-war change in the economic geography of Great Britain is evidently the subject for a separate substantial volume. Part Two must stand, therefore, as a monumental contribution to the economic geography of Great Britain at about the time of the Second World War, and of its immediate antecedents: as such it will retain a permanent value.

It began with a discussion of the complex agricultural landscape of the country centring mainly on the varying farming systems. While Smith was clearly conscious of the land use approach, and had played his part in the Land Utilisation Survey of Britain, he chose, in keeping with changing thought among economic geographers of his time, to focus the discussion on farming systems. These were modelled by management decisions—by the farmer's choice—in the circumstances of his own technical resources and of the prices and markets available to his products. The physical environment offered possibilities and set limits to the range of choice, but evaluations of land resources changed from time to time, sometimes with revolutionary speed.

A broad division was made into Arable Farming and Grassland Farming. In discussing Arable Farming,[1] the chalklands offered good examples of changes in land use in response to economic and technical change. He went on to distinguish the arable regions first of the eastern side of Britain, and later of the Midlands, the West and Scotland, indicating the characteristics of each in turn. Major distinctions were drawn between arable farming in England and Scotland, primarily the result of climatic conditions. In England the differences between east and west again reflected climate, but soil type was also a main differentiating agent, especially in the English Plain.

Grass farming,[2] he found, presented no less variety than arable farming. He employed the evidence of Stapledon's work

---

[1] *An Economic Geography of Great Britain*, London, 1949, Chapter IV.

[2] *Ibid*. Chapter V.

and of the Grassland Map of England and Wales on regional variations in the quality of grassland: he considered the effects on farming of regional differences in the cycle of grass growth which, in the main, reflected climatic conditions. He attempted to show how nutritional factors influenced the concentration of stock rearing in the uplands and of dairying and fattening in the lowlands. He gave a comprehensive analysis of the regional types of grass farming parallel to that of arable farming, and concluded with a brief discussion on land productivity to which further reference is made later.

Smith next went on to consider the geography of coal mining,[1] emphasising the effects of geological structure on the patterns of coal production but putting his discussion into the context of changes in the economy of the industry from the year of peak production, 1913. Changes in the distribution of mines and of production reflected changes in market conditions for different types of coal. The geographical problem of changes in production patterns was the central theme, the fullest possible explanations were needed of the general tendency for movement from exposed to concealed coalfields and for fluctuations in the fortunes of individual fields. Output per man employed was regarded as the most suitable index of efficiency of production, for that period, in comparing coalfields one with another. Why should there be such great variations between coalfields in output per man-shift and what was the relationship of such variations to those of costs of production? While much of the material is descriptive, Smith's questioning mind constantly reveals itself: how far, for example, did output per man-shift increase with size of mine? No conclusive answer was possible: the evidence was uncertain.

It may well be that the chapter on Iron and Steel Manufacture[2] has been one of the most influential upon a number of generations of students and teachers. Underlying it, quite evidently, is Smith's interest in location theory, especially in Weber. Also important is the distinction, drawn from the locational standpoint, between the iron and the steel industries. Attention must further be drawn to the discussion of the relevance of technical change to an appreciation of locational

[1] *An Economic Geography of Great Britain*, London, 1949, Chapter VI.
[2] *Ibid.* Chapter VII.

values. There was the necessary regional analysis by types of iron and steel. Usefully, Smith discussed and illustrated the distinction between geographical integration and economic integration. His account of the industry included an examination of the distribution of rolling mills and of the several forms of finished steel production. The great diversity in types of location in the industry was dissected, revealing a complete range from material sites to sites at consumption points, embodying the effects of past as well as of present factors. The location of an industry, it was made clear, was often a legacy from former times, reflecting past economic and technical conditions and past appraisals of site value.

A treatment of Engineering[1] followed naturally upon that of iron and steel. By contrast with iron and steel this was a secondary industry and, locationally, it was dispersed rather than localised, though the West Midlands, in particular, had a greater share of employment in engineering than in industry generally. The problem of distinguishing the factors responsible for the dispersed character of the industry, had, in accordance with his method, to be seen in the context of change in the several sections of the industry. The principal groups examined were Agricultural, Locomotive and Textile Engineering; Ships, Motor Vehicles and Aircraft; and Electrical Engineering.

The chapters on Wool Textile[2] and Cotton Manufacture[3] are certainly among the most interesting in the book, reflecting Smith's detailed involvement in the history and geography of the industries. The characteristics noted for other chapters are here present also, but special interest attaches to his analysis of location factors. The textile industries, less dependent locationally than the metal industries upon sources of raw materials, were more affected by the conditions required for the manufacturing processes and the other materials employed in those processes. Thus, especial attention was given to analysis of the effects of the demand for water power, the need for supplies of soft water, and the supposed effect of humidity. The broad conclusions were that the effect of the water and humidity factors (and also of coal) on the woollen and worsted

---

[1] *An Economic Geography of Great Britain*, London, 1949, Chapter VIII.
[2] *Ibid*. Chapter IX.
[3] *Ibid*. Chapter X.

industries was 'to favour districts in the north and west, external to the English Plain'. But as between one coalfield area and another in the north and west these factors had had little significance and the explanations for regional industrial differentiation had to be sought in historical circumstances and in the process of 'competition between different kinds of industrial employment for the labour and inventiveness available in the district'. In the case of the cotton industry, he argued, 'the physical factors of soft water, water-power, and coal thus limit the industry to the eastern side of Lancashire'. Humidity had been an additional factor at the formative period of localisation. 'It is in reference to conditions at that time rather than at the present day that the close localisation of the industry is to be understood. Once established and once it acquired an economic momentum, it persisted on its original site.' The analysis was not narrowly deterministic: it was illuminated by his discussion of the socio-economic conditions of the Pennine borders at the relevant periods. He showed the importance of the emergent transport system in the process of industrial concentration and of the links with the ports. In detail the localisation of the various trades within the woollen and cotton districts could only be appreciated in the light of a knowledge of the organisation of the industries. How far did the horizontal organisation of the cotton industry find geographical expression? Finally, the industries must be studied not merely in relation to the local environments which provided the suitable physical and economic conditions for their development but also in relation to the world environment from which they drew raw materials and to which they exported significant proportions of their product.

The treatment of the clothing trades[1] was a natural sequel to that of the textile industries. As the character of the industry had changed from that of handwork and homeworking to a factory industry, so geographical concentration had become established. Tailoring offered a good example. He suggested the concept of 'stage' in the emergence of a location pattern, considering the textile clothing industries to be at the same locational stage which the manufacturing textile industries had passed through a century ago. Further attention to this

[1] *An Economic Geography of Great Britain*, London, 1949, Chapter XI.

B

concept of 'locational stage' could well be rewarding in the study of the geography of industry. Among other questions raised was the contrast between the increasing urbanisation and concentration of textile clothing manufacture into a few districts (Greater London, the West Riding, Lancashire) and the increasing dispersion of hosiery production.

Smith was attracted to the study of the leather industries[1] providing as they did 'as neat an example as the iron and steel trades of the diminishing effects of source of materials on locali-sation as the product diverges progressively from its original form'. Port sites had become increasingly important locations for tanneries, and Merseyside and the lower Mersey valley was the largest single centre of hide tanning in the country. The dominance of the ports was a function of the import of hides and skins and of tanning agents as well as of the specialist character of British tanning. The former, small, widely dis-persed rural tanneries were greatly diminished in number. The growth of the industry, the emergence of the transport net, the expansion of sources of raw materials and the widening of markets had brought increased size of plant and greater specialisation of area. Thus, this study exemplified one of Smith's principal arguments. It remained to measure the degree of specialisation, to distinguish the principal areas as precisely as possible and to indicate the nature of contemporary change and the influences forming change.

In a somewhat similar way, Smith found the milling and baking trades[2] useful case studies 'of the factors influencing industrial location, of the changes consequential on the adoption of a commercial economy, of the balance of advantage between location at the point of production and location at the point of consumption, and of the variation in this balance of advantage between primary and secondary food industries'. Theory had to be tested in the hard light of observed facts and distributions. Each chapter was, in essence, a thesis in itself.

The geographical structure of the economy had been built upon a system of exchanges and flows of goods and services. 'Means of transport are a pre-requisite of specialisation.'

---

[1] *An Economic Geography of Great Britain*, London, 1949, Chapter XII.
[2] *Ibid.* Chapter XIII.

Moreover the means of transport often conditioned the nature of the specialisation. From that point of view the distinguishing characteristics of canal, road and rail transport[1] were considered, and the resultant effects of the growth of areas of specialisation upon the nature of the transport net were suggested. Each type of terrain and each type of economic region was likely to develop its own variety of transport pattern. He went on to suggest, in the case of the railway net, the general characteristics of the nets exhibited by manufacturing regions and by mining regions. As in so many chapters, while the actual data are now outmoded, such probings recur: suggestions to the modern reader for further thought and inquiry, lines of investigation that remain to be followed. In pursuit of the initial aims of the chapter, coastal and ocean shipping services were also studied and a brief indication given of the coming importance of air transport to the economic geography of Great Britain.

In his final chapter, Smith reminded us of the relative neglect by geographers of the study of foreign trade, a neglect which the years since his death have done little to remedy. 'An analysis of foreign trade,' he wrote, 'is not an appendage to, but an integral part of, an economic geography of Great Britain.'[2] The intricate inter-digitation of home production and overseas trade was a vital element in the British economy and a part of the great story of the growth of an economic geography made up of related but specialised regions.

The concluding paragraph of the book is, perhaps, worth quoting in full. He wrote:

'The land of Britain offers resources for human use, but the precise employment made of these resources has varied from time to time with changes in human equipment and technique. Regions vary in physical resources and they vary in the efficiency by means of which these physical resources are utilized. Variations in efficiency are, up to a point, within human control. A low level of efficiency can dissipate even natural advantages, a high level of efficiency can make effective use of even mediocre material equipment. The economic geography of Great Britain is modelled not only by the physical resources

---

[1] *An Economic Geography of Great Britain*, London, 1949, Chapter XIV.

[2] *Ibid.* Chapter XV, p. 654.

of the land of Britain, but also by the knowledge and efficiency of its people.'

The picture of the economic geography of Great Britain that we would draw today would differ in many respects from that delineated by Smith. Many new industries have grown while others have declined; further regional shifts have taken place. But his main themes hold good and are as much in need of urgent study in the 1960s as they were in the years before 1948. His book had its critics: it was too long, said some, or not easy to read: the statistics did not relate to common years and contained inconsistencies. But as a work of scholarship it stands, in the main, unchallenged, holding throughout to a common group of problems; the discovery of economic distributions and the relationships between them, the explanation of how those distribution patterns had come into being, the problem of the location of industry, the processes by which increasing specialisation of area had become characteristic of modern industry. Though he was not always successful, he aimed consistently to draw out the long-term rather than the short-term trends. He did not aim to be comprehensive: what was important for the scholar was to analyse the fundamental properties of the economic geography of a country or area. And this is, perhaps, the simplest, and yet the most necessary, lesson for his successors.

IV

THE LOCATION OF INDUSTRY

In view of Wilfred Smith's long interest in this field of study and of the centrality of the location problem in his work, mention must be made of his individual contribution. He had closely studied Alfred Weber's work[1] and was familiar with the studies of E. M. Hoover.[2] It must be remembered, however, that Smith's work was mainly accomplished before A.

[1] Alfred Weber: *Über den Standort der Industrien* (Tubingen, 1909): translated by Carl J. Friedrich as *Alfred Weber's Theory of the Location of Industries*, Chicago, 1929.

[2] Notably, *Location Theory and the Shoe and Leather Industries*, Harvard University Press, 1937.

Lösch's work on *The Economics of Location*[1] was available in England and before the publication of most of Walter Isard's important contributions.[2]

In his inaugural lecture, *Geography and the Location of Industry*,[3] Wilfred Smith summarised his approach to the problem of the regional location of industry. The three general factors of location, the location of raw materials, the location of industrial techniques including both skills and equipment, and the location of markets, coincided only infrequently. The location pattern was the result of a balance of the patterns of resources, skills and markets, varying in dominance from industry to industry, from time to time, and from place to place. Particular interest attaches to his discussion of location in relation to the distribution of skills and equipment, a relationship, he wrote, 'built on what are, in the long run, shifting sands whose distribution pattern changes with comparative rapidity'.

Careful consideration of the economic conditions under which location patterns developed was clearly essential. The theory of comparative costs, operating both as between countries and as between regions within a country, assisted him to explain the growth of specialisation of area in the nineteenth century. Reciprocally, the study of geography helped him to explain the patterns and distributions that arose as nations, and areas within nations, differently endowed, strove to obtain comparative advantages. These are themes that recur throughout *An Economic Geography of Great Britain*. But not all the factors influencing industrial location were economic in nature; the role of government policy had increasingly to be considered and the basis of policy was often social rather than economic.

The technical context was also important. Generally speaking, handicraft, by reason of its small workshop character, its limited need of power and the high percentage which labour costs bore to total costs, was usually widely dispersed. By contrast, factory industry was dependent on power: labour

---

[1] A. Lösch: *The Economics of Location*, translated by W. H. Woglom and W. F. Stolper, New Haven: Yale University Press, 1954; first published in German at Jena, 1940.

[2] Brought together in Walter Isard: *Location and Space-Economy*, New York and London, 1956 and subsequent works.

[3] Published by the University Press of Liverpool, 1952.

costs were a lower percentage of total costs and, consequently, raw material costs became relatively more important as elements in the location decision. More clearly defined patterns, with larger units in more intense clusters, replaced the dispersion of the handicraft stage. The process of transformation did not proceed at uniform speed in all industries and in all areas: relict sites persisted.

Smith then went on to formulate the location problem in terms of the current British economy, in 'a technical context of factory industry with relics of handicraft manufacture and an economic context of regionally specialised systems of production but overlain by a veneer of diversification'.[1] Instead of adopting the customary formulation of the problem as location at material versus location at market, Smith chose to state it as location at material versus location elsewhere, for location at market was not the only alternative. Industries fixed in their location by materials displayed certain measurable qualities— a high weight of material per operative, low values of material and of product per ton, and low labour costs as a proportion of total costs. Alfred Weber had, of course, considered large loss of weight in the main product in the course of manufacture to be an important quality of material-oriented industries. Smith found two difficulties: first, the problem in modern industry of defining the main product; second, that Weber had defined loss of weight by including coal among the materials, thus confusing the issue when his theoretical analysis came to be applied to actual cases. Smith was to consider this problem in a later paper.[2]

Market-oriented industries could be classified in three ways. Some made a perishable product, others were tied to the market by the need for personal contact with the consumer, a third type located near to markets by reason of increase in weight or bulk.

The location of regional skills was a factor also of the first importance, although, he observed, its significance was tending to decrease in many industries as capital equipment came to be substituted for local skill.

There remained an important residue of industries, not

[1] Published by the University Press of Liverpool, 1952. p. 11.
[2] *Transactions and Papers of the Institute of British Geographers*, 21, 1955, pp. 12–15.

rooted in materials nor tied to markets or to labour. These were, in general, mobile industries. Many of them were attracted to the large cities, or found there conditions particularly favourable to further growth. He had in mind the contemporary industrial growth of London and the Birmingham district. Other mobile industries were attracted to low cost labour. Though this was not a current factor in Britain, it had formerly been so and the residual effects on the location pattern could be discerned. A third factor was the exercise of legislative or administrative action by government.

Such was Smith's schematic framework for the study of industrial location. At least two reservations needed to be made. Not all industries, nor all plants, were efficiently located. Efficiency in organisation and management could, at least for a time, compensate for inefficient location. Further, industrial landscapes reflected the operation of past as well as of present conditions: relics of archaic distributions remained and the momentum of established businesses enabled them to survive, for a period, on anachronistic sites.

It was within this framework that Smith undertook the detailed studies of industries such as coal-mining, the iron and steel industries, the woollen and cotton textile industries, flour milling and baking, leather and boot and shoe manufacture which made up the bulk of Part II of *An Economic Geography of Great Britain*. But the historical approach was indispensable, the understanding of the antecedents essential. In addition to those studies, themselves a major contribution to economic geography, Smith made at least two important contributions to the methodology of industrial location study and these now deserve specal mention.

While he was well aware of the increasing importance of the 'servicing' group of industries and regarded them as indubitably of geographical interest, his own interest was held mainly by the extractive and manufacturing groups. One particular aspect of the industrial location problem particularly grasped his attention, namely the extent to which industry is located by raw materials.

His interest in this problem arose in the course of his study of *The Distribution of Population and the Location of Industry on Merseyside* (1942). In studying the types of industries located on

Merseyside he devised a number of tests with a view to quantifying the degree of fixation to materials. These were:

(1) The weight of material handled per operative;

(2) The value of a given weight of product;

(3) The cost of materials as a proportion of the gross value of an industry's output;

(4) The proportion of males in the total number of operatives.

The value of these tests was also recognised in a related problem, that of distinguishing between heavy and light industries. The lack of clarity in making such distinctions was thrown into focus during the discussions on the formulation and application of a government policy for industrial location in Great Britain. How far was it true that heavy industries were immobile, light industries mobile? Were all light industries suitable for dispersion to areas of industrial decline? Tests were needed to distinguish heavy from light industries. In this context Smith's four tests were taken up by P. Sargant Florence, who himself added a fifth, the horse power capacity in use per operative worker. Sargant Florence's conclusion, based on calculations of all five tests for fifty-five industries, was that the ratio *weight of material per operative is clearly the most representative*.[1]

Wilfred Smith retained his interest in the devising of tests, the better to throw light on, and to explain, the locational patterns exhibited by different industries and with the object of drawing out general principles of location, or at least general tendencies. The second edition of *An Economic Geography of Great Britain*, published in 1953, contained a new Appendix on 'Location of Industry by Materials' in which he set out the strengths and weaknesses of the five tests and constructed a table placing seventy-two industries in order of fixation by materials.[2] Students of industrial location problems will still find this Appendix of notable value.

We must now turn to Smith's interest in Weber's theory of industrial location. The theory of industrial location seems never to have been far from his mind. 'The economic geographer,' he wrote, 'needs theoretical analysis to clarify his mind,

[1] P. Sargant Florence, assisted by W. Baldamus: *Investment, Location and Size of Plant*, Cambridge University Press, 1948, pp. 8–9, and Appendix I, pp. 160–7.

[2] *An Economic Geography of Great Britain*, 2nd Edition, 1953, Appendix C, pp. 709–17.

to define his problem and to strip it of irrelevancies; but in order to arrive at solutions theoretical analysis must run in harness with the examination of evidence. . . . Only by the marriage of theory with concrete fact can the principles of industrial location be formulated.'[1]

Smith had long been interested in Weber's theory[2] and in one of his most interesting contributions to economic geography made an attempt to test one of Weber's main propositions against the observed facts of industrial location in Britain.[3] The proposition in question was that industries whose produce weighs less than the materials from which it is made (weight-losing industries) are tied in location to raw materials. As Weber argued, in such cases it is in theory cheaper to manufacture at the site of the material rather than at the market, other things being equal, for the cost of transporting the smaller weight of product is less than the cost of transporting the larger weight of materials.

Without doubt, Smith found, some industries fulfil Weber's requirements. The cases of sugar beet factories (material index 8), manufactured milk products (material index 6), blast furnaces (material index 3–4) were convincing. All these were primary industries. It was also worthy of note that, in calculating the loss of weight, by-products were ignored though, in the cases studied, these were bulky, low value products used within a short distance of the processing plant, and so did not invalidate the general conclusion.

Of more interest were the cases of a large number of weight losing industries in which the weight loss was not overwhelming; for example, grain milling, fish curing, mineral oil refining, leather tanning. In the main these industries also demonstrated the value of Weber's proposition and also showed that the strength of the link with materials varied with the amount of weight loss.

Smith then attempted to test the hypothesis against a much greater range of British industries, drawing his data from the Census of Production, 1948. Owing to the inadequacies of the data only sixty-five industries could be examined: these varied

[1] *Transactions and Papers of the Institute of British Geographers*, 21, 1955, p. 2.
[2] A. Weber, *op. cit.*
[3] *Transactions and Papers of the Institute of British Geographers*, 21, 1955, pp. 1–18.

from those whose product was less than one-fifth of weight of materials (including coal) to those whose product was more than twice the weight of materials (including coal). The analysis showed Weber's argument to have some general, though only very broad, validity. The ratio of weight of materials to weight of product (the material index) was only a blunt tool, effective only at the extremities of the classification. For 49 out of the 65 industries with material indices in the middle range, the index offered no certain guide.

A second tabulation was made excluding coal from industrial raw materials. Weber's inclusion of coal was open to criticism: coal ties industry to coalfields, not necessarily to raw materials. On this basis the effectiveness of the material index as a tool was improved; the 'middle range' of industries was narrowed. But the middle range still included half of the 65 industries and it was clear that in these ranges 'the material index jostles with other conditions to determine location'.

Were there other tests which might usefully be employed to sort out the industries in the middle ranges of the loss of weight classification? A new test was suggested, that of the weight of materials per operative. This test was found to be effective not only for the 65 industries previously examined but for an even wider range. It appeared that weight of material per operative was a sharper tool than loss of weight during manufacture for sorting industries into those located by materials and those located independently of materials. This led Smith to adumbrate what may be regarded as a useful addition to the Weberian principles: 'loss of weight has significant locational effects only when it is combined with large weight per operative, for variations in transport costs are substantial enough to affect location only if weights handled are large. A combination of large loss of weight and large amount of material per operative ties an industry in location to its raw materials: a combination of large gain in weight and small amount of material per operative frees an industry from location at its raw materials: where the two conflict ... it is the weight of material per operative which is the more significant in its effect on locational ties to material.'

Smith went on to illustrate his contention in relation to a number of examples, pointing out the general tendency for the earlier processes in the manufacturing sequence, where primary materials are used, to be attracted more strongly to the sources of materials than the later processes. The iron, steel, engineering sequence afforded a good case for demonstration. The chief difficulty in applying his suggested test, weight of materials per operative, as he himself recognised, was the unavailability of accurate data for many industries.

V

MERSEYSIDE

A brief review of Wilfred Smith's contribution to the economic geography of Great Britain is not the most appropriate place in which to make a full assessment of his studies of the geography of Merseyside. Yet any review of his work would give a false picture unless some mention were made of the care and detail with which he studied his own district. It was the starting point for many of his inquiries into industrial location: he was especially interested in the industries of seaports and, most probably, it was through studies of the economic geography of Merseyside that he came to develop his interest in statistical tests of localisation. *The Distribution of Population and the Location of Industry on Merseyside*, published in 1942,[1] was a factual survey of the economic geography of Merseyside in mid-1939 on the eve of the war. It displayed the background against which war-time changes were proceeding. It suffered in presentation from war-time conditions which totally prevented the inclusion of the map evidence. The substantial body of work which was summarised might well, nowadays, be the product of a research team or group. It has been too little regarded by those who have recounted the history of regional surveys. Smith attempted to study the inter-relationships of population change and employment change; he was one of the first geographers to employ the 'location factor'.[2] He stressed the importance in regional planning of establishing efficient

[1] *The Distribution of Population and the Location of Industry on Merseyside*, The University Press of Liverpool, 1942.

[2] A method of measuring the degree of localisation of an industry within an area first suggested by P. Sargant Florence: the term was later changed to 'location quotient'.

locations for industries; of the need for satisfactory location of housing relative to workplaces and amenities; of the relief of traffic congestion; and of the improvement of amenities, including open space. It was with the first two of these aims that he was principally concerned: the lack of satisfactory data on journey to work was a particular problem that he later tried to solve and on which he was, indeed, engaged at the time of his death.

Three important conclusions emerged from his work which had immediate bearing upon the formulation of planning policies for Merseyside.[1] These were that too high a proportion of the working population was engaged in shipping, in the port, and in port-oriented industries; that there was too great a preponderance of unskilled male employment; and that it was unlikely that the existing industries would be able to provide employment for all the insured workers. There was a good case for encouraging the growth on Merseyside of industries with a high degree of mobility, making goods for consumption and assembling their materials from many sources.

There followed, in 1946, a *Physical Survey of Merseyside*,[2] which he described as 'a geographer's contribution to the data available to the landscape planner. Different sites possess different qualities and these different qualities are not all equally adaptable to every kind of use'. The delineation of areal variations in site values, and of the extent to which they had been recognised by past and existing land uses, were objects of the work. The Physical Survey represented part of a Report that had been commissioned by the Ministry of Town and Country Planning and was another indication of Smith's conviction that, to be successful, town and country planning must rest upon the best possible description and analysis of geographical characteristics. Necessarily, the scope of the survey was limited: it concentrated on the surface forms of the landscape which had influenced the urban lay-out and on those aspects of climatology which had a bearing upon agricultural land use and the siting of housing and of industry. Climate was indeed shown to be a factor of importance in causing variations

[1] See, for example, F. Langstreth Thompson: 'An Outline Plan for a Region: Merseyside', *Journal of the Town Planning Institute*, XXXI, 1945, p. 95.

[1] *Physical Survey of Merseyside: a background to Town and Country Planning*, The University Press of Liverpool, 1946.

in land use within south-west Lancashire and Wirral, 'variations which are sufficient to give different qualities to different
types of position and site and which are, therefore, of importance to the landscape planner'.

The work which best reflects Wilfred Smith's view of the
importance in geographical study of the understanding of the
individuality of place is the Scientific Survey which appeared,
under his editorship, at the time of the meeting in Liverpool
in 1953 of the British Association for the Advancement of
Science.[1] The editor himself contributed a number of chapters
including the introductory review on 'Merseyside and the
Merseyside District' and those on the 'Present Distribution of
Population', 'The Location of Industry', 'The Urban Structure
of Liverpool', 'The Agricultural Geography of the Merseyside
District' and, with R. Lawton, 'The West Lancashire Coalfield'
and 'The North Wales Coalfield and Chester'.

Without doubt, these chapters contain some of Smith's best
writing. It was as though he was now able to throw off some of
the constraints imposed by the economy measures of wartime
publication as well as by his self-imposed discipline of careful
factual statement and to express his mastery of the geography
of his own region and of geographical method: Merseyside—
'a little world in itself, and a little world which can be fully
comprehended only by reference to many fields of knowledge'.
Smith's editorship brought coherence to the survey. His own
contributions studied the uniqueness of Merseyside and
recognised areas that fulfilled specific economic or social
functions within the body of the region and the city: but he also
sought opportunities to establish wider truths, especially
about the location of industry and the character of large urban
areas. Those who attended the meeting in 1953 will remember
his opening lecture to Section E of the Association on the
character of the region and will see him, in the mind's eye, over-
coming his lameness as he communicated his delight in field
study and the depth of his field observations to enthusiastic
field parties.

---

[1] Wilfred Smith (ed.): *A Scientific Survey of Merseyside*, University Press of Liverpool, 1953.

VI

AGRICULTURE AND THE COUNTRYSIDE

While, in retrospect, it may be seen that Smith's more important contributions to knowledge were made through his work on manufacturing industries, his interest in and writings on the agricultural landscape must not be neglected. His feeling for land, for the problems of the farmer and for the rural landscape of Britain were never so clearly expressed as when writing of the agricultural landscape. For example,

'It embodies the very substance of geography. It is rooted in the physique of the land, its bed rock, its morphological surfaces, its soil profiles, and, as these vary, so also does the farmer's employment of the land. It reflects the weather and the climate: for those who can read the signs, it mirrors the heavens. Farming is modelled, moreover, not only by soil and climate but also by human intelligence and efficiency and on many a British hillside the bright green of one farmer's fields stands out sharply from the dull hues of those of his neighbours. An agricultural landscape adapted to current farming practice is not infrequently also an open-air museum of former systems of land use, preserved unconsciously here and there in the long, curved lands of a field, in the lie of a hedge, in the field shapes of a moorland margin. Farmhouses melting into the landscape with sites carefully chosen for shelter and water, the conscious design of field and garden and park, the plant communities of wide open moorland shaped not so much by man as by nature, all present a functional yet decorative scene which it is a delight to study, to view the sweep of the landscape in panorama and to dissect it piece by piece in detail.'[1]

His studies of farming, Chapters I, IV and V in *An Economic Geography of Great Britain*, while revealing his interest in the emergence of the landscape through time, showed most clearly his desire to disentangle long-term from short-term trends and his skill in analysing in detail the varied regional patterns of British farming. He was especially happy in his demonstration of the trend to regional specialisation of farming during the nineteenth century, the response, as he wrote, on the agricultural side 'to the specialist economy which developed in

[1] *Geography and the Location of Industry*, 1952, pp. 2–3.

Britain . . . in industry even more than in farming'. The arable districts remained largely arable, the grass districts became more completely under grass, devoting themselves more exclusively to *one* form of stock economy. The changes in the economy, the growth of new markets, new methods of farming led, his work implied, towards a more intimate adjustment to physical conditions, not, as was superficially supposed, to a diminution in the importance of the physical factor. The significance of his chapters increases when it is remembered that these were written before the results of the Land Utilisation Survey were made available by L. Dudley Stamp (as he then was) in *The Land of Britain: its Use and Mis-use.*

Smith's interest in measurement in economic geography found expression also in his work on agriculture. In a short section on Land Productivity,[1] he commented on, and criticised, M. G. Kendall's celebrated paper on 'The Geographical Distribution of Crop Productivity in England'.[2] In his studies of the Fylde he devised an index of land productivity based on the density of the stocking of grassland.[3] There are indications that this is a problem to which Smith would have made further contributions had he lived longer. Only a brief reference could be made to it in his report on the Land Utilisation Survey of Lancashire, a report which was, in the circumstances of the war, necessarily brief.[4]

Not surprisingly, Smith's dual interests in industry and in the countryside led him to participate, to some extent, in discussions on competing claims for use of the limited land of Britain. In his paper on 'Industry and the Countryside'[5] he attempted, dispassionately, to weigh the arguments for and against the introduction of manufacturing industries into rural areas. The concluding paragraph is characteristic of the realistic and practical man that he was:

'I am as attracted as anyone to an undespoiled countryside

[1] *An Economic Geography of Great Britain*, pp. 267–9.

[2] *Journal of the Royal Statistical Society*, CII, 1939, pp. 21–62.

[3] W. Smith: 'The Agricultural Geography of the Fylde', *Geography*, XXII, 1937, pp. 29–43 and 'A Live-Stock Index for the Fylde District of Lancashire', *Empire Journal of Experimental Agriculture*, VII, 1939, pp. 63–75.

[4] Land Utilisation Survey of Britain, *The Land of Britain*, Part 45, Lancashire, 1941.

[5] Wilfred Smith: 'Industry and the Countryside', *The Town Planning Review*, XXV, October 1954, pp. 207–15.

and I yield to none in my appreciation of the beauty of the face of nature. But we cannot attempt to preserve the entire countryside as a museum piece, pleasant to live in and interesting to visit on vacation. . . . It is a place to work in as well as to live in and a place whose resources must be utilized to the maximum extent in the national interest.'

VII

How can Wilfred Smith's achievements as an economic geographer be summarised?

By patient and long continued work he clarified our knowledge of the distribution of industries in Great Britain. His achievement rested on careful use of the geographer's traditional techniques of cartography and field survey: to these he added the critical analysis of statistical data; he devised statistical tests and applied them to geographical problems.

He showed that, geographically, manufacturing industry could not be regarded as a single unit: rather it was a collection of diverse and highly differentiated parts, each with its own locational requirements and its own particular relationships to its materials and its markets. He made a special contribution in showing how the closeness of fixation to materials could be measured. He helped to give form, coherence and discipline to the new economic geography of his time, the geography of production rather than of commerce.

Wilfred Smith was a man of wide learning, with a grasp of disciplines other than his own. His studies of industry were informed by his knowledge of history, by his acquaintance with statistical techniques, and by his interest in economic theory, and in location theory in particular. He attached importance to a close understanding of the processes, techniques and management decisions of the industry under study. It was necessary always to keep in mind the national economic and political context. His studies thus contributed to knowledge of society in its spatial aspects, of how society organised itself territorially, and he may be regarded as one of the pioneers in this field of study which, ten years after his death, has blossomed with new contributions from many workers.

The breadth of his grasp is especially well seen in his close studies of Merseyside societies; always penetrating, firmly rooted in the physical conditions of the region, consistently related to the themes of changing distribution and areal differentiation.

He found satisfaction in learning, in building patiently on discovered facts and distributions, in seeking to explain to fellow scholars the origins and character of the economic geography of the country. In the traditions of his University he threw light on hitherto dark aspects of knowledge. Professor R. H. Kinvig, who was Roxby's first assistant, and thus a teacher at Liverpool when Smith was an undergraduate, has written: 'I know that the transparent honesty of his approach to geography won respect from most who came into contact with him. He was a stickler for detail and had a great mastery of facts. He was suspicious of all broad generalisations until he had familiarised himself with the essential details and he had a well developed and logical mind.' Nowhere better are these characteristics expressed than in *An Economic Geography of Great Britain*.

C

AN

HISTORICAL INTRODUCTION
TO THE
ECONOMIC GEOGRAPHY OF GREAT BRITAIN

CHAPTER 1

Agriculture

I

THE MIDDLE AGES

In the Middle Ages a type of farming with self-sufficiency as its main objective was common to all parts of the country.[1] The agricultural unit, the village or hamlet, produced the greater part of its own requirements—of corn for bread and drink, of beasts for meat and clothing. The only articles of necessity which every unit could not itself produce were salt and iron. The self-sufficiency of the medieval village must not, however, be over-emphasised. It is true that extreme local self-sufficiency was general even in the English Plain until the beginning of the twelfth century and in the more remote parts of the country even later still. It had been the custom for noble families to migrate to each of their estates in succession in order to consume the production of the estate on the spot— 'this perambulatory feeding', as Prof. N. S. B. Gras describes it.[2] But during the twelfth and thirteenth centuries the lord's estates were in many cases farmed by bailiffs who sent the produce of the demesne to the lord's main establishment or else the monetary proceeds of its sale instead. From this time onwards trade in corn and in other products of the farm gradually developed. By the end of the thirteenth century the manors of the Bishopric of Winchester were selling 70 per cent. of their wheat, 67 per cent. of their rye, 40 per cent. of their barley, and 30 per cent. of their oats.[3] These were from the demesne and the percentage sold from the villein's holding would be very much less. In the more remote parts, such as

---

[1] Treatment throughout is of agricultural and not of tenurial or of social conditions.

[2] N. S. B. Gras: *The Evolution of the Corn Market* (1926), p. 5.

[3] N. S. B. Gras, *op. cit.*, Appendix A.

South Wales, farming for market did not begin to emerge until the fourteenth century.[1] The areas of excess wheat production appear to have been the Oxford Clay Vale, the southern part of the Lias Clay Vale, and the loams of East Norfolk. The growth of the towns, which involved a demand for corn beyond the production and capacity of the burgesses' own fields, created internal local markets, and in years of good harvest there was sporadically an export abroad from coastal regions such as Kent, East Anglia, or the East Riding of Yorkshire.

Self-sufficient agriculture implies the production in every locality of the main staples of food whether the quality of the soil be suitable or not. This is the geographical significance of the system. Regional agricultural specialisation, whereby one district is almost wholly in arable and another almost wholly in grass in accordance with the qualities of the regional environment and which is possible under a system of commercial farming, was then impossible in any complete form. Corn must have been grown on land more suited to other agricultural employment, and there was, in fact, a low average level of productivity. The average yield of wheat, for example, in the Middle Ages was well under 10 bushels per acre,[2] as compared with 32 bushels, which was the average for the inter-war period of the present day.[3] Better seed and improved technique of cultivation, of course, are also responsible for the increase.

While subsistence farming was everywhere the main objective, there were differences between different parts of the country in

---

[1] W. Rees: *South Wales and the March, 1284–1415* (1924), p. 191.

[2] The calculation of the average yield per acre in medieval times presents a difficult problem and involves many statistical adjustments. In the thirteenth century Walter of Henley considered 6 bushels per acre, a threefold increase, a fair return (*Walter of Henley's Husbandry*, ed. by E. Lamond (1890), p. 19), and the author of the anonymous *Husbandry* bound up with it states that wheat 'ought by right' to yield fivefold, but admits that unfavourable weather and poor soil would diminish the yield. Sir William Beveridge calculated the average yield of wheat per acre, 1200–1450, from some hundreds of returns to be just under fourfold (3·89:1) or 9·36 bushels (approximately 7·5 modern bushels). See Sir W. Beveridge: 'Yield and Price of Corn in the Middle Ages', *Economic History*, No. 2 (1927); M. K. Bennett: 'British Wheat Yield per Acre for Seven Centuries', *Economic History*, No. 10 (1935); R. Lennard: 'Statistics of Corn Yields in Medieval England', *Economic History*, Nos. 11 and 12 (1936 and 1937). See also Sir W. Beveridge: *Prices and Wages in England from the Twelfth to the Nineteenth Centuries* (1939).

[3] This is the average for the ten years, 1924–33; it was 32½ bushels for the ten years, 1929–38.

field systems, in the relative importance of corn and beasts, in
the particular crops grown, and in the particular beasts kept.
These variations to a large extent were regional, and they are
of considerable geographical interest. There was a varied
geographical pattern of agricultural activity. It is not, however, by any means a simple task to substantiate these variations
owing to the many difficulties involved in the interpretation of
medieval records, and it will be necessary to quote a certain
amount of evidence.

The regional field systems which will be distinguished here
are, first, the two- and three-field system of midland England;
second, the Kentish and East Anglian; and third, the systems
of western and northern Britain. The first was essentially an
arable system and the last largely pastoral. No attempt will
be made to discuss the antecedents of these, for it is with the
agricultural geography as developed by the thirteenth century
that this account deals.

The main outlines of the two- and three-field system were
delineated by F. Seebohm in his classic description in *The
English Village Community*.[1] Although Seebohm's interpretation
of evidence, some of which referred to the Hitchin tithe map of
1816, has been criticised, the reality and antiquity of the system
are unquestioned. Prof. H. L. Gray has collected evidence
dating from the late twelfth, the thirteenth, and the fourteenth
centuries from 422 townships in twenty-four counties to show
the practice of a two- or three-field system specifically during
the Middle Ages.[2] It was a common-field system, though
cultivation in common was not peculiar to it. This characterised, to a greater or less degree, most of the other agricultural
systems of medieval Britain; it was the rule in medieval Europe,
and it has often been encountered elsewhere in the world among
peoples at a somewhat comparable stage of culture. Although
bound up, no doubt, with the political and social conditions
of the period, common cultivation, or co-aration strictly so-
called, was certainly required by the ploughing technique of the
time. The heavy plough, with its plough team of eight oxen,
the commonest implement of the period, was beyond the means

[1] F. Seebohm: *The English Village Community* (1883).

[2] H. L. Gray: *English Field Systems* (1915), Appendix II. This appendix includes
228 references to the fifteenth century and later, in addition to the 422 references
of the twelfth to fourteenth centuries.

of all but the lord in most communities and beyond the means of all who held by villein tenure in every community, so that joint-ploughing with oxen assembled from several tenants was unavoidable.[1] Co-aration was, therefore, the rule.

The particular form which common cultivation took in the two- and three-field system was that of intermixed and unfenced strips[2] in two or three arable fields, all strips in each field growing the same crop in any particular year. The intermixture was probably the result of the practical exigencies of working with a common plough, as described by Dr. C. S. Orwin, but it incidentally ensured to each peasant samples of each type of land. During any one year, where there were three fields, one was in winter-sown corn (wheat or rye), a second in spring-sown corn (barley, bigg, or oats) or pulses, and a third in fallow. Each field grew a different crop each successive year and was fallow every third year: thus was the fertility of the land maintained. Experiments at Rothamsted have demonstrated the value of bare fallow for increasing yield in the immediately succeeding year.[3] The fields had to be roughly equal in size or, where the soil varied in quality, of roughly equal productivity,

---

[1] G. C. Homans gives specific examples. In Bransdale, in North-east Yorkshire, an extent of 10 Edward I required four neighbours, each holding two ox-gangs, to contribute their oxen to make up a plough-team. This was a relatively simple case and the proportions only occasionally worked out so neatly. Moreover, as Homans observes, these arrangements were those made for tilling the demesne and that the tenant associated with his neighbours in an identical fashion when working his own land is an assumption, albeit a reasonable assumption (G. C. Homans: *English Villagers of the Thirteenth Century* (1942), pp. 75–82).

[2] The dimensions of the strips, which might include one or more *lands*, varied enormously. For Bedfordshire, G. H. Fowler states that they 'were typically not less than a rood nor more than an acre in area; an acre strip was usually ploughed in four selions, a half acre in two, a rood as one' (*Quarto Memoirs of the Bedfordshire Historical Record Society*). The rood was here approximately 220 yards by 5½ yards, the acre 220 yards by 22 yards, but these are purely generalised figures and it may be asserted that the medieval farmer understood linear measurement and a day's work, but not areal measurement. The average size of parcels listed in a survey of *c.* 1745 of Apsley Guise in Bedfordshire, in each of four open fields, was 0·27, 0·29, 0·30, and 0·28 acre: these were virtually quarter-acre strips. A dowry comprising sixty strips in a total of 32 acres in the North Field at Harleston in Northamptonshire at the beginning of the fourteenth century consisted predominantly (53 out of 60) of half-acre strips (*The Estate Book of Henry de Bray* (Camden Society)), Vol. 27 (1916). Later surveys show that this regularity of strip size disappeared with the incidents of inheritance and division. It is often stated that an acre was ploughed in a day's work, which ended at noon, for plough oxen were grazed during the afternoon, but Dr. C. S. Orwin states that a day's ploughing to-day varies between two-thirds and three-quarters of an acre: this is with the aid of lighter and sharper ploughs, and the swifter traction of horses as compared with oxen (*The Open Fields* (1938), p. 36).

[3] *Report for 1936* (Rothamsted Experimental Station), pp. 49–50.

for the same amount of food was required each year. Prof. Gray lists the following from an extent of the demesne arable of Brompton, in Somerset (16 Edward III): 49 acres sown with wheat *in campo occidentali*, 60 acres with spring corn *in campo boriali*, and 39 acres fallow *in campo orientali*.[1] Brompton had three fields. *The Estate Book of Henry de Bray* gives an example of a two-field system for Harleston, in Northamptonshire: 50 acres *in campo boriali* and 50 acres *in campo australi*.[2] Where the arable was in two fields only, one was in fallow and the other partly in winter corn and partly in spring corn. The crops were all for human consumption, except some of the oats as provender for horses and perhaps occasionally for other stock.

This arable cultivation seems to have been the chief objective of land utilisation in the two- and three-field system, and of the farm stock the most important were the plough oxen. It was an arable rather than a pastoral system. Nevertheless, pasture arrangements were carefully regulated. Stock were depastured on the waste the whole year through, on the fallow until ploughed for winter corn, on the unploughed pieces within the arable fields for tethered stock even when crops were growing, and on the stubble and after-grass of the meadow after corn and hay had been led. Meadow hay, the chief winter stock food, was very valuable and meadow was usually rented higher than arable.[3] The number of animals which each tenant was permitted to graze was often carefully stinted and the dates on which corn and hay stubble could be opened to stock were strictly regulated. The depasturing of stock on the fallow had some manurial value and assisted in maintaining fertility. The importance of the stubble grazing naturally varied inversely to the quantity and quality of natural grazing available. In those areas where the greatest proportion was under the plough the

---

[1] H. L. Gray, *op. cit.*, Appendix II, p. 496.

[2] *The Estate Book of Henry de Bray*, pp. 33–5.

[3] 'On the demesne at Apsley in 1295 arable land was valued at only 3d. per acre, but the 12 acres of meadow at 2s. an acre' (G. H. Fowler: *Quarto Memoirs of the Bedfordshire Historical Record Society*, p. 26). A. Savine (*English Monasteries on the Eve of the Dissolution* (1909), p. 171), extracts from the *Valor Ecclesiasticus* of 1535 particulars of monastic income from several types of land. The average income per acre was 5s. 9d. for arable, 11s. 1d. for pasture, and 19s. 6d. for meadow. These are post-medieval and refer to only a few of the monastic properties, and they must be regarded with further qualifications, but they show the same order of variation as the Apsley values, which are specifically medieval.

right of pasturage over the arable fallow was, after the Middle Ages, held so tenaciously that it became perhaps the chief buttress of the system,[1] for the insistence on this right of pasturage prevented the introduction of improved rotations which would eliminate fallow. Such pressure on pasture was, however, probably post-medieval.

Both two- and three-field townships existed side by side by the end of the twelfth century, and Walter of Henley mentions them both in the thirteenth century, but it may be that the two-field was the earlier and more primitive and the three-field the later and more advanced, developed owing to the growth of population. I have classified the references prior to the fifteenth century for 422 townships given in Gray's Appendix II according to the century to which they refer. These are set out in Table I in the form of percentages.

TABLE I

CLASSIFICATION OF REFERENCES TO
TWO- AND THREE-FIELDS

| | CENTURIES | | | |
	Twelfth	Thirteenth	Fourteenth	Twelfth to Fourteenth
Two-field	7	53	40	100
Three-field	1	26	73	100

Source: Calculated from H. L. Gray: *English Field Systems*, Appendix II.

These frequencies suggest an earlier date for the two-field arrangement. There are a few examples of a two-field township becoming a three-field[2] and a few of two-field townships becoming four-field, but the nature of the evidence is such that only occasionally are there data for the same township at two different dates. The one change happened, according to Gray, in the thirteenth and fourteenth centuries, the other in the sixteenth and later centuries. It is possible that the two- and three-field systems had each different frequencies not only according to date, but also according to soil. Gray discovers that in Oxfordshire the three-field townships were on the clays and the two-field on the brashy soils of the Cotswolds. The

[1] E. C. K. Gonner: *Common Land and Inclosure* (1912) and H. L. Gray, *op. cit.*, pp. 47–8.

[2] An example is also given by T. A. M. Bishop: 'Assarting and the Growth of the Open Fields', *Economic History Review*, Vol. 6 (1935), p. 19.

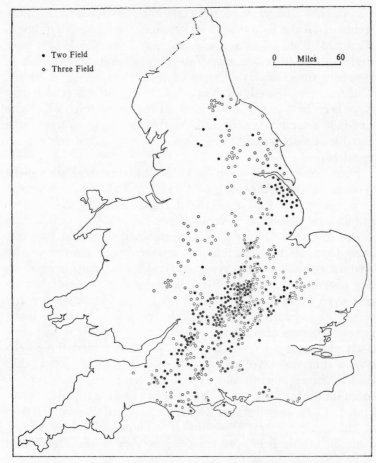

Figure 1. Two- and Three-Field Townships in England

Map drawn from evidence collected by H. L. Gray and printed in his *English Field Systems* (1915), Appendix II. Evidence relates to period extending from the thirteenth to the seventeenth centuries. The open circles mark the three-field townships, the dots the two-field townships.

other counties which contained two-field in excess of three-field townships (according to the evidence which Gray collected and which I have plotted on Figure 1) all have considerable stretches of chalk and Jurassic upland. Although it would be unwise to strain the evidence too far, it may be that, within the area covered by the two- and three-field system, the three-field was the more frequent on the clays and the two-field the more frequent on the lighter soils of the chalk and Jurassic uplands. T. A. M. Bishop has asserted that the Yorkshire Wolds were under a two-field and the Vale of York under a three-field system:[1] there was the same coincidence of soil contrast. Under medieval methods of arable farming the lighter soils may have been held to require more frequent fallow rests, which the two-field system allowed, and the stronger clays to have been capable of more frequent cropping, which the three-field system required.

Such were the characteristics of the two- and three-field system. It was not the only system of land utilisation practised in the country. I have prepared Figure 1 to display its geographical distribution.[2] According to the evidence of this map it was to be found only in a long midland stretch of England from Durham to Dorset and from the Welsh Border to the western bounds of East Anglia. Gray's own map generalises this distribution. Orwin also has mapped its extent,[3] but he employed in addition to medieval sources, Enclosure Awards of the eighteenth and nineteenth centuries. Though there were important differences, especially in Norfolk, it was precisely the same area which practised the two- and three-field system that was involved in the enclosure of common arable field in the eighteenth and nineteenth centuries. Enclosure of common arable field by Act as such has been mapped by both Prof. E. C. K. Gonner[4] and Dr. G. Slater,[5] and they both arrive at the same general distribution.[6] Those townships whose common arable field was enclosed by Act in the eighteenth

---

[1] T. A. M. Bishop, *op. cit.*, p. 17. But see Figure 1.

[2] This map has been constructed from the full list of townships in Gray's Appendix II, 422 of which refer to the twelfth to fourteenth centuries and 228 to the fifteenth century and later. It includes the post-medieval as well as the medieval references. In each of the twenty-four counties in which these townships lie there are, however, examples prior to the fifteenth century. Of the post-medieval references some 22 were drawn from Enclosure Awards.

[3] C. S. Orwin, *op. cit.*, p. 65. Only in respect of Norfolk does this map differ from that based on Gray's evidence and this difference is due to Orwin's use of Slater's lists.

[4] E. C. K. Gonner, *op. cit.* Map A in Appendix.

[5] G. Slater: *English Peasantry and the Enclosure of Common Fields* (1907). Map opposite p. 73.

[6] Slater maps the total area of individual townships involved in enclosure by Act irrespective of the proportion of the area involved, while Gonner maps the proportions enclosed for registration districts, but not for individual townships.

and nineteenth centuries were those which had longest resisted enclosure and where, by inference, the medieval arrangements had longest retained their vitality. The coincidence is so striking that it cannot be wholly fortuitous. Regional differences in agricultural systems operative during the Middle Ages continued thus to have significant consequences well into the nineteenth century.

The second set of field systems was that of the extreme south-east of England—Kent, East Anglia, and, perhaps, the lower Thames Valley.[1] There are many apparent resemblances to midland practices and their identity as distinctive systems must not be overstressed. Yet the enclosure maps of Slater and Gonner point to the existence of some post-medieval individuality in their agricultural arrangements, for these areas were enclosed before the period of Parliamentary enclosure (indeed, largely before the end of the sixteenth century), and it is necessary to inquire wherein this individuality lay. The individuality of their field systems in the Middle Ages has been discussed in detail by Gray. Later workers—Miss N. Neilson[2] and J. E. A. Jolliffe[3]—confirm the distinctiveness of the agricultural arrangements as they were manifested in Kent, and Prof. D. C. Douglas[4] the distinctiveness of those of East Anglia.

Kent had unquestionably an individuality in its pre-feudal institutions,[5] and these persisted into the Middle Ages as the tenure of gavelkind shows.[6] It is not certain that Kentish medieval cultivation was strictly a common field one, but, as Jolliffe points out, and as a perusal of the *Black Book of St. Augustine* and of the *Cartulary of Bilsington* shows, the holdings were often too small for it to be possible for each peasant to

[1] For the position of Buckinghamshire see W. E. Tate: *A Hand-List of Buckinghamshire Enclosure Acts and Awards* (1946).

[2] N. Neilson: *The Cartulary and Terrier of the Priory of Bilsington, Kent* (1928).

[3] J. E. A. Jolliffe: *Pre-Feudal England: The Jutes* (1933).

[4] D. C. Douglas: *The Social Structure of Medieval East Anglia* (1927).

[5] J. E. A. Jolliffe, *op. cit.;* also R. G. Collingwood and J. N. L. Myres: *Roman Britain and the English Settlements* (1936).

[6] Gavelkind permitted the division of the holding between heirs, but in practice a holding was often in the hands of a group of heirs or relatives, which contrasted strongly with midland England. The following are examples from *The Black Book of St. Augustine* (1915), ed. by G. J. Turner and H. E. Salter: 'Heredes Philippi de Faireport et heredes Wilhelmi de Boyton tenet XXV acras' (Pt. 1, p. 117) and 'Heredes Alexander de Gluocestria et pares de terra Rische tenet XXVIII acras et dimidiam perchiatam' (Pt. 1, p. 108).

possess a plough-team of his own and co-operation in practice, if not in law, was probable. Land was, in fact, frequently held jointly by co-heirs.[1] A peasant's arable holdings were not, however, as in midland England, in two or three great open fields each bearing a simple descriptive name and following a clearly defined system of farming, but in 'a bewildering number of field divisions . . . giving little clue to the husbandry employed'.[2] Moreover, Jolliffe argues that the agrarian unit was the hamlet rather than the village, an additional point of distinction from the area practising the two- and three-field system. Further, much arable in the middle of the fourteenth century appears to have been sown annually.[3] This land was more valuable, rising to 12d. per acre per annum, than the land fallow every second or third year of the midland system, whose value ranged from 3d. to 8d.[4] The practice was not general, however, and the records refer only to demesne so managed, but it indicates a greater flexibility of the Kentish as compared with the midland field systems, a flexibility which facilitated early agricultural improvement. Continuous cropping of this kind necessarily implied differences in pasture arrangements for there would be no fallow grazing on such land. The mast of the Weald woods was used for pigs and the coastal marshes of Romney, the lower Stour, and the Thames for sheep and cattle.[5] These were not infrequently many miles removed from the village and physically detached from it. With subsequent increase of population these detached portions achieved independence of their parent and became townships in their own right.

---

[1] This holding of land jointly by *heredes, fratres, socii,* or *pares* was well developed by the end of the thirteenth century. *Heredes* and *fratres* were clearly groups of relatives and *pares* may have described 'still more remotely connected groups' (J. E. A. Jolliffe, *op. cit.*, p. 24). Whatever the relationship of the individuals in these groups, it appears to have been convenient to keep the holdings together, despite the partible inheritance and division of holdings which the custom of gavelkind permitted. There were holdings by *heredes* as late as the fifteenth century constituting 'perhaps 10–20 per cent. of the whole' (J. E. A. Jolliffe, *op. cit.*, p. 22), but they were then less numerous than in the thirteenth century. The fifteenth-century *Survey of Bilsington* also lists holdings by *heredes,* though in this instance they would appear to be considerably less frequent than 10 per cent. of the whole.

[2] H. L. Gray, *op. cit.,* pp. 281–2.

[3] 'possunt seminari quodlibet anno' (H. L. Gray, *op. cit.,* p. 302).

[4] H. L. Gray, *op. cit.,* pp. 301–2.

[5] N. Neilson, *op. cit.,* Introduction, pp. 2–56.

In East Anglia conditions were less distinctive. There was partible inheritance[1] in some communities, it is true, and the holdings were described in terms other than the virgates or yardlands of the two- and three-field system; but these differences relate to tenure. A three-course rotation of crops on the arable has been established for the fifteenth century for Northwest Norfolk,[2] but a three-course rotation does not necessarily imply a three-field system, for the rotation may have been applied to the holdings of individuals and not to the village fields as a whole. Features of agricultural (as distinct from tenurial) individuality were not lacking, however. The pasture arrangements were of a special kind. A single township was often divided up into a number of 'fold-courses', each having its own sheep flock which was folded on the arable fallow. Evidence of this dates back to the twelfth century.[3] Though it involved extra labour in moving hurdles, this practice of folding on particular parts of the fallow was a more efficient way of manuring the land than the indiscriminate wandering over the fallow field under the midland system. It was a practice which later proved to be of great importance in the evolution of the Norfolk system of arable husbandry during the eighteenth century. It appears to have been sheep rather than cattle which were involved in this folding, and this implies a further point of contrast with the midland system in which plough oxen had the chief grazing privileges. Folding of part of the fallow appears also to have been the practice in some Essex townships, according to a lease of the twelfth century. At Walton, in Essex, the demesne had 180 acres of fallow, of which 28 acres were twice ploughed (*rebinata*), 33 acres sown (*seminata*), and 11 acres *faldata*, which Hale translated as 'folded with sheep for manure'.[4] Both Gray and Douglas[5] advance the view that the arrangement of arable holdings within the lands of the township in East Anglia was distinctive and different from the

---

[1] G. C. Homans, *op. cit.*, pp. 113–17.

[2] For example, George Elmdon of Weasenham, in Norfolk, had 61½ acres under winter corn, 54½ acres of barley (the greater part had had winter corn the year previous), and 48 acres of fallow in 1584 (H. L. Gray, *op. cit.*, pp. 318–26).

[3] The evidence from which Gray deduces this is on pp. 341–4.

[4] Leases of manors during the twelfth century bound up with *The Domesday of St. Paul's*, ed. by W. H. Hale (Camden Society) (1858), p. 131.

[5] D. C. Douglas, *op. cit.*, p. 45.

scatter of strips in each of the fields which was the rule in the Midland system.

The third group of agricultural systems was that of northern and western Britain, but these northern and western systems were by no means uniform. The evidence for each area must be considered in turn.

In Wales the position was complicated by the Anglo-Norman conquest and the semi-manorialisation which followed it. In the *Black Book of St. David's*, which refers to South Wales, the distinction is frequently drawn between land held by the law of England and land held by the ancient tenure.[1] Whether the land in the Englishry, however, was cultivated according to the practices of midland England is by no means certain. At Llantrissent, near Usk on the English Border, which Prof. W. Rees quotes as a typical case, the demesne arable had, it is true, the same acreage under corn each year and in three out of four years had equal acreages of winter-sown wheat and of spring-sown oats, but the fields which grew the corn were individually under a two-course, a three-course, and a four-course rotation.[2] The field system was an irregular one. Of the seven manors in the *Black Book of St. David's* whose demesne arable was attributed to fields specified by name, two had two fields, two had three fields, and three had many fields up to twelve in number.[3] The same irregularity is evident. None of the fields had the simple descriptions, such as East Field or West Field, common in midland England. In the Welshry conditions were very different. Land was held not by individuals, but by a group of relatives, the *gwely*.[4] This was the ancient tenure. The difference was not tenurial alone. The amount of land held by a *gwely* varied greatly: in the 'Country of

[1] *The Black Book of St. David's*, ed. by J. W. Willis-Bund (Cymmrodorion Record Series) (1902).

[2] W. Rees, *op. cit.*, pp. 192–3. The particulars relate to the successive years 1323–6.

[3] *The Black Book of St. David's*, pp. 73, 109, 119, 137, 171, 229, and 293.

[4] Even in the Englishry much land held by tenants was in the name of co-tenants. In North Wales, at any rate, the gwely organisation sometimes cut across the settlement of hamlet organisation. A Crown Rental of the sixteenth century relating to Llysddulas in Anglesey reveals seven gwelyau distributed over upwards of twenty-five hamlets: in one of the hamlets each gwely had rights, but at the other extreme some hamlets were in the sole possession of single gwely (T. J. Pierce: *Bulletin of the Board of Celtic Studies* (1940)). In Chirkland, the Llangollen district, the joint family organisation was beginning to decay, however, by 1390 (G. P. Jones: *The Extent of Chirkland* (1933)).

Landeilo' the arable was as low as four acres, though there was meadow and pasture in addition. The arable, cropped mainly for oats, could not have been the mainstay of the group. Stock rather than corn provided the basis of subsistence and the rent payable to the lord often took the form of cattle or sheep. The Welsh districts were mainly in the hills where arable farming would in any case be limited to small patches. Of a later date (1603), George Owen's *Description of Pembrokeshire* describes practices similar to contemporary outfield cultivation in Scotland, to be described later, although it must not be inferred that the Scottish infield-outfield system was practised in its entirety. There was the night-time folding of stock in summer on land about to be ploughed; there was the sowing of oats 'eight or ten yeares together till the lande growe so weake and baren that it will not yeald the seede: and then let they that lande lie for eight or ten yeares in pasture for their Cattell'.[1] In Cornwall, at the end of the eighteenth century at any rate, similar practices were common.[2]

For North Wales, the *Survey of the Honour of Denbigh, 1334,* gives evidence of somewhat similar conditions to those of South Wales. There was the same distinction between farming in the manors and on the tribal land. There was but a handful of manors and even these exhibited no uniformity in their arable arrangements. Two had arable *in tres seisonas*.[3] But in another the arable is stated *not* to be cultivated in three seasons, and in still another a few acres were noted as sown annually and as having a higher value than the rest. Even the three-course rotation did not necessarily imply a three-field system. In the middle of some of the arable fields was land not worth plough-ing through exhaustion[4] and given over to sheep pasture, and among the new meadows was land *in campo*. There was clearly no lack of flexibility and there was no imposition of a rigid field system from England. The tribal land was held similarly

[1] G. Owen: *The Description of Pembrokeshire*, ed. by H. Owen (Cymmrodorion Record Series) (1892–97), p. 62.

[2] 'Arable is sown with wheat, barley, or oats, as long as it will bear any; and then grass for eight or ten years, until the land is recovered, and capable again of bearing corn' (R. Frazer: *General View . . . Cornwall* (1794), p. 33).

[3] At Kilforn, 66 acres in the first, 69 in the second, and 66 in the third (*Survey of the Honour of Denbigh, 1334*, ed. by P. Vinogradoff and F. Morgan (1914), p. 4).

[4] 'non valent converti cum aliis seisonas terre arabilis propter eorum debilitatem' (*Survey of the Honour of Denbigh, 1334*, p. 230).

D

in Denbigh to that of the Welshry in South Wales, and stock rather than corn was the main objective of farming.[1]

Medieval evidence for Scotland is not extensive. Down the eastern side of the country land was held in bovates and occasionally it is described as lying *in campo*.[2] The bovate was a common descriptive name in the North of England also, as will appear later: it was a measure of ploughing capacity rather than of a precise area and the acreage of a bovate did, in fact, vary within wide limits. The heavy eight-ox plough[3] was here customary, and in the more remote places was in use until the Improving Movement of the Agrarian Revolution. But there is no mention of field names of the *genre* of those of the two- and three-field system and the phrasing in the charters might be held to imply that the bovate formed a compact block of land.[4] In other parts of Scotland there were substantial divergences from this general pattern. In western Scotland and in the Highlands horse-gangs and not bovates or ox-gangs were specified, the plough employed was small and light and the traction was provided by four small horses or ponies. In parts of the Highlands it is probable that even the light plough was replaced by the *càs chrom*, or foot plough, which permitted only a small plot or croft as distinct from a field type of cultivation. The small horse plough and the foot plough of these districts, although probably also of cultural significance, were bound up with the rough and broken relief and with the existence here and there of patches of soil too small in size and too irregular in shape to permit the use of a large plough and of a large

---

[1] It may be that this was also true of some of the manorialised land. Lay Subsidy Accounts of the reign of Edward I for Lleyn in Carnarvonshire give some data in this connexion. The taxable properties included 352 *boves*, 897 *vaccas*, and 897 *oves*, valued at 5s., 3s. 4d., and 6d. per head respectively. It will be noticed that the cows were numerically more important and in the aggregate were worth more than the oxen. The entries for arable produce were considerably smaller in value than the entries for stock (T. J. Pierce: *Bulletin of the Board of Celtic Studies* (1929 and 1930)).

[2] *Chartulary of Lindores Abbey, 1195–1479*, ed. by J. Dowden (Scottish History Society), Vol. 42 (1903). *Charters of Inchaffray Abbey, 1190–1609*, ed. by W. A. Lindsay, J. Dowden, and J. M. Thomson (Scottish History Scoiety), Vol. 56 (1908). *Charters of the Abbey of Inchcolm*, ed. by D. E. Easson and A. Macdonald (Scottish History Society), Third Series, Vol. 32 (1938).

[3] Its beasts might be increased to ten or twelve on heavy soils and reduced to six on light soils (J. A. S. Watson: 'The Scottish Plough Team in History', *Scottish Journal of Agriculture*, Vol. 14 (1931), pp. 143–5).

[4] The possibility that the bovate and the carucate were merely fiscal tenements must not be excluded.

plough-team. In the extreme North-east, but especially in the Orkneys and Shetlands, was a peasantry largely of Norse extraction, practising partible inheritance (though with certain qualifications) and an extensive form of land utilisation with only limited acreages under tillage.[1]

In post-medieval times Scottish farming exhibited the two characteristics of run-rig and of infield-outfield cultivation. Run-rig was the joint cultivation in intermixed parcels of the lands of a farm or of a small hamlet. In Strath Spey, in the late eighteenth century, William Mackintosh of Balnespick sub-let three farms in this way:[2] one of 40 acres with joint-tenants, a second of 40 acres with three joint-tenants, and a third of 50 acres with two or three joint-tenants. The farms and the number of joint-tenants, however, were usually larger than these. The system tended to be associated with a hamlet rather than with a village form of settlement. Similarly, almost every farm on Lochtayside, according to the *Survey* of 1769, had several joint-tenants who worked the farm as a unit. Thus, to take a random sample, Ballemore had two ploughs, upper and nether, the upper being in the hands of three tenants with one-third of a plough each and the lower being in the hands of three tenants, one with half a plough and the other two with a quarter of a plough apiece.[3] The second characteristic was the infield-outfield arrangement. The arable was divided not into two or three fields, one of which was fallowed annually, but into infield and outfield, each of which was managed differently. The infield was cropped continuously without fallow rests and on it all the dung accumulated during winter stall-feeding was concentrated. The corn grown was nearly all spring-sown, bigg being sown on land freshly dunged and followed by oats–oats or oats–pease.[4] Corn cultivation was thus continuous, or nearly so. The outfield was divided into five, six, seven, or ten parts called folds, faughs, or brakes, one of which was broken up annually and cropped until the return barely repaid the amount

[1] A. W. Brøgger: *Ancient Emigrants* (1929).

[2] I. F. Grant: *Everyday Life on an Old Highland Farm, 1769–82* (1924), p. 103. These acreages refer to improved land and there was muir in addition.

[3] *Survey of Lochtayside, 1769*, ed. by M. M. McArthur (Scottish History Society), Third Series, Vol. 27 (1936).

[4] This convention is employed throughout to indicate the succession of crops in rotation. Thus, in this instance, oats in one year was followed by pease in the next year.

of seed sown. It was then left to reclothe itself as best it might and used as rough pasture. The only manuring the faughs received was from the droppings of stock folded in the summer during the night and at midday on that faugh whose turn it was to be sown the following spring. Of the antiquity of the infield-outfield arrangement there is little certain evidence. Miss I. F. Grant traced it back no farther than the seventeenth century,[1] but there is a reference in a sixteenth-century charter (1541) of the Abbey of Inchcolm to 'infeyld outfeyld' and to a 'broume fald'.[2]

Continental travellers in Scotland during the sixteenth century were not impressed by the quality of the arable cultivation, but they were impressed by the abundance of stock.[3] Sample entries in thirteenth-century charters relating to Inchaffray Abbey specify 13 acres of land, that is, arable land, but 41 cows, 120 sheep, and 7 horses. Medieval Scottish agriculture, it would appear, stressed stock at least as much as crops.

It is not easy to discover the nature of the field systems of North-west England. There was land in common-field cultivation: medieval records cite land *in campo* or, to avoid any possible doubt, *in communibus campis*, and arable holdings were frequently in bovates or ox-gangs. The *St. Bees Register* lists bovates, but there is no mention of fields, the land being described as *in territorio de Bolton*, or simply *in Gosford*.[4] The *Furness Abbey Rental* of 1537 specified two fields of almost equal size at Bolton-in-Furness, but of the thirteen tenants only two had holdings in both fields.[5] Unless the system was in decay, the reference being post-medieval, this would not be a workable two-field system if each field was fallow every alternate year, for eleven out of the thirteen tenants would have a crop only one year in two. Liverpool had its Townfield with each man's holdings in scattered strips, but it appears to have been only a

[1] I. F. Grant: *Social and Economic Development of Scotland before 1603* (1930), p. 287.

[2] *Charters of the Abbey of Inchcolm*, pp. 71–2.

[3] I. F. Grant: *Social and Economic Development of Scotland*, p. 290.

[4] *The Register of the Priory of St. Bees*, ed. by J. Wilson (Surtees Society), Vol. 102 (1915).

[5] *Furness Abbey Coucher Book*, Vol. 2 (Chetham Society), New Series, Vol. 78 (1919). See also H. L. Gray, *op. cit.*, and *A Middlewich Chartulary*, ed. by J. Varley (Chetham Society) New Series, Vol. 105 (1941).

single field for agrarian purposes with sub-divisions of the dimensions of furlongs or shots for tenurial purposes.[1] Quite generally the settlement unit was small. This was especially so in the hill country where the place-name fold later became very common, but even in Cheshire the average rating per manor in the *Domesday Survey* was rather less than $1\frac{1}{2}$ hides,[2] which has been taken to mean land for approximately $1\frac{1}{2}$ plough-teams,[3] obviously a small agrarian unit. The inferences to be drawn from the above samples of evidence are, firstly, that the field system was on a different and much less regular pattern to that of midland England, and, secondly, that the settlement unit was frequently small with fields adjacent to it also small.[4] The highly accidented character of the relief and, even in the lowlands, the hummocky distribution of boulder clay with marsh and moss in the hollows, permitted fields for tillage to be available only in relatively small parcels, each insufficient in size to form a large field according to the requirements of the midland system. The names[5] infield and outfield were recorded in Cumberland in the reign of Elizabeth, and the name infield in the Fylde in West Lancashire in a tithe map of the early nineteenth century.[6] The references, it will be noted, are post-medieval, as in Scotland. Cultivation in the Fylde at the end of the eighteenth century, though then in severalty, was an almost continuous round of corn crops with only an occasional fallow:[7] it was reminiscent of the Scottish infield. In Cumberland and Westmorland[8] at this time the common practice was to crop with oats and barley continuously for nine or more

[1] In Cheshire reference appears to have been also to the Townfield in the singular and unless they were much shrunken remnants those Townfields recorded on the tithe maps were of quite small size even in comparison with population. D. Sylvester: 'Rural Settlement in Cheshire', *Trans. Historic Society of Lancashire and Cheshire*, Vol. 101 (1950).

[2] *The Domesday Survey of Cheshire*, ed. by J. Tait (Chetham Society), New Series, Vol. 75 (1916). Introduction, p. 13.

[3] *Domesday Survey of Cheshire*, Introduction, p. 5. There were 500 plough-teams and 540+ hides for Cheshire as a whole, excluding uninhabited land. It cannot be assumed, of course, that each manor was invariably a separate settlement unit.

[4] In *A Middlewich Chartulary* there are references to grants of half a field (*dimidio unius campi*) which imply fields of quite small dimensions.

[5] H. L. Gray, *op. cit.*, p. 232.

[6] I am indebted to Miss A. M. Moss for this reference.

[7] J. Holt: *General View . . . Lancaster* (1795), p. 51.

[8] J. Bailey and G. Culley: *General View . . . Cumberland* (1797), pp. 188–9; A. Pringle: *General View . . . Westmorland* (1797), pp. 270–1.

years, and to leave it for almost as many years to recover by self-sown grass: this was reminiscent of the Scottish outfield. North-west England, unlike midland England, was early enclosed.

The names infield and outfield[1] are recorded, and there are also traces of the continuous cultivation and of the temporary cropping which these names respectively may be held to imply, sporadically elsewhere far removed from Scotland and Wales and in the heart of the English Plain. At West Wretham, in Breckland in East Anglia, a terrier of 1612 specifies infield and outfield. There is no certainty that the infield was cultivated continuously and of the outfield all that is known is that it was divided into seven *breks*, described as arable lands and folded with sheep each apparently once in seven years.[2] It looks as though this was similar to the system of contemporary Scotland. Traces of temporary 'outfield' cultivation have also been met with on the Yorkshire Wolds[3] and in the poor sands of the Forest District of Nottingham.[4] On the Lincoln Wolds, in the Lincoln Fens, and in the Isle of Axholme there was temporary cultivation until the land was worn out:[5] similar practices were reported on the heaths and moors of Stafford,[6] in Salop,[7] and on the Mendips.[8] There was 'every year's land' in the Vale of Gloucester,[9] and in Oxfordshire 'the more homeward or bettermost land is oftener cropped, or sometime cropped every year'.[10] It is to be noticed that the traces of 'outfield' cultivation in the English Plain refer mainly to upland wold or heath, to forest or moor; that is, to land of a special character, some of which

---

[1] Inland and outland must not be identified with infield and outfield. They had quite different meanings.

[2] J. Saltmarsh and H. C. Darby: 'The Infield-Outfield System on a Norfolk Manor', *Economic History*, Vol. 3 (1935), p. 36.

[3] I am indebted to H. King for this reference.

[4] *Breaks* were taken up for five to six years, cropped in succession with oats (or peas)–barley–rye–oats–skegs, and then left to recover by rest (R. Lowe: *General View . . . Nottingham* (1798), p. 20).

[5] T. Stone: *General View . . . Lincoln* (1794).

[6] On the heaths of Staffordshire R. Plot described temporary tillage for up to five years (rye–barley–peas–oats–oats), after which the land was 'thrown open to the commons again' (R. Plot: *Natural History of Staffordshire* (1686), p. 343).

[7] J. Bishton: *General View . . . Salop* (1794).

[8] J. Billingsley: *General View . . . Somerset* (1794).

[9] G. Turner: *General View . . . Gloucester* (1794).

[10] R. Davis: *General View . . . Oxford* (1794).

under the agricultural practices of the day was not capable of continuous or even of frequent cropping. In any case, these references are all post-medieval.[1]

It is thus clear that there was great variety in systems of cultivation and in relative emphasis on crops and stock in different parts of medieval Britain. It is tempting to read a cultural provenance into these, but, though there are traces of this in some of the tenurial features, cultural and agricultural distributions do not always coincide. The well-defined two- and three-field system, often assumed to be the *English* system, prevailed in an area much less than the area of the English settlement. The systems of west and north Britain, in their various forms, which have been labelled *Celtic* on the grounds that they were practised in those parts of Britain not involved in the English settlement, did not coincide either with the area of Celtic survivals. There is rather more justification to read a cultural provenance into the Kentish system, but the cultural relationships of the East Anglian are as baffling as those of the rest. The truth of the matter does not seem to lie along these paths. The rigid two- and three-field system, on the one hand, and the flexible temporary cultivation system on the other, were alternative methods of solving the farmers' problem of maintaining the fertility of the land. They may, as Dr. Orwin argues, be arranged in order of more primitive and more advanced means to this end,[2] but they also show signs of some relationship with the regional environments of the country.

[1] The name *breche* (O. E. bræc and M. E. breche) is common in many Midland counties and is noted in the reports of the English Place-Name Society on the counties of Northampton, Buckingham, Bedford, Huntingdon, Warwick, Worcester, Surrey, Hertford, Essex, Cambridge, Middlesex, Nottingham and Wiltshire. The interpretation of the name there given is 'land broken up for tillage', but this does not necessarily imply land broken up for *temporary* tillage and then abandoned. It would be incorrect to assume that where the name appears an 'outfield' type of cultivation is implied. Similarly, Bishop finds the term *brek* to be a synonym for *assart* in Central and East Yorkshire in the thirteenth century. In districts with Norse place-names the modern *breck* is usually derived from O.N. *brekka*, a slope. Thus Breck Shutes in the Liverpool Townfield were on the slope of Everton Hill. Breck is a common place-name element in West Lancashire. G. G. Homans (*op. cit.*, p. 84) regards *intake* as descriptive of land temporarily broken up for tillage, though he admits that some of these intakes later became permanently arable. In the North of England the term *intake* has been customarily applied to land permanently reclaimed from the waste.

[2] The more primitive is the temporary cultivation. In his book *The Open Fields*, a reference to the siting of strip-holdings in Cornwall prompts the comment, 'This is further support for the theory which suggests topographical and technical, rather than ethnic, limitations to the evolution of the Open Fields', p. 65.

This is the justification for a somewhat prolonged discussion and quotation of evidence.

Nasse pointed out that the 'field-grass husbandry',[1] as he described the temporary cultivation, was suited to areas having a considerable rainfall where, during the years of recovery after exhaustion from continuous cropping, a tolerably good grass sward could naturally develop. This line of argument is capable of extension and further application. In western Britain, where this system was common, grass-fed beasts were as important as corn, and at its best it was a form of convertible husbandry. The Scottish infield-outfield was, perhaps, a specialised practice which allowed full use to be made of the best crop land. In the lowlands of the English Plain, on the other hand, where the climate was drier and more suited to corn, it was at once more profitable to have a greater acreage under corn and more difficult to grow a good grass sward. The two- and the three-field system was primarily a corn-growing system, and the one-year fallow was insufficient to grow a tolerably good grass sward. If the ideas put forward by Nasse may thus be extended, the two systems may be interpreted as adaptations to the conditions of their respective climatic environments. The argument may be taken further. The traces of 'outfield' cultivation within the English Plain are mainly in areas of poor soil, and Marc Bloch noted that in France 'dans les pays de sol pauvre, l'Ardenne, les Vosges, les zones granitiques ou schisteuses de l'Ouest, pratiquaient sur toute leur étendue la culture temporaire'.[2] Finally, it may be asserted that the two- and three-field system with its requirement of large fields of more or less uniform soil was suited to the English Plain, but not to the accidented surface of the west and north, to whose varied relief was added the local variation of soil as a result, directly or indirectly, of glaciation. If these arguments are valid, the variation in medieval methods of land utilisation as between the two- and three-field system and those of the west and north was related to regional differences in physical environment. The effect of physical environment on the distinctive qualities of medieval Kentish and East Anglian

[1] E. Nasse: *On the Agricultural Community of the Middle Ages* (1871). Trans. by H. A. Ouvry.

[2] M. Bloch: *Les Caractères Originaux de l'Histoire Rurale Française* (1931), p. 27.

farming is not so clear, unless it can be argued that the continuous cultivation of some of Kent was related to the fertility of its soil—it was the 'garden' of England—and that the sheep-folding of East Anglia was related to its dry soils, naturally 'sound' for sheep liable to be infested with the liver fluke on damp ground. It may be, as Bloch argues for France, that these cultivation systems were related also to particular forms of plough.[1] And it may be that they were associated with particular forms of settlement, as Meitzen argues for North-west Europe as a whole.[2] Some investigations along these lines have been collected by the Commission de l'Habitat Rural of the Union Géographique Internationale.

There was no more uniformity in the particular grains grown than there was in methods of land utilisation. The grains were winter corn, wheat and rye, and spring corn, barley, bigg, and oats, together with pease and beans.[3] Winter corn and spring corn were both grown throughout the English Plain and in western lowlands such as Pembroke in South-west Wales. But there was little or no winter corn in upland Wales,[4] in the higher Pennine uplands,[5] and in Scotland (except the South-east). In upland Wales, though some wheat was grown, it was spring wheat sown in late March–early April.[6] In these uplands the chief corn crops were oats and bigg, the northern form of barley. In this, the effect of the lower temperatures and shorter growing season of the uplands can be easily discerned. In South Wales the distinction between those communities which grew winter corn and those which did not was heightened

[1] M. Bloch, op. cit., pp. 51–7. Also J. B. P. Karslake: The Antiquaries Journal (1933).

[2] A. Meitzen: Siedelung und Agrarwesen de Westgermanen und Ostgermanen (1895), 3 Vols.

[3] They were not always sown separately. Wheat and rye were often mixed, and this was maslin or mancorn (W. J. Ashley: The Bread of Our Forefathers (1928)); barley and oats were mixed as in the South-west Peninsula to-day. Whether the pure or the mixed grain was sown depended partly on the season, for, if sowing was late, rye might be sown along with wheat or even instead of it, and partly on the policy of the farmer, for rye often succeeded in a year when wheat failed and the sowing of wheat and rye together was a form of medieval insurance. Wheat, rye, barley, and oats were all used for bread and in times of scarcity pease and beans would be mixed in as well.

[4] W. Rees, op. cit., pp. 187–8.

[5] G. H. Tupling: The Economic History of Rossendale (Chetham Society), Vol. 86 (1927), p. 40.

[6] G. Owen, op. cit., pp. 60–1.

by the cultural distinction between English and Welsh. Within the areas climatically suitable for winter corn, the choice lay between wheat and rye. The effect of the space-relations of Britain at the terminus of the Mediterranean–Atlantic and of the North European Plain routes alike is evident, for wheat is dominant in the Mediterranean and France, rye in the North European Plain. It is very difficult to determine the geographical distribution of wheat and rye respectively in medieval Britain.[1] There is no doubt that wheat was gradually increasing at the expense of rye even in the Middle Ages; it indicated the growth of capitalist farming and the modification of the medieval economy.[2] There is some evidence, however, to indicate that particular areas did concentrate on particular crops. In the Hundred of Blackbourne in West Suffolk tax assessments of 1283 show no wheat but much rye in the westernmost parishes, much wheat but little rye in the easternmost.[3] The west part of the hundred has the light poor soils of Breckland, the east part the stiffer richer soils of High Suffolk (studied in Part II). An examination by Dr. Pelham of a Kent account roll of 1297 giving the hundreds from which grain was supplied for an expedition to Gascony affords another illustration that this variation of grain grown sometimes, at any rate, coincided with differences of soil, if it be assumed that contributions from each area accorded in kind with the local production. He finds that the chalk loams, particularly those of East Kent and the Isle of Thanet, contributed mainly wheat and barley, while the forest soils of the Weald and the marsh soils of Romney contributed mainly oats with only a little wheat.[4]

---

[1] Detailed records refer mainly to demesne farming which was then devoted (in part) to the growing of corn for sale and for this purpose wheat was the grain chiefly in demand. Wheaten bread was eaten by the upper classes, rye bread by the lower. The peasant might grow rye for his own household, but it was not sold extensively and was not therefore favoured by the capitalist farmer. Hence, so W. J. Ashley argues (*op. cit.*, pp. 83–94), the fact that wheat figures much more prominently than rye in Thorold Rogers's material (J. E. Thorold Rogers: *A History of Agriculture and Prices in England*, Vols. 1 and 2 (1866)) does not prove that wheat was grown more extensively than rye, for his material was drawn chiefly from bailiffs' accounts.

[2] W. J. Ashley, *op. cit.*, p. 137. It also registers improved farming by liming and draining.

[3] E. Powell: *A Suffolk Hundred in the Year 1283* (1910). It would be possible by working through the detailed acreage and production statistics of the manors of the Bishopric of Winchester to give many more examples.

[4] R. A. Pelham: 'Grain Growing in Kent in the Thirteenth Century', *Empire Journal Experimental Agriculture* (1933), pp. 82–4.

Finally, there were regional variations in stock farming. It has already been pointed out that in the uplands of the west and north (and in some of the western lowlands as well) pastoralism rather than corn-growing dominated the agricultural geography. What corn was grown was mainly, if not invariably, spring corn. The better land, though under corn in spring and summer, was thus available for stock grazing in winter when pasture was scarce. In this sense the choice of spring corn rather than winter corn was an adaptation to pastoralism. The stock kept included both cattle and sheep. Sheep were fewer than to-day. It is true that they figured numerically rather prominently in the *Black Book of St. David's*, for example, yet if they be equated with cattle at the rate of ten head of sheep to one head of cattle[1] (the ratio there adopted in measuring pasture values) they become roughly equal in importance. Sheep were kept as much for their milk[2] as for their wool, a practice which remained in the Highlands and Southern Uplands of Scotland[3] until the end of the eighteenth century and in upland Wales until the end of the nineteenth century.[4] The milk was made into cheese in which form summer-produced food could be stored for winter use. The keeping of sheep primarily for wool was a late development, and its arrival marked the emergence of capitalist farming. In some upland districts cattle alone were kept. Many parts of the Pennines were managed as vaccaries or cattle-breeding farms. In Blackburnshire, on the slopes of Rossendale, Pendle and Boulsworth Hills, there were in 1296 28 and in 1305 29 vaccaries with 2,423 and 2,397 head of cattle respectively. There were similar breeding farms in adjacent parts of the West Riding. When they reached maturity, the beasts were sold into the lowlands, the young oxen for the plough and the heifers for the dairy. Cattle were

---

[1] The same proportions of cattle to sheep were employed in the stints of common pasture at Apsley Guise in Bedfordshire in 1633–34. The *Survey of Lochtayside, 1769*, in Scotland equated five sheep to one cow, ignoring followers in each instance.

[2] *Walter of Henley's Husbandry*, p. 27. Ten sheep were reckoned to produce the same quantity of cheese or butter as one cow.

[3] In the English Plain, sheep milking, though common in the Middle Ages, died out earlier. In parts of the English Plain, in the Cotswolds and Herefordshire Ryelands at least, sheep were 'cotted' or housed and fed under cover in winter.

[4] J. H. Clapham: *An Economic History of Modern Britain: Free Trade and Steel* (1932), p. 277.

similarly exported from North Wales into the Cheshire Plain.

It appears to have been on the abbey lands that sheep-farming for wool first developed on a large scale. Pegalotti's list (c. 1315) of houses supplying wool to Flemish and Italian merchants shows that the largest producers lay on the western fringes of the English Plain, especially those in relatively remote districts. But numbers of sheep increased at a later date in South Wales and in the manors of the Bishopric of Winchester, and Thorold Rogers quotes wool prices for almost every county in the English Plain. Sheep-farming thus became widespread. Whether wool sheep were kept mainly on particular types of land is not altogether clear, but there is some reason to suppose that sheep were more plentiful on the South Downs than in the Weald, on the Mountain Limestone than on the Millstone Grit. They were kept frequently on heaths and downs and almost every writer in the sixteenth century ascribed the finest wool to such sheep.[1]

The yield from farm stock was low. They were small beasts. Thorold Rogers notes that in the sixteenth century oxen bought for victualling the Navy weighed no more than 4 cwts.,[2] and the average sheep fleece weighed little more than 1 lb. in South Wales,[3] but nearer 2 lbs. was probably the general average.[4] The yield of milk by the dairy cow was low, a wey (224 lbs.) of cheese[5] being made from each beast during each season lasting from Easter to Michaelmas, and she was not expected to yield much milk outside this period.[6] This gives a lactation little more than 6 months long, as compared with the 10½ months, which is the average at the present day.[7] These low yields reflect the lack of good pasture and the scarcity of winter feed. Meadow hay was valuable and fed sparingly and many

[1] There is modern evidence to show that a sheep fed on a deficient diet gives a finer and shorter fleece than if fed on an adequate diet (W. C. Miller: *Empire Journal Experimental Agriculture* (1933), p. 173).

[2] J. E. Thorold Rogers, *op. cit.*, Vol. 1, p. 328. This may have been carcase weight and not live weight.

[3] W. Rees, *op. cit.*, p. 197.

[4] J. E. Thorold Rogers, *op. cit.*, Vol. 1, p. 53.

[5] This was only on good pasture. Walter of Henley notes a yield in addition to the wey of cheese, of half a gallon of butter a fortnight, but it was probably whey butter. This implies a yield of milk in the season of approximately 224 gallons.

[6] E. Lamond, *op. cit.*, pp. 27 and 77.

[7] H. G. Sanders: 'Variations in Milk Yield and their Elimination', *Journal Agricultural Science* (1927 and 1928).

beasts had necessarily to be killed in the autumn because there was no winter feed for them.

II

THE NEW HUSBANDRY

The agricultural geography of medieval times was in process of gradual modification during the fifteenth, sixteenth, and seventeenth centuries, but it was not *replaced* until the Agrarian Revolution, which, as will appear, was a geographical as well as a tenurial and technical revolution. It would be interesting to trace the progress of change, but limitations of space will not permit. The upshot was a very different geographical distribution of farming types, almost exactly the reverse of the distribution pattern of medieval times. The foundations of this new distribution pattern had been laid in the seventeenth century, and it did not finally take shape until the nineteenth century, but its outlines were already established by the end of the eighteenth.

The new technique of farming involved both arable and stock. The improvement of both crops and beasts was intimately related. The New Husbandry, the new arable technique, was gradually formulated as the eighteenth century wore on. In order to appreciate its significance in effecting the revolution in the distribution of arable farming, it is necessary to consider its main characteristics. The first was the principle of cultivation embodied in Jethro Tull's horse-hoeing husbandry—constant tillage of the soil, not only before seeding, but when the crop was growing, in order to destroy weeds which robbed the soil of nutriment and competed with the growing crop. With seed sown broadcast, hand-hoeing of a growing crop is difficult, but horse-hoeing impossible. The complementary aspect of Tull's constant tillage was, therefore, the sowing of seed in drills, in straight lines sufficiently far apart to permit a horse-drawn hoe to cultivate the rows between them.[1] He

---

[1] Horse-hoeing husbandry was the description which Tull gave to his methods, but it was often known to contemporaries as the drill husbandry, a description which W. Cobbett later also employed (W. Cobbett: *Rural Rides, 1821–32*, ed. of 1908, Vol. 2, p. 184). Tull invented and used a drill which, though possibly not the first of its kind, was the first to achieve practical success. The drill effected a very considerable saving in the amount of seed sown.

himself practised horse-hoeing with wheat, but this involved very thin sowing, and it was with roots that the method was most successful. Constant tillage is easier in light than in heavy soils, for these cannot be worked in very wet or in very dry weather, and horse-hoeing husbandry was therefore better adapted to light than to heavy soils. This was of considerable geographical significance, as will appear later. During the eighteenth century an improved plough was introduced. The Rotherham plough, patented in 1730, 'shows a great advance in the improved form of its frame and had a profound effect on plough design in this country'.[1] Not only was ploughing more effectively done, but the easier traction permitted a given number of animals (and of ploughmen) to do more work and made constant tillage correspondingly more easy. The smaller plough-team also rendered co-operative ploughing largely unnecessary except for the very small copyholders.

The second characteristic of the New Husbandry was the field cultivation, as an integral part of the rotation, of the new crops introduced on the farm in the seventeenth century— turnips, potatoes, temporary grasses. The crops under medieval systems of farming were mostly 'white' crops, grain of various kinds. These all exhausted the soil and a fallow was necessary to permit the land to recuperate. The stirring of the soil during the summer fallow encouraged nitrogen accumulation, but summer cultivation of the fallow does not in practice seem to have been very clean, and the summer fallow was regarded chiefly as pasture for stock. The only non-grains cultivated in medieval times were pulses, pease and beans, which were some-times substituted for the spring-sown corn. Though sometimes reckoned as 'white' crops, pulses 'tend to increase the soil reserves of nitrogen',[2] and in this sense are recuperative and not exhaustive crops. The medieval farmer's preoccupation was the growing of bread corn (and drink corn) and, as pulses were inferior in this respect, spring corn was favoured in their stead.[3] Of the new crops, seed grasses served the same purpose as

[1] A. J. Spencer and J. B. Passmore: *Agricultural Implements and Machinery* (1930).

[2] J. A. S. Watson and J. A. More: *Agriculture. The Science and Practice of British Farming* (1933), p. 277.

[3] C. S. Orwin, however, remarks: 'It would be more correct, instead of talking of the "bread corn" and the "drink corn", to speak of the "bread field" and the "fodder field" ' (C. S. Orwin, *op. cit.*, p. 168).

pulses in accumulating nitrogen when the grass sward was ploughed under and decomposed. Moreover, a grass seeds mixture, if suitably selected, gives a heavy yield of hay, considerably heavier in its first and second years than from a permanent grass sward. One of the greatest problems of the medieval farmer, one which he never solved, was the provision of winter food for stock. The sixteenth century saw no improvement in this respect, but seeds hay, which, if a one-year sward, could usually be cut twice, helped considerably in its solution.[1] The significance of the roots, turnips and potatoes, was different. These are cleaning crops or, as they were described in the eighteenth century, fallow crops. Being drilled or set in rows, they permitted constant tillage between them during the summer: the land was thoroughly aerated and thoroughly weeded. They served the same purpose as a frequently stirred bare fallow and there was a crop in addition. Roots thus eliminated the need of fallow on land where potato or turnip cultivation was possible. The soil could now be cropped continuously without fear of exhaustion. This form of husbandry with turnips instead of fallow was invariably described at the end of the eighteenth century as the turnip husbandry. Neither crop, however, was suited to heavy land: mangolds, which are, were not introduced until nearly the end of the eighteenth century. Potatoes were largely human food, but field turnips were food for stock and, together with seeds hay from the temporary grass, provided that winter food hitherto lacking. Temporary grass and roots were incorporated into a rotation which, developed in Norfolk, came to be known as the Norfolk system. Winter corn was sown in autumn or early winter on a ploughed-in grass sward; in the second year, the soil was well tilled in the spring and early summer and turnips were sown in June; in the third, barley was sown in spring and a few weeks afterwards grass seeds for the following, the fourth, year. This rotation incorporated an important principle, the alternation of a recuperative with an exhaustive crop. No two corn crops followed each other, temporary grass followed the spring corn and roots the winter corn. Thus was continuous cultivation

---

[1] When a one-year sward was the object, the seeds sown in the eighteenth century were mainly red clover and trefoil. Lucerne and sanfoin, on the other hand, are deep-rooted grasses and were sown on land intended to be in grass for six to seven years.

practised and the fertility of the soil maintained.[1] The aggregate production from a given unit of land was increased.

The third characteristic of the New Husbandry was the close association of crops and stock. Nathaniel Kent described the similar rotation of Flanders as 'an alternate crop for man and beast'.[2] Seeds hay and turnips provided an abundance of winter food.[3] Turnips were either lifted or fed to stock on the ground. When intended for cattle feeding, they were usually fed in the stall or yard; when for sheep feeding, the crop was usually fed off to sheep folded on the turnip field. Bullocks fattening on turnips, straw, and hay yielded vast quantities of manure which were carted back on to the land to return fertility to it. Bullock feeding, unlike the grazing of dairy cows or ewes in milk, takes relatively little out of the land if manure is thus returned. Where oil-cake was fed—Coke of Holkham is reported to have introduced it into Norfolk at the end of the eighteenth century—the manurial residue was a net gain to the soil. Sheep were folded on the turnip field and the fold was moved until the whole crop was eaten: folding enabled the land to be systematically and evenly manured and, on light land, the treading of the sheep consolidated the soil.[4] Stock, therefore, not only enabled a profitable use to be made of hay and roots, but, by manurial residues, the fertility of the land was maintained and, in some cases, positively increased.

[1] Subsequent experience made it clear that continuous cropping was possible only with heavy manuring and that land became clover-sick if sown regularly every fourth year (J. Caird: *English Agriculture in 1850–51* (1852), pp. 501–3). Modifications of the strict four-course developed in consequence, though the principle of this alternate husbandry, the alternation of exhaustive with recuperative crops, remained.

[2] N. Kent: *General View . . . Norfolk* (1796).

[3] Where the farm consisted very largely of arable, as was common in East Anglia, there was little summer food available, and the bullocks and the sheep were bought in at the fall of the year. 'East Norfolk farms', says Marshall, writing in 1787, 'are in the months of July, August, and September as free from sheep as elephants.' Many bullocks, however, were grazed in summer on the marshes about the Broads.

[4] It was not inappropriate that the New Husbandry should be associated so closely with East Anglia, for medieval East Anglia had given special grazing privileges to sheep in the custom of fold-courses. Sheep-folding on the fallow was not, however, peculiar to East Anglia. Best records it in the East Riding in the seventeenth century (H. Best: *Rural Economy in Yorkshire in 1641*, p. 17), Plot in Oxford and Stafford, and the county reports record it at the end of the eighteenth century in Lincoln and Gloucester, *inter alia*. Defoe reported it on the Central Downlands as a new method of husbandry contributing to a great increase in fertility (D. Defoe: *Tour thro' the Whole Island of Gt. Britain*, ed. G. D. H. Cole (1927), Vol. 1, pp. 187, 285–6).

Closely associated with the New Husbandry and its provision of more and better stock food was an improved breeding of stock. This was not possible until seeds, hay and turnips had increased the supply of winter fodder. Hitherto such stock as could not feed itself in winter on the fallow or the commons was slaughtered in the fall of the year. The plough-oxen and horses and some breeding stock were given what hay was available, but there was little left for growing beasts. Tusser's descriptions make clear the poor condition of stock at the end of winter in the sixteenth century.[1] Any careful breeding and rearing was impossible. The founder of modern stock-breeding was Robert Bakewell, whose work began in the 'forties of the eighteenth century. It is very significant that he made full use of the turnip husbandry and that he was as much an expert in irrigating meadows[2] as in selecting stock from which to breed. The improvement of fodder and the improvement of stock went on hand in hand. His object in selecting breeding stock was not the perpetuation of 'fancy points', but, to use Youatt's words, 'the greatest propensity to fatten, . . . the largest proportion of valuable meat, and the smallest quantity of bone and offal'.[3] His greatest success was with Leicester sheep, the Dishley Leicester, as it was known to contemporaries. It was an economical feeder on good lowland grass or when folded on arable crops, and in Bakewell's hands it developed into a very effective mutton sheep, but it was not suited to poor land. Sheep had previously been kept almost entirely for wool (and milk) and the rapid extension of the improved Leicester, a mutton and not a wool sheep, in the latter part of the eighteenth century indicated to what extent increased food production had become a prime object of British farming. His experiments with Longhorn cattle were not quite so successful: he produced a better beef animal, but at the sacrifice of milk production. Bakewell's work was quickly followed by others, for once the improved methods of breeding had achieved success they came

[1]   'From Christmas, till May be well entered in,
          Some cattle waxe faint, and looke poorely and thin.'
T. Tusser: *Five Hundred Pointes of Good Husbandrie*, ed. of 1580 reprinted by English Dialect Society (1878), p. 142.

[2] Bakewell's methods of watering meadows are described by W. Marshall: *The Rural Economy of the Midland Counties* (1796).

[3] W. Youatt: *Sheep* (1837), p. 314.

E

to be applied later to the numerous regional breeds of Britain, each of which developed during the course of the nineteenth century some special excellence or some special adaptation to the qualities of the local environment. The production of food from British stock was greatly increased. Sir John Sinclair reported to a Parliamentary Committee in 1795 that the average weight of beeves at Smithfield in 1710 was 370 lbs., in 1795, 800 lbs.; of sheep in 1710, 28 lbs., in 1795, 80 lbs.[1] These weights cannot be accepted without reserve, and if the 1795 figures represented live weights and the 1710 carcass weights dressed for the butcher, the increase would become of more reasonable dimensions.

At the very end of the eighteenth century the first Board of Agriculture was founded, with Arthur Young as its secretary, and commissioners were appointed to report on the farming of each county of Great Britain. These reports[2] are a mine of information, and it is possible with their aid to reconstruct the agricultural geography of the time. For the first time it is possible to make a systematic survey of the whole country. Contemporary with these county reports was a series of surveys made by William Marshall, first of counties, Norfolk and Yorkshire, and later of large regions of England, the West of England, the Midlands, the West Central, the Southern. The object of these single-handed surveys was the delineation of the regional agriculture of England within the natural framework of the land as distinct from the artificial framework of the counties. Marshall has been hailed, with some truth, as the founder of modern agricultural geography.

The New Husbandry had made considerable progress by the end of the eighteenth century, but it was often practised only in part and not in its entirety. The turnip husbandry had spread widely and the sowing of clover more widely still, but turnips were very frequently sown broadcast, and, if hoed at all, only by hand.[3] The new crops, it may be inferred, were adopted more readily than the improved methods of tillage. The turnip

---

[1] Quoted by Lord Ernle: *English Farming Past and Present* (1932), p. 188.

[2] The earliest were issued in 1794 in quarto for comments and additions. In most cases a revised report in octavo was issued subsequently.

[3] The Cornwall report, for example, noted that turnips were grown only by the larger farmers and that even they cultivated them badly, neither drilling nor hoeing (R. Fraser, *op. cit.*, p. 43).

husbandry was found down the entire eastern side of England
from Northumberland to Kent, but only on light and medium
soils and not on heavy.[1] In Marshall's Midland Department,
a region[2] of relatively strong soils and 'a grassland country',
turnips were not common except on light soils, and it was
admitted that their cultivation presented 'difficulties ... on
strong retentive land'.[3] The turnip husbandry was not practised extensively in North-west England or in the South-west
Peninsula, and only to a very small extent in Wales. In some
Welsh counties field turnips were apparently unknown, and in
others, as Pembroke,[4] only lately introduced. All the reporters
were convinced of the value of the turnip husbandry for light
soils. Most were also of the opinion that, however excellent
the turnip husbandry was for light soils, it was not suited to
deep clays and that on these soils an occasional bare fallow
was still essential to clean the land. The sowing of clover and
rye grass was more widespread, both as to soil and as to region,
than the turnip husbandry. It was suited to heavy as well as to
light soils and to western as well as to eastern districts. In the
west, where the long ley was common, the better farmers
sowed down clover as a preparation for it, although the poorer
farmers continued to sow seeds taken at random from the hay-
rick if, indeed, they sowed grass seeds at all. Many allowed
their land to seed itself. The western districts adopted even the
clover husbandry less extensively than the eastern; it was not
because the clover husbandry was unsuited to their soil and
climate, but because they were still culturally remote and their
farming methods relatively old-fashioned.[5] The value of the
clover and rye grass husbandry was very substantial when
properly practised. In Cheshire it provided spring grazing a
week or ten days earlier than any other pasture, and was ready
to be cut for hay by mid-June, at least a month earlier than the

[1] In Nottingham, for example, turnips were grown on the soils of the Forest
District, but not on the clays of the Vale of Belvoir (R. Lowe, *op. cit.*, pp. 10 and 28).

[2] Leicester, Rutland, Warwick, together with South Derby, South Nottingham,
East Stafford, and North Northampton.

[3] W. Marshall: *Rural Economy of the Midland Counties*, Vol. 1 (1796), pp. 203–6.

[4] C. Hassall: *General View ... Pembroke* (1794), p. 17.

[5] Artificial handicaps were also imposed on its practice, for in Buckingham many
leases forbade the sowing of clover or of any green crop (W. James and J. Malcolm:
General View ... Buckingham (1794), p. 22).

natural meadow.[1] In Northumberland old natural meadow usually gave 1–1½ tons of hay per acre, clover and rye grass 2 tons.[2] Arthur Young placed clover after turnips as the greatest of 'modern improvements'.[3] Like turnips, potatoes were mainly suited to light and medium soils, but, unlike turnips, they were to be found mainly in western districts—in Lancashire, Cheshire, Cumberland, Somerset, West Cornwall, to give a few examples. In most of these districts they had become the staple diet of the poor. In Wales they had only recently been introduced and were absent in some counties: their cultivation was, however, increasing and taking the place of potatoes imported from Ireland.[4] Potatoes were not, however, confined to western districts. They were grown in Northumberland and in the West and North Ridings, and they had become an export crop from the Humber marshes,[5] an important potato district to-day, but there is no mention of them at all in the Fens of the Holland division of Lincoln. The geographical distribution of potato cultivation, like that of turnips and clover, was to change very considerably during the course of the nineteenth century.

In previous centuries wheat had hitherto been sown to only a limited extent in the north-western parts of England and on the edges of many upland areas. This was true of the sixteenth century as well as of the Middle Ages. The county reports give evidence of expanding wheat cultivation in several areas in the late eighteenth century. In Cumberland it was reported, 'Wheat is a modern production here; a general opinion used to prevail, that wheat could not be grown in many parts of this county'.[6] It was into the Carlisle Plain and the West Cumberland coastlands that wheat had been introduced. In Lancashire wheat was now grown in the south-west, the Fylde, and Low Furness, but not on the higher land towards the moors. Upper Ryedale, in North-east Yorkshire, was formerly supplied with wheat grown in Cleveland, but this import had ceased and

[1] H. Holland: *General View . . . Cheshire* (1808), p. 184.

[2] J. Bailey and G. Culley: *General View . . . Northumberland* (1797), pp. 96–101.

[3] A. Young: *General View . . . Suffolk* (1797), p. 83.

[4] G. Kay: *General View . . . Anglesey* (1794), p. 14.

[5] Rennie, Brown, and Sherriff: *General View . . . West Riding* (1793) p. 99; T. Stone, *op. cit.*

[6] J. Bailey and G. Culley: *General View . . . Cumberland* (1797), p. 190.

wheat was then being sent from Upper Ryedale to the manufacturing districts of the West Riding.[1] In Flintshire wheat was
taking the place of rye and barley.[2] This extension was, in a
sense, into areas climatically marginal to wheat, encouraged
by high prices and an increasing demand, but it also reflected
a modification of the spring corn complex of many of these
districts, associated with their pastoralism and convertible
husbandry.[3]

At the end of the eighteenth century there was considerable
variation of rotation, and this usually coincided with differences
of soil and climate. The Norfolk system was practised on light
soils in the eastern drier half of England: it was associated with
heavy winter feeding of stock whose manure was essential for
the maintenance of land fertility. On the clay soils of the
English Plain, where the turnip husbandry was impossible,
either the traditional common-field cultivation was retained
or corn was alternated with clover and beans. In western
districts, with a moist climate naturally favouring grass,
the long ley was common, either in its unimproved form
of a rest for exhausted land or else associated with improved
arable rotations which were gradually being adopted. This
summary of the distribution of crop rotations has been drawn
from the eidence of the county *General Views*.

As a result of improved cultivation the yield of corn had
risen considerably. Particulars of yield for wheat, barley, rye,
and oats have been abstracted from the county reports, and
these are set out in Table II.[4] In the mid-seventeenth century
Hartlib reported a six- to eight-fold increase as a good crop of
wheat, and King, at the end of the century, a five-fold increase.
If seeding was at the rate of 2–2½ bushels per acre, this would
give crops of 12–20 and 10–12½ bushels per acre respectively.
The returns in Table II indicate that the yield of wheat at the

[1] Tuke: *General View . . . North Riding* (1794), p. 35.

[2] G. Kay: *General View . . . Flint* (1794), p. 10.

[3] In 1758 Charles Smith estimated that more ate oats and barley bread than
wheat bread in North England and Wales, but that few ate other than wheat bread
in the English Plain. Quoted by J. Percival: *Wheat in Great Britain* (1943).

[4] The list does not pretend to be complete, but samples are given of different
parts of the country. The figures must be regarded as only very approximate.
On account of the statistical difficulties involved, no attempt has been made to
calculate a figure for the country as a whole. One such difficulty is the uncertainty
as to whether the statute acre or a local acre was employed, another is the uncertainty as to the weight of the bushel in each case.

end of the eighteenth century was probably between 20 and 25 bushels per acre.[1] The increase was substantial. In 1771, Arthur Young estimated the yield of wheat to be 23 bushels per acre. Bennett is of the opinion that Arthur Young's estimate was too high for the mid-eighteenth century,[2] but it accords for the end of the century with the estimates in the county reports.

TABLE II

YIELD OF GRAIN PER ACRE
AT THE END OF THE EIGHTEENTH CENTURY

| | IN BUSHELS PER ACRE | | | |
	Wheat	*Barley*	*Oats*	*Rye*
Cumberland	16–30	21	15–40	—
Lancashire	24	30	40	—
Cheshire	20	25	30	—
Stafford	25	30	30–40	—
Worcester	15–20	25–45	—	—
Gloucester	20–24	20–25	24	—
Carnarvon	32	28	32	—
Montgomery	27½	29	34	25
Northumberland	24–30	30–60	20–60	20–30
West Riding	20–30	30–44	48–70	—
Nottingham	16–32	24–56	32–56	24–32
Northampton	26	34	36–40	—
Rutland	24–32	28–36	36–64	—
Cambridge	23	36	26	20
Norfolk	24	32	—	—
Suffolk	22	28	32–36	16
Essex	24	33	36	20
Kent	22	26	12–56	—

Source: Compiled from the county reports to the Board of Agriculture, 1794 onwards.

Although it is not possible to use Table II[3] to indicate regional differences of yield owing to innumerable statistical difficulties, it is possible in certain cases to discover variations between small areas within individual counties, for it may be presumed that within a single county there was a more uniform statistical

[1] It is not possible to compare the yield in one county with that in another at all closely, as there were wide differences in methods of estimation, varying from detailed estimates for the districts or parishes, as in Essex and Cambridge respectively, to very general estimates for the county as a whole, in addition to differences in size of acre and weight of bushel.

[2] M. K. Bennett, *op. cit.*, pp. 25–6.

[3] See footnotes on this and previous pages.

presentation. In East Norfolk the yield of wheat was 48 bushels per acre, but in the 'very light parts of the county', that is, in West Norfolk, only 16 bushels per acre.[1] In Suffolk the yield of wheat varied from 32 to 40 bushels on the best soils to 12 bushels on poor sands, which were really rye and not wheat soils.[2] In Kent the yield of oats was sometimes as low as 12 bushels per acre on poor down, but on good land it was up to 56 bushels per acre.[3] In Essex the alluvial lands along the coast gave as high as 30 bushels of wheat per acre and 40 bushels of oats, but the chalk soils in North-west Essex gave only 20 bushels of wheat and 24 bushels of oats.

During the course of the seventeenth century, as the topographers pointed out, many of the heavy clay soils were beginning to develop into grass districts. The process was continued during the eighteenth century, and it was not to be finally completed until the close of the nineteenth. At the end of the eighteenth century much clayland arable remained, but Arthur Young admitted that the arable management of heavy soils was not as well understood as that of light soils. The New Husbandry, with its emphasis on turnips and constant tillage, was essentially a light land system. The clay which remained in arable often followed traditional medieval rotations whether it was enclosed land or common field, and it is not surprising that it immediately became more profitable when laid down to grass, provided it was laid down with an appropriate seeds mixture and was not allowed to tumble down unaided. Nathaniel Kent, after writing of the improvements in productivity after the adoption of turnips and seeds, goes on 'to say nothing of the wonderful improvements which sometimes result from a loam or clay; which will, when well laid down, often become of twice the permanent value in pasture, than ever it would as ploughed land. Most striking effects of this sort are to be seen in Leicestershire, Northamptonshire, and other midland counties'.[4] It is possible from the accounts given in the county reports to construct in outline the geographical distribution and character of grass farming at the end of the eighteenth

[1] N. Kent, op. cit., p. 56.
[2] A. Young, op. cit., p. 53.
[3] J. Boys: General View . . . Kent (1796), pp. 87–90.
[4] N. Kent, op. cit., pp. 73–4.

century. It was clearly becoming identified with clay, as arable was with light, soils.

The standard of grass husbandry was admittedly low in East Anglia and Kent, the very areas where the arable New Husbandry was most successfully practised. 'Upon the same farms,' says Arthur Young, writing of Suffolk, 'where almost every effort is made upon the arable, the grass is nearly, or quite neglected. . . . Our sister county of Norfolk is, if possible, yet worse in this respect.'[1] Similarly, Boys reports that 'the hay-meadows of Kent are much inferior to those of many other counties'.[2] Marshall confirms the poor standard of grassland management.[3] The reason for the neglect was partly environmental, for the dry climate (and largely light soils) of these districts were unsuited to grass, and it was partly due to the concentration of attention on the arable, here the main object of husbandry. The marshlands, particularly Romney Marsh and the Norfolk Broadlands, however, provided excellent grazing. The latter could fatten a bullock on $1\frac{1}{2}$ acres of summer grazing. The former was an object of excellent management. The grass was grazed short by breeding ewes and fattening wethers and the only cattle brought on to the sheep pastures were lean stores to eat off the spring and early summer flush when the grass was running away from the sheep flock.

Grass farming was of better quality in many western, northern, and midland districts. The physical environment was more suited to grass and these districts were not preoccupied to the same extent with the new arable techniques. The methods of making hay practised in Cheshire were recommended to Suffolk farmers. The best Cheshire pastures were on 'a tolerably stiff clay soil'.[4] In Craven 'the old rich pastures about Skipton, Settle . . . makes a hay of great repute, and is generally used over the whole Riding'; and again, 'the graziers in general are very expert at their business'.[5] In North Stafford the valley of the Dove was 'extraordinarily fine grassland', and a footnote comment adds, 'The farmers are accustomed to say, that it is

[1] A. Young, op. cit., p. 138.

[2] J. Boys, op. cit., p. 105.

[3] W. Marshall: The Rural Economy of the Southern Counties, Vol. 1 (1798), pp. 163–6.

[4] H. Holland, op. cit., p. 170.

[5] Rennie, Brown, and Sherriff, op. cit., pp. 116–17, 119–20.

scarce possible to over-stock a few acres of Dove land'.[1] This was the same district that Leland had noticed nearly three centuries before. The clay soils of Leicester, Northampton,[2] Warwick, Oxford, and Buckingham had become famous feeding districts which drew in stock from Wales, the Welsh Border, and the South-west Peninsula. The Buckingham reporter wrote of the Vale of Aylesbury: 'Its amazing fertility soon makes a visible alteration in the appearance of the animal . . . a proof of the quality and ability of the land'.[3] Many of the county reporters quote these Midland clays as essentially grass soils and as examples of improvements effected by laying deep clays down to grass.

In the extreme western districts of Wales and the Lake District grass farming was the main form of land utilisation and stock rather than crops the main object of management. It had been so in the Middle Ages, but arable had fallen to even lower levels by the end of the eighteenth century. Many Welsh counties imported corn for human requirements and some districts limited their arable to the production of winter stock food. This was equally true of Cumberland and Westmorland.[4] The management of the grass was designed largely to secure as much winter grazing as possible. In Anglesey, and perhaps elsewhere also, cattle were kept out of doors the winter through.[5] Fogging pastures was widely followed. The pastures were shut up early in the grass season and were not opened to stock until late autumn: in these mild, moist western districts, where grass could continue to grow until Christmas, it was held that an acre of fog was better than an acre of the best hay.[6] There was some butter-making and a little cheese, but the demand for Welsh store cattle on the deep Midland clays was too considerable to permit dairying to develop on any scale.[7] The Welsh

[1] W. Pitt: *General View . . . Staffordshire* (1796), p. 69.

[2] Norden, writing of Northampton in the seventeenth century, had referred to 'Meadowes and deepe feedings' in the valleys and to 'the Feelds on the Hills above' (*Speculi Britanniae Pars Altera* (1620)).

[3] W. James and J. Malcolm, *op. cit.*, p. 17.

[4] J. Bailey and G. Culley: *General View . . . Cumberland* (1797), p. 202; Pringle, *op. cit.*, pp. 272–5.

[5] This was possible also in Somerset.

[6] T. Lloyd and Turnor: *General View . . . Cardigan* (1794), p. 18.

[7] In Pembroke the soil was good enough for fattening, but there were no markets for fat stock near by and for economic reasons only young stores were kept (Hassall, *op. cit.*, p. 12).

mountain pastures and the Lake District fells were stocked with sheep in summer and a transfer up on to the mountain and fell in summer and down into the dales and valleys in winter was a regular rhythmic movement. Stock (cattle as well as sheep) were sent up in spring, the date varying according to the date when grass began to grow, and brought down about Michaelmas. The Carnarvon reporter had been informed that 'it was a common practice in this county, for families to go up to the mountains, in the summer season, to attend their flocks, and to reside in huts, in which they made cheese',[1] but he himself failed to find any traces of such transhumance in his day. It may be inferred that it had been practised earlier in the eighteenth century, but had since ceased. The decline of transhumance in Wales was linked with the substitution of sheep for cattle and with the enclosure of hill grazing.[2]

It would be interesting to analyse the geographical distribution of the several improved and unimproved breeds of stock at the end of the eighteenth century. I will confine my attention to cattle as an example. Although the old controversy of horse *versus* ox was still active in some districts, the Weald, for example, cattle were now bred primarily for meat and milk and not for muscle. The Longhorn still dominated North-west England and the West Midlands. The best Longhorn stock seems to have been in Lancashire and Craven, but Longhorns were found from Cumberland to Gloucester and Oxford. The Shorthorn had, in contrast, an eastern distribution, and it was still sometimes called the Dutch breed. But, as its milking qualities were becoming known, it was gradually spreading into other districts where dairying was the main objective. There were Shorthorns in Cheshire and in Somerset. They gave more milk than the Longhorn—3–4 cwts. of cheese[3] or 3 firkins of butter[4] in the season as compared with 2½ cwts. of cheese[5]

[1] G. Kay: *General View ... Carnarvon* (1794), p. 17.

[2] R. Alun Roberts: 'Trends in Semi-Natural Hill Pastures from the Eighteenth Century', *Report Fourth International Grassland Congress* (1937), pp. 150–1. He has discovered traces of transhumance in a modified form in Snowdonia as late as 1861.

[3] J. Billingsley, *op. cit.*, p. 15.

[4] J. Bailey and G. Culley: *General View ... Northumberland* (1797), p. 121.

[5] W. Pitt, *op. cit.*, pp. 131–3.

or 1–2 firkins of butter[1] of the Longhorn. The Shorthorn was clearly the more successful dairy cow. A few Channel Island cattle were found in Kent 'in dairies of gentlemen's families'. In the South-west Peninsula and in the south-west counties generally, the dominant breeds were red in colour, whether the Devon or the Hereford. These were good beef animals and were kept by graziers for fattening in these districts or for finishing on the deep clay pastures of the Midlands. The small black cattle of Wales were graziers' beasts also, and were brought by drovers to the Midlands and Kent. They were not good milkers, and when kept for milk yielded little more than 1 firkin of butter in the season. The bullocks fattened in the winter on the arable crops in East Anglia were mostly Scotch.

Contemporary with these improvements in crops and stock, there was proceeding a gradual reclamation of the waste. Light dry soils in western East Anglia and in Lincolnshire, which had hitherto been poor sheep pasture or rabbit warren, were improved and brought into cultivation through the agency of turnips and clover and the winter feeding of bullocks and sheep. Much open down was ploughed in the Central and Western Downlands (Hampshire, Berkshire, Wiltshire, and Dorset) and brought into arable cultivation with the help of sheep folded on the thin chalk soil. Defoe had noticed this in progress early in the eighteenth century, and it was active also at the end of the century.[2] The draining of the Fens,[3] though begun in medieval times, was not completed until the nineteenth century, and the draining and reclamation of much of the mossland of the Lancashire Plain had also to await the nineteenth century. But Pennine moor was being as actively improved as the open down of the English Plain, and it had been in progress early in the sixteenth century.[4] At this time population was attaining its highest altitudinal distribution. Small farms, which practised textile crafts and lead-mining (as at Alston) as well as farming, formed intakes around the moor edge. The farming of these small holdings was of a semi-subsistence type, though inadequate to supply the family, but

[1] J. Bailey and G. Culley: *General View . . . Cumberland* (1797), p. 210. The firkin was a measure of capacity (7½ gallons) and not of weight.

[2] A. and W. Driver: *General View . . . Hampshire* (1794), p. 23.

[3] H. C. Darby: *The Medieval Fenland* (1940) and *The Draining of the Fens* (1940).

[4] G. H. Tupling: *The Economic History of Rossendale*, p. 42–69.

away from the industrial and mining districts larger farms were being created. The bleak and exposed Forest of Knaresborough, for example, was brought into convertible husbandry, arable for a number of years succeeded by grass grazed by young growing stock.[1]

This increase in arable on down and moor compensated for the decline in arable on the deep clays of the Midlands. The total arable acreage probably did not decline,[2] but its geographical distribution was changing. The Midland clays had probably been in the Middle Ages the chief corn-growing districts of the country, but they had since been largely laid down to grass, though they still displayed the high ridge and furrow, whose ridges were possibly the lands or selions of the open fields and which were certainly designed to assist the drainage of these heavy soils. The light soils, many of them in upland areas relatively devoid of population since the English settlement, were, on the contrary, being transformed from sheep pasture to arable, though their sheep husbandry was being incorporated into the arable system with sheep folded on the arable. The light soils were the beneficiaries of the New Husbandry, the heavy soils of the new grazing and dairying. Nathaniel Kent, writing of Norfolk corn production, recognised this reversal in the geographical distribution of arable farming. 'It is evidently so great,' he says, 'that no part of England, not even the famous vales of Taunton, White Horse, and Evesham are supposed to exceed it in proportion of corn.'[3] The 'famous vales' had stiff or relatively stiff soils and had been heavy producers of corn. The same reversal was noticed, on a smaller scale, in the Vale of Belvoir. It was an agrarian revolution geographically as well as technically.

The new and improved methods of farming were most successful on enclosed land. Though much of the evidence is not of such a nature as to be incontrovertible, there was probably a difference in yield of corn between enclosed land and open field.[4] The average crop of wheat on the common fields of Nottingham was 16–24 and on the enclosed land 20–32

[1] Rennie, Brown, and Sherriff, *op. cit.*, p. 142.

[2] J. Caird was of the opinion that the arable acreage in 1850–51 was considerably greater than it had been in 1770 (J. Caird, *op. cit.*, pp. 475–6).

[3] N. Kent, *op. cit.*, p. 150.

[4] C. Vancouver: *General View . . . Cambridge* (1794), p. 192.

bushels per acre. The enclosed land had the advantage. Many other similar examples might be given. These returns do not, however, necessarily prove the point, for there may have been a difference in the intrinsic quality of the soil as between open and enclosed, that is, the addition of a second variable.[1] However this may be in respect of *yield*, almost every county report gives particulars of the higher *rent* of enclosed arable land as compared with common field arable. The increase was stated in particular counties to be one-quarter, one-third, one-half, two-thirds, and double the rent of open field arable. In Cambridgeshire the average rent of enclosed arable was 18s. and of open field arable 10s. per acre;[2] in Essex, 14s. 8d. and 10s. 2d.;[3] in Northampton, 20s. and 11s. respectively.[4] The average increased rent of enclosed arable thus appears to have been about two-thirds or three-quarters of the rent of open field arable. This higher rent was due to a greater profitability of farming on enclosed land, but it was also due to the customary character of common-field rents which held such rents down.

I will not attempt to examine the distribution of enclosure by Act. It is discussed at considerable length by Prof. E. C. K. Gonner and Dr. G. Slater in the works referred to earlier in this chapter. The enclosure of common field was in that stretch of midland England where the two- and three-field system had been practised in its most accentuated form: elsewhere common field had been enclosed long before. The enclosure of common waste by Act was in contrast most prominent in the Pennine and Welsh uplands. In the English Plain common waste had been enclosed piecemeal previously as a result of pressure of population.

The form of agricultural use adopted after enclosure by Act varied widely. It is certain that enclosure was not all intended for laying down arable to grass. This did happen extensively on the deep clays of the Midlands which had already become famous grazing districts. But much enclosure of the chalk was unquestionably for arable cultivation. The success of the New

[1] N. Kent (*op. cit.*, p. 73) seemed to have no doubts that enclosed land actually yielded more.

[2] C. Vancouver: *General View . . . Cambridge* (1794), p. 193.

[3] C. Vancouver: *General View . . . Essex* (1795), p. 115.

[4] J. Donaldson: *General View . . . Northampton* (1794), p. 14.

Husbandry ensured that all enclosed light soils would pass under the plough. Enclosure, therefore, was not only a tenurial change: it had profound geographical effects on the landscape and on the use of the land. It greatly altered the face of the countryside. Common-field cultivation was open and un-hedged and only the coppices broke the sweep of the wind. It was a naked landscape, as Cobbett frequently described it, but it allowed sun and air to get to the growing crops. The chequer-board of the modern British countryside, with its hedges, fences, and walls, is a product of long-continued enclosure. It is a handicap to the ploughman, but it has its advantages to the stockman, for it enables him to manage both stock and grazing more efficiently. The open fields of the Middle Ages and the enclosed fields of to-day are, in fact, indicative of largely arable and largely pastoral types of farming respectively.

III

THE IMPROVING MOVEMENT IN SCOTLAND

The Improving Movement in Scotland came relatively late. In the seventeenth and eighteenth centuries there was a general air of agricultural backwardness. Celia Fiennes crossed the Border beyond Carlisle at the end of the seventeenth century, but she was glad to return:[1] she had the prejudices of the Southern English of the time. But Defoe was also struck by agricultural backwardness. Writing of the Lothians, one of the best cultivated parts of Scotland, he said, 'thus a good Soil is impoverish'd for want of Husbandry', and he specified the improvements required as enclosed pastures, better winter feeding of cattle and sheep-folding in order to accumulate dung, and fallowing to permit the cleaning of the land.[2] Accustomed to the improved arable methods of the English Plain, he had put his finger on the weaknesses of Scottish arable practice. Defoe visited Scotland in the 'twenties of the eighteenth century and the Improving Movement did not substantially take shape, as Dr. Hamilton shows, until after the middle of the century.[3]

[1] C. Fiennes: *Through England on a Side Saddle in the Time of William and Mary* (ed. of 1888), pp. 170–1.

[2] D. Defoe, *op. cit.*, pp. 699–700.

[3] H. Hamilton: *The Industrial Revolution in Scotland* (1932), p. 36.

By the time of the county reports at the end of the century, Scottish farming was a varied pattern of old and new. Writing in 1813, Sir John Sinclair remarked on the improvement in the last forty-four years.[1]

The process of change was, in general terms, similar to the process of change in South Britain, the specialisation of production and the disappearance of common-field cultivation; and the agents of change were similar also, improved methods of tillage and the introduction of roots and seed grasses. There were legal and tenurial differences, of course, owing to the different character of Scots law.

Even before the middle of the eighteenth century there was a not inconsiderable regional specialisation of agricultural production. East Lothian had a substantial corn surplus, wheat being sent to Portugal and Spain, oats to the Western Highlands and Ireland. This, according to the East Lothian reporter, was between 1720 and 1740.[2] Defoe reported a surplus of corn from the Carse of Gowrie and the Vale of Strathmore and an export from Dundee to England and Holland;[3] and he reported also an export from Aberdeen, 'but they generally bring it from the Firth of Murray or Cromarty, the Corn coming from about Inverness, where they have great Quantities'.[4] It will be noticed that these (East Lothian, Carse of Gowrie, Moray Lowlands) are all dry eastern districts of fertile soil and that export was not only to other parts of Britain, but also to continental Europe. Wheat was grown in all these eastern districts, indeed possibly as far north as Caithness.[5] On the other hand, much of the west of Scotland was a stock rather than a corn country. Even the lowland of Ayr, which Defoe described as 'rich and fertile', and which, after travelling through Galloway, reminded him of England again,[6] imported corn before 1750 across country from the Lothians.[7] Galloway was essentially a stock district,

[1] J. Sinclair: *An Account of the Systems of Husbandry adopted in . . . Scotland* (1813), vol. 2, p. 72.

[2] G. Buchan-Hepburn: *General View . . . East Lothian* (1794).

[3] D. Defoe, *op. cit.*, p. 806.

[4] D. Defoe, *op. cit.*, p. 812.

[5] D. Defoe's reference to Caithness—'Very good Bread, as well Oat Bread as Wheat'—does not necessarily imply that wheat was grown there, for it may have been imported (D. Defoe, *op. cit.*, p. 825).

[6] D. Defoe, *op. cit.*, pp. 740–1.

[7] W. Aiton, *General View . . . Ayr* (1811), p. 533.

rents were paid in stock and beasts were sent into England in great numbers. A Cheshire man travelling in Galloway in 1635 noted the absence of wheaten bread.[1] The Western and Central Highlands, as may be readily expected, were not self-supporting in corn except in years of good harvest,[2] and they also sent droves of cattle into England for fattening. Like Wales, Scotland contributed cattle to the English grazier and feeder.

The county reports at the end of the eighteenth century permit, as in England, the reconstruction of the agricultural geography of the time. There is additional evidence for Scotland in the *First Statistical Account*, published contemporaneously.[3] The most improved districts were East Lothian and Berwick;[4] they were the districts most closely in touch with England and they had the dry climate and (in part) the light fertile soil suitable for the New Husbandry. The effect of both space-relations and of local physical environment is clear. They both used Small's plough, an improvement, its users claimed, on the Rotherham plough.[5] This needed only two horses and one ploughman in place of the four horses or eight oxen with a driver as well as a ploughman which the old Scots plough required.[6] Small's plough was passing into general use throughout the Central Lowlands of Scotland by the end of the century, but the old Scots plough was still common in South Perth[7] and in Aberdeen.[8] Improved forms of plough had been introduced also into the lands around Moray Firth,[9] which in Defoe's time was an outlier of good cultivation. It is an outlier too of dry climate and mild weather. Clover and rye grass had been introduced into East Lothian in the 'twenties, turnips some twenty years later, and the Norfolk system about 1750. Both

[1] *North Country Diaries* (Surtees Society), Second Series, Vol. 124 (1915), p. 45.

[2] I. F. Grant: 'Some Accounts of Individual Highland Sporting Estates', *Economic History*, No. 3 (1928), p. 406.

[3] *The Statistical Account of Scotland*, Vols. 1–21 (1791–99).

[4] Hamilton, *op. cit.*, p. 46.

[5] In the districts using improved ploughs Tull's principles of drilling and horse-hoeing were also employed.

[6] The Scots plough was sometimes used for working strong land, even in districts using a lighter plough for other purposes (B. Johnston: *General View* . . . *Dumfries* (1794), p. 41).

[7] J. Robertson: *General View* . . . *Southern Districts of Perthshire* (1794).

[8] J. Anderson: *General View* . . . *Aberdeen* (1794).

[9] J. Donaldson: *General View* . . . *Elgin* (1794).

the clover and the turnip husbandry appear to have been adopted in Berwick about or just before 1750. Once proved successful, these new crops spread rapidly throughout the entire eastern side of Scotland.[1] In the west they were grown in Dumfries,[2] but in Ayr turnips were grown only in gardens in 1773, though rye grass and clover were frequently sown preparatory to a ley,[3] and they were almost unknown in Argyll and the Central Highlands at the end of the century.[4] The potato had, however, come into general cultivation in both western and eastern districts, in both highland and lowland. In many cases it had been introduced in a famine year and had proved so successful that it had become a staple article of diet. 'This valuable exotic' was recognised to be useful in improving moss soils and was usually cultivated in a rotation as a fallow crop, though it was sometimes grown year after year in the same ground.[5] In eastern districts potatoes were planted alongside turnips and in the Carse of Gowrie replaced turnips in the fallow break.[6] It was cultivated much more generally than in England.

Those districts which practised the turnip and clover husbandry rarely, however, followed the Norfolk rotation. Only on the dry 'turnip and barley' soils of the Merse of Berwick[7] was it common, and it was occasionally encountered in East Lothian. In the Merse of Berwick the grain sown after clover was usually oats rather than wheat. When wheat was grown it was sometimes spring sown. These conditions reflect the cooler summers of North Britain. A common rotation on the dry coastal soils of East Lothian, where seaweed could be used for manure, was turnips–barley–clover (two years)–oats–pease or beans–wheat. But one reporter after another in these eastern districts made the statement that no regular system of rotation was followed. Perhaps there can be detected

---

[1] North of the Highland line improvement was far from complete at the end of the eighteenth century. In the parish of Cabrach in Banff rye grass was sown only in yards (*First Statistical Account*, Vol. 7, p. 362).

[2] H. Hamilton, *op. cit.*, p. 47.

[3] *First Statistical Account*, Vol. 7, pp. 30 and 355 (Ayr).

[4] W. Marshall: *General View . . . Central Highlands* (1794).

[5] D. Ure: *General View . . . Dumbarton* (1794), pp. 52–3.

[6] J. Donaldson: *General View . . . Carse of Gowrie* (1794), p. 15.

[7] A. Lowe: *General View . . . Berwick* (1794), p. 28.

in this the persistence of the flexibility which was a mark of the old Scottish system. A rotation rigidly followed was more common of England, whose medieval agriculture had been dominated (in the midland belt) by the rigid two- and three-field system.

The alternation of white and green crop was not everywhere the rule. On heavy soils unsuited to turnips the old exhaustive rotation of fallow–wheat–pease–barley–oats was still to be found, but clover was in many cases being intercalated between the barley and oats. In Clydesdale, a moist western district, the clays were usually in convertible husbandry, an arable shift similar to the above, followed by a long ley.[1] The long ley was common also in western England. But Sir John Sinclair recognised that 'in soft soils and moist climates . . . the dairy ought to be the principal object of the farmer'.[2] In many districts the infield-outfield system still persisted. It is described in the reports on East Lothian, the Carse of Gowrie, and Elgin as the old system which had gradually fallen into disuse since the middle of the eighteenth century. In the form of continuous cropping for corn, followed by years of recovery under self-sown grass, it was to be found in Tweeddale and Galloway. But in the Central and Western Highlands the infield-outfield system persisted almost unmodified.[3] Marshall estimated that on the sides of Loch Tay the 'nominal farms', that is, the farms of joint-tenants, had each 20 acres infield, 15 acres outfield, 10 acres meadow, 35 acres green pasture, and, beyond the head dyke marking the limit of the 'improved' land, 250 acres of muir. It was the Highlands that were most backward in methods of land utilisation.

The increased winter food provided by turnips, seed grasses, and, to a smaller extent, by potatoes, effected in Scotland, as in England, a revolution in stock husbandry.[4] Winter food had been scarcer, so writers seem agreed, than in England, and it

---

[1] J. Naesmith: *General View . . . Clydesdale* (1798), p. 69.

[2] J. Sinclair, *op. cit.*, Vol. 2, p. 119. There was a good deal of dairying near Glasgow—milk selling within two miles, butter making over two miles, and cheese making over ten miles distant (Vol. 1, pp. 116–17).

[3] J. Smith: *General View . . . Argyll* (1798), p. 30; J. Robertson, *op. cit.*, p. 24; W. Marshall: *General View . . . Central Highlands*, pp. 30–1.

[4] In Berwickshire good grass would now support an ox or five adult Leicester sheep per acre and ordinary grass a bullock or four and a half shearing Leicesters per one and a half acres (J. Sinclair, *op. cit.*, Vol. 1, pp. 110–12).

was not uncommon for one-fifth of the young stock to die during the winter and for stock to be lifted or carried in the spring, so weak had they become.[1] Marshall describes the paring of land 'to the quick' in the efforts to gather wisps of hay from roadsides, from wood bottoms, and from rushy patches in the pastures which stock would not touch in summer when better herbage was available. Straw was not infrequently more nutritious. The large-scale export of cattle in the eighteenth century, from the Highlands and Galloway particularly, but from the far corners of the Hebrides and Caithness as well, was in autumn at the end of the grass season. With free access to the English market after the Union, export of cattle to England grew in volume as the population of England grew, but especially as the New Husbandry with its demand for cattle for winter feeding gradually spread over the light soils of East England. At the end of the century Sir John Sinclair estimated the annual export to England at 100,000 head. Both the Galloway and the West Highland Kyloe were good feeding animals. They were, however, small, Galloways in Ayrshire weighing when fat 18–27 stone only.[2] The Scottish Improving Movement, with its roots and hay, ultimately decreased this export of lean stores, but not until the first half of the nineteenth century. By the time of the *New Statistical Account* (*c.* 1840) large numbers of cattle were being fattened on turnips and clover within Scotland and exported by steamship coastwise as fat beasts. The steamship, with its short journeys of a day or two, replaced the long months along the drove road when stock inevitably lost condition. It was not until the nineteenth century that the black polled Aberdeen-Angus beef breed took shape in its present-day form,[3] though the Galloway and the West Highland Kyloe were in existence in the eighteenth century.

By the end of the eighteenth century there had begun the great transformation in the land utilisation of the Highlands whereby the cultivation of corn and the rearing of cattle came to be replaced by the keeping of sheep for wool and mutton. The Highlands had been relatively highly populated, 'over-

[1] H. Hamilton, *op. cit.*, p. 21.

[3] These would presumably be carcase weights (*First Statistical Account*, Vol. 1,) p. 107).

[4] Wallace: *Farm Live Stock of Great Britain* (1923), pp. 161–4.

stocked with inhabitants', in Marshall's opinion,[1] owing to the clan system and its demand for men to bear arms. As much corn for local consumption was grown as possible by the infield-outfield system, cattle were bred, and sheep were kept mainly for milk. Highland cattle do not yield much milk and, although for suckling only one calf was allowed to two cows, little was available for cheese or butter.[2] It was the custom to transfer stock to the summer shielings for six to seven weeks in order to save the pasture near the homestead as much as possible. The practice had been abandoned within living memory around Loch Tay, but it was still followed in Glen Garry.[3] The shielings have continued to be used in the Hebrides almost to our own day. The milked sheep were being replaced by the Blackface, a North Pennine and South Upland stock, more capable of grazing on the bleak mountain pastures. The milked sheep had always remained near the homestead. First, the southern fringes of the Highlands were affected, in Dumbarton and Perth, then Argyll and Inverness, and before the end of the century Cromarty and Sutherland. The Cheviot had spread with the Blackface, but on the less bleak and more grassy slopes. These sheep were grazed on the mountain in summer and were wintered in the straths and glens. Their summer grazing displaced cattle and their wintering displaced much arable cultivation. Although the depopulation of the Highlands had begun before sheep-farming had become at all extensive,[4] sheep greatly accelerated the movement. The clearances for deer forests and grouse moors did not come until later in the nineteenth century. Some of the displaced population was settled in crofter communities, but most went to the Lowlands or overseas.

The Southern Uplands had become almost entirely a sheep district. The county of Selkirk had only three or four farms wholly in arable at the end of the eighteenth century, and two dozen which might be described as semi-arable sheep farms. Of the rest some grew just sufficient oats for the household and the horses, but others grew no corn whatever. The Blackface

---

[1] W. Marshall: *General View . . . Central Highlands*, p. 21.

[2] W. Marshall: *General View . . . Central Highlands*, p. 45.

[3] W. Marshall: *General View . . . Central Highlands*, pp. 45-6.

[4] H. Hamilton, *op. cit.*, p. 68-9; I. F. Grant: *Economic History*, No. 3 (1928), p. 407.

was here confined to the bleaker uplands, the rest being grazed by a white-faced cross-bred (Blackface ewes × Cheviot tups). The flock was kept on the uplands except in bad weather, and was stocked in summer at the rate of one to two sheep per acre. The Southern Uplands provided fairly good grass pasture and even the rocky Highlands yielded better summer grazing than Blackamore in North-east Yorkshire, in Marshall's opinion. The Peebles reporter gave particulars of three type farms in Tweeddale as an example of variations in seeding and yield at different altitudes. From these particulars Table III has been constructed. Farm A was a valley farm, farm B on the lower slopes, and farm C on the upper slopes. Wheat and barley were grown only on the lower and better ground and bere only on the upland farms. Yields gradually decreased, when reckoned as a return on seeding, with elevation.

TABLE III

CROP YIELDS AND SEEDING PER ACRE IN TWEEDDALE, 1794

SEEDING AND YIELD IN BOLLS

| | Farm A | | Farm B | | Farm C | |
	Sown	Yield	Sown	Yield	Sown	Yield
Wheat	10	90	—	—	—	—
Barley	22	210	—	—	—	—
Bere	—	—	7½	68	5	40
Oats	90	540	40	200	32	130
Potatoes	6	150	4	60	2	20

Source: T. Johnston, General View ... Tweeddale (1794).

The Improving Movement in Scotland, like the New Husbandry in England, was accompanied by, if it did not cause, the disappearance of cultivation in common. The open unfenced landscape cultivated in run-rig was replaced by the rectangular enclosures of the new system.[1] It often involved a quite considerable replanning of the settlement sites, the field pattern and the roads, some examples of which have been worked out by Dr. Geddes.[2] In the Highlands the only new

[1] At the time of the First Statistical Account, the parish of Linton in the Southern Uplands had, according to the terms used by the minister reporting on it, its croftlands 'enclosed' and its outfield 'uninclosed' (Vol. 1, p. 140). The croftland was under continuous cultivation: the outfield under occasional.

[2] A. Geddes: 'The Changing Landscape of the Lothians, 1600–1800', Scottish Geographical Magazine, Vol. 54 (1938).

fences were the straight lines up the mountain-sides. The small size of the agrarian unit, the hamlet rather than the village, presumably facilitated agreement amongst its members and the flexibility of the field systems, as in the early enclosed parts of England, presumably facilitated the replanning of cultivation. Every reporter who discussed the point was agreed that enclosure increased the value of the land, the amount of the increase varying, as in England, from one-third to double the previous figure.

IV

THE NINETEENTH CENTURY

The replacement of the old by the new agriculture was not by any means complete by the beginning of the nineteenth century, but by this time the new order was dominant and the old recessive. The new order had certain economic implications which it is necessary to notice. The full delineation of these is the province of the economist, but as they reacted on geographical distributions they are germane to the present treatment. The economic environment, at all stages in the evolution of the economic geography of Britain, had differential reactions on different regions of the country.

In the first place, farming for a market implied dependence on the price fluctuations of the market. As long as subsistence farming was practised and the produce of the land consumed on the farm, price fluctuations had only a limited significance. Under the new order, high prices for a particular commodity implied an extension of the area producing that commodity into lands normally marginal.[1] Conversely, low prices meant a contraction of the area of production into those regions where the optimum *economic* conditions for the production of that commodity obtained. The districts presenting optimum economic conditions were not necessarily those with the highest yields per acre (in the case of arable crops), but those with the maximum return for effort expended. Light soils often did not produce as heavy crops of wheat per acre as stiff clays in a

[1] For an application of this principle to world wheat production, see R. O. Buchanan: 'Some Features of World Wheat Production', *Scottish Geographical Magazine*, Vol. 52 (1936).

favourable year, but they were much easier and less expensive to work and the financial return, balancing expenses and returns, was greater. Medieval farming, prodigal of labour, grew its wheat mainly on stiff soils which gave the highest yields under medieval methods, even though they were laborious to work. The revolution in the distribution of British arable farming, from stiff to light soils, has already been noticed as in progress by the end of the eighteenth century. It was to become much more pronounced, as will appear, during the course of the nineteenth century.

In the second place, the price fluctuations of the market were no longer determined simply by British conditions alone, by the relation between supply and demand within Britain, by good and bad harvests in the case of crops and arable-fed stock or by abundance and scarcity of grass in the case of grass-fed stock. William Cobbett insisted that good and bad harvests in Britain had ceased by the time of the *Rural Rides* to be the sole factor determining the price of corn. The effect of the season continued to operate, but British wheat production had ceased to be sufficient, except after an exceptionally good harvest, for the consumption needs of the country.[1] As the manufacturing population of Britain grew and as the gap between corn production and corn consumption widened, import increased. Costs of production and variations in harvest in the remote corners of the world began to effect corn prices and the acreage under crop in Britain at home.

In the third place, exposure to market conditions and later to 'the world price' required great elasticity of farming practice and great mobility of labour. The conservatism and rigidity of medieval farming and the fixity of the medieval population, though neither were complete, were unsuited to the new conditions. Elasticity of farming was at times an essential condition of economic survival. Enclosure greatly increased the mobility of labour, though in the South of England its effects in this respect were masked for a time by the Speenhamland policy.[2] On enclosure, many small freeholders sold their holdings as, deprived of common rights, their few arable acres ceased to be

[1] *Minutes of Evidence*, Select Committee on Agriculture, 1833. Evidence of W. Jacob, D. Hodgson, T. Oliver, and J. Sanders.

[2] J. H. Clapham: *An Economic History of Modern Britain: The Early Railway Age* (1926), p. 131.

an economic unit under methods of capitalistic farming. The mere expense of hedging was sometimes beyond their pockets. Many copyholders ceased to farm.[1] The cottagers with an acre or less filched from the waste, who had no legal title to any land and who were admitted to the commons on sufferance and not by right, frequently became landless, though in some enclosure awards they were allotted substantial gardens and occasionally small commons were preserved for their sole use. Many of the smaller cultivators and all the cottagers thus became landless labourers dependent entirely on wage labour on farmers who, in their turn, had become dependent largely on price fluctuations. When prices fell, labourers fell out of employment and, as they had no land to tie them to any particular village, they were free to migrate elsewhere, except when tied by poor law regulations.

As the price of corn affected arable farming so profoundly, it is necessary to analyse briefly the course of corn prices during the nineteenth century as a preliminary to an examination of their effects on the geographical distribution of arable farming within Britain. Of the four grains, wheat was the most involved in commercial farming and most affected by price fluctuations. Rye had become less and less important.[2] Oats was a staple bread corn in the North of England and in Scotland, witness Dr. Johnson's famous definition of oats as food for men in Scotland but for horses in England. The substitution of horses for oxen in the eighteenth century had greatly increased the demand for oats, but oats did not enter largely into trade. The better qualities of barley were grown for malt and the rest fed to stock.[3] The average annual price of wheat per imperial quarter in Britain from 1771 to 1939 is set out in Figure 2. Certain phases are easily discernible.

(a) Before the Revolutionary Wars prices were arranged in cyclical fluctuations with minima of 35–40s. and maxima of 54–55s. per quarter, an average of 47s.

[1] The yearly tenants had little claim on the land and the holders of lease or life interests could be bought out.

[2] A witness before the Select Committee of 1833 stated that a little rye was consumed as bread corn in North-east Yorkshire and in North Wales, but not apparently to his knowledge elsehwere. Q. 85.

[3] The consumption of barley for bread was also rapidly on the decline. Select Committee of 1833. Q. 88 and 3431.

(*b*) During the Revolutionary and Napoleonic Wars the price of wheat rose to very high levels, to 119s. in 1801 and to 126s. in 1812. It was still subject to fluctuations, but these had become irregular.

(*c*) After 1820 and until the end of the 'fifties, prices fell to more normal levels, an average of 56s. per quarter, which was higher than the pre-war average. It fluctuated between minima of 40–50s. and maxima of 68–75s., exhibiting the same regularity of arrangement as in the pre-war period.

(*d*) In the 'sixties and 'seventies the amplitude of fluctuation was greatly reduced. Minima remained at similar levels as in period (*c*), but maxima did not rise beyond 64s. per quarter. The average for the period was 51s.

(*e*) After the 'seventies prices fell steadily, with only a slight recovery in 1891, to a minimum of 23s. per quarter in 1894–95. From this trough the price of wheat gradually recovered, passing 30s. in 1907 and remaining above this level until the outbreak of the war of 1914–18. The cyclical fluctuation, so marked in earlier periods, had been damped down and had practically disappeared.

It was possible during the eighteenth century for Britain to produce all the corn required for home consumption, except in years of bad harvest. Increase in production was proceeding both by the adoption of improved methods of farming and by the bringing of new land into cultivation. Fluctuations in price were determined by harvest conditions within Britain. Improvement in farming method and reclamation of down and moor were most active during the wars when prices were especially high and when obviously marginal land was sown— chalk down with only a few inches of soil and Pennine moor at an altitudinal limit for the ripening of corn.

After the wars, it was gradually realized that conditions were changing. The gap between consumption and production was widening, and it was becoming clear that additional supplies would be forthcoming from abroad, not only from Europe, but also from overseas, particularly North America. There was no fear that the population of the country would starve. The anti-Corn Law League, representing the manufacturers, began its agitation for free trade in corn in order to assist the development of a reciprocal trade of British manufacturers for overseas wheat and in order to lower the cost of living for the workers in their employ.[1] Repeal was not supported by the manufacturers alone, for many held that the admission of foreign corn would reduce the fluctuation of corn prices incident upon good and bad harvests.[2] William Cobbett, who was no friend of the manufacturers, opposed the corn laws on the grounds that they 'could do us no good'. Nevertheless, the repeal of the corn laws did represent the victory of the manufacturing over the

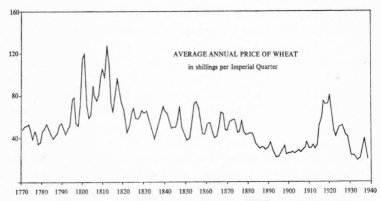

AVERAGE ANNUAL PRICE OF WHEAT
in shillings per Imperial Quarter

Figure 2. Average Annual Price of Wheat, 1771–1939
In shillings per Imperial Quarter

agricultural interests. The Select Committee of 1833 was concerned about the relative proportions of the agricultural and industrial elements in the English population, and it was reported in evidence that even in 1811 the 'extraordinary and unexpected' conclusion was that of the total number of families 34·7 per cent. were employed in agriculture and 45·9 per cent. in trade and manufacture.[3] Britain was becoming primarily

[1] D. G. Barnes: *A History of the English Corn Laws from 1660 to 1846* (1930), p. 288.

[2] The burden of many of the questions asked of witnesses appearing before one Select Committee after another was the price at which corn-growing could be profitably carried on. One witness before the Select Committee of 1833 was asked the question, 'What would be the price of corn . . . supposing the trade in corn were entirely free?' The reply was 38–40s. per quarter (Q. 3205–8). With wheat at 56s. per quarter, a Wiltshire witness held that the minimum yield per acre to pay expenses, exclusive of rent, would need to be 24 bushels on stiff and 16 bushels on light soils (Q. 1221–3). This was a very significant statement.

[3] *Report*, Select Committee of 1833, p. 7.

industrial and its economic policy was coming to be modelled on that basis. The repeal of the corn laws had for a time the effects that Cobden and Peel hoped. The average price fell from 56s. in period (c) to 51s. in period (d) and the amplitude of fluctuation was damped down considerably. These were not years of depression. Lawes and Gilbert imply that the 'sixties were years of 'great prosperity'.[1] But imports were increasing and in 1872–73 for the first time the net imports of wheat exceeded home production and, save for the good harvest

TABLE IV

ACREAGE, PRODUCTION AND IMPORT OF WHEAT IN THE
UNITED KINGDOM, 1852–78

	Acreage	Yield (bushels) per acre)	Home Production (quarters)	Net Import (quarters)
1852–59	4,092,160	28	14,310,779	4,652,784
1860–67	3,753,011	28⅜	13,309,247	8,097,761
1868–75	3,792,636	26⅝	12,699,155	10,745,568
1876–78	3,266,335	27¼	11,116,910	13,700,386

Source: From J. B. Lawes and J. H. Gilbert: 'On the Home Produce, Imports, Consumption and Price of Wheat, 1852–53 to 1879–80', Journal Royal Agricultural Society, Second Series, Vol. 16 (1880), Table V. The figures are annual averages.

season of 1874–75, they continued to do so from that time onwards.[2] These figures, calculated by Lawes and Gilbert, are set out in summary form in Table IV. The acreage began to contract in the 'sixties, according to this table, before the catastrophic fall in prices began, but the acreage figures for England prior to 1866 (and for some of these years for Scotland) are estimates. The increased import was not from Europe, but from North America, and from quite a different type of farming. The virgin lands of the Middle West could, worked by family labour, produce wheat cheaper than the English farm. Production per acre may not have been high, but costs of production were low. In the early part of the nineteenth century shipments from North America had been mainly of

[1] J. B. Lawes and J. H. Gilbert: 'Our Climate and our Wheat Crops', Journal Royal Agricultural Society, Second Series, Vol. 16 (1880), p. 173.

[2] J. B. Lawes and J. H. Gilbert: 'On the Home Produce, Imports, Consumption, and Price of Wheat, 1852–53 to 1879–80', Journal Royal Agricultural Society, Second Series, Vol. 16 (1880), Table V.

flour, for cost of transport by land in the pre-railway age and by sea in sailing vessels was relatively high. But the development of the steamship and railway greatly reduced transport costs and raw wheat could enter the British market freely and cheaply.[1] The price of wheat fell catastrophically and until the war of 1914–18 remained at levels lower than the average for the whole of the eighteenth century. Although other corn crops were involved in this fall of prices, their price did not collapse to the same extent. The price of oats during the 'nineties and first decade of the twentieth century did not fall below the level of the 1770–90 period. The Select Committee of 1833 was set up specifically to inquire into agricultural distress. Some whole districts, it discovered, had fallen out of cultivation altogether and elsewhere the general standard of farming had deteriorated. This was not true of all arable farming, however. There was a striking contrast between light soils, where the standard was maintained, and heavy clays, where deterioration was universal. The contrast had been heightened by a series of wet seasons immediately prior to 1833, when the crops on the wet retentive land had suffered badly, but the contrast was more deep-rooted than that. It has been pointed out that at the end of the eighteenth century the improved system of the New Husbandry had been adopted extensively on light soils within the English Plain and that the heavy soils, to which the turnip husbandry was unsuited, were not cultivated to the same extent on the new principles, and that many retained, even when enclosed, the old medieval rotation. The contrast at the end of the eighteenth century was due chiefly to the fact that the new arable technique was a light-land technique. But in the nineteenth century an additional differential began to emerge. By 1833 it had become clear that light soils were cheaper and heavy soils more expensive to till. Relative expense of cultivation was becoming an important factor in proportion as commercial farming became dominant. A heavy soil was more expensive to work as it often required double the number of horses in a plough-team and as it needed elaborate draining which involved not only capital expenditure in laying the

[1] In 1878 J. Caird calculated that 'the cost of transporting a quantity equal to the produce of an acre in England is seldom less than 40 sh., . . . an advantage equal to the present average rent' (General View of British Agriculture', *Journal Royal Agricultural Society*, Second Series, Vol. 14 (1878), p. 280).

drains, but also recurrent expenditure in scouring the ditches.[1]
Its yield was also more uncertain.[2] The loss of crop on clay in a
wet season owing to defective drainage was placed as high as
4–12 bushels per acre in the North Riding, a very substantial
proportion of the total crop.[3] Every witness was of the opinion
that the clays would go out of cultivation first, and in fact the
concentration of the arable on the light soils was progressive
during the whole of the nineteenth century. A member of the
Committee, having in mind the concentration of medieval wheat
farming on clay and the suitability of wheat to a stiff soil, asked
the significant question, 'Do not we rely for our supply of wheat
mainly on these clay soils?' He received the equally significant
reply, 'No; the supply of wheat for the last thirty years has been
very much increased from the sand lands, and from the strong
loam.'[4] In the west deterioration was not noticeable. In some
districts, South Salop[6] and Cornwall,[5] progress was even
reported, but it is clear that this progress represented a lag in
improvement. The principles of the New Husbandry were still
in process of adoption. But even here some of the heavy land
was ceasing to be arable.[7] These western districts, when in
arable, did not rely on wheat to the same extent as the arable
districts of the east.

Within a few years of the repeal of the corn laws, there
appeared a first-hand account of English agriculture by James
Caird.[8] Caird's survey has a distinctly modern flavour. In the
course of his tours he came across an instance of common field
in Berkshire. He placed it in inverted commas and considered
it necessary to explain to his readers what a common field was,

---

[1] As indicative of the higher costs of working, a Wiltshire witness held that, in
order to meet expenses (exclusive of rent) the heavy land must yield 24 bushels
of wheat per acre as compared with 16 bushels on the light land. The implication
was that heavy soils cost half as much again to work as light soils (Q. 1221–3).
There was much poor clay that yielded only 16 bushels of wheat per acre. In
Clun Forest there was poor clay yielding only 9 bushels per acre (Q. 606).

[2] Q. 228 and Q. 1046.

[3] Q. 2398.

[4] Q. 1047.

[5] Q. 375–8.

[6] Q. 3361.

[7] Q. 478.

[8] J. Caird: *English Agriculture in 1850–51* (1852). See also L. de Lavergne: *The
Rural Economy of England, Scotland, and Ireland* (1885), a more general account of
the British Isles based to a less extent on first-hand knowledge.

such an historical curiosity had common-field cultivation become.[1] In reporting methods of crop cultivation, he added a specification of the artificial fertilisers employed[2] and discussed their relative merits for different crops and under different conditions of soil and climate.[3] Similarly, in reporting stock rations, Caird frequently registered the feeding of oil-cake in winter to fattening beasts and to dairy cows at the rate of 3–4 lbs. per head per day. This use of artificial fertilisers for crops and of concentrated foods for stock freed the farmer from the necessity of adhering rigidly to the standard rotations laid down some generations previously.

It is clear from Caird's regional survey that in many districts there was an approximation to modern forms of land utilisation. The more general points only will be considered here, and only in so far as they bear on the evolution of the agricultural geography. Caird was fully aware of the changing agricultural distributions of his day and, in particular, of the changing character of clay-land farming from arable to grass and of the increasing tendency for market gardening and milk production to develop on suitable soils near the large centres of consumption, the market gardening on sand and the dairying on clay. He was not only aware of these changes, but he specifically encouraged them in certain cases as more profitable uses of the land.

Most of the bad arable management was in clay districts. Old fashioned rotations of fallow–wheat–beans or fallow–wheat–oats were still encountered and Caird asserts that in some of these cases the yield per acre was actually declining.[4] The Oxford Clay was described to Caird as 'too strong for cultivation, and too weak to carry crops'.[5] Of the South Essex Clay, he writes, 'that great exertions are necessary to render its

---

[1] J. Caird: *English Agriculture in 1850–51*, p. 115.

[2] The early work at Rothamsted was largely concerned with manures and fertilisers. Lawes himself was a manufacturer of superphosphates. He entered into the occupation of Rothamsted in 1834.

[3] In this railway age, when the railway was gradually spreading its tentacles over the countryside, some farmers experimented with a light portable tramway for carting turnips in order to prevent poaching of the land by horses, in much the same way as in the present motor age farmers have fitted pneumatic tyres to their farm carts.

[4] J. Caird: *English Agriculture in 1850–51*, p. 340.

[5] J. Caird: *English Agriculture in 1850–51*, p. 113.

cultivation profitable',[1] and he advises the Essex clayland farmer, within easy rail distance of London, to supply London with milk. He does not suggest grass dairying, however, in this instance, but house-feeding on clover and tares in summer, mangolds and cabbage in winter.[2] In reference to the stiff Lias Clay in Warwickshire, which was rented as low as 15s. per acre while sandy loams were at 25–45s., Caird makes the comment that the stiff soils were even then rented too high.[3] The clay had fallen into disrepute as an arable soil. At the end of the eighteenth century the clay was not adapted to the turnip husbandry, but in 1850 mangolds were being grown on many relatively heavy soils. The expense of working them rather than the lack of a suitable improved rotation had now become the chief deterrent to their treatment as arable.

The second change in progress which Caird noticed was the growth near the large towns of market gardening and of dairying for the sale of liquid milk. There had been market gardening on the outskirts of London since the seventeenth century, fostered by, as Cobbett put it, 'the demand for crude vegetables, and repayment in manure'.[4] But elsewhere it was relatively new. By the side of the Bridgewater Canal at its Manchester end and on sandy soils in North Wirral, near Birkenhead,[5] an early and a main crop of potatoes were lifted from the sand

---

[1] J. Caird: *English Agriculture in 1850–51*, p. 134.

[2] J. Caird: *English Agriculture in 1850–51*, p. 142.

[3] J. Caird: *English Agriculture in 1850–51*, pp. 221–2. Another example of the same difference is furnished by the following table:

Region	Type of soil	Arable acreage	Costs per acre		Yield per acre (bushels)		
			Rent, taxes, etc.	Working expenses	Wheat	Oats	Barley
			s. d.	s. d.			
Howdenshire	Poor clay	149	19 3	47 6	20	28	24
Holderness	Good clay	326	31 11	49 5	33	50	—
York Wolds	Chalk	618	31 10	51 5	30	48	35
Lincs Wolds	Chalk	1,541	33 10	62 2	33	61	42

The table has been constructed from particulars of individual farms collected by J. Caird (p. 320). The poor clay of Howdenshire (within the East Riding but west of chalk scarp) had working expenses almost as high as the other soils, but a yield very much lower.

[4] W. Cobbett, *op. cit.*, Vol. 1, p. 57.

[5] This dated back to the end of the eighteenth century.

land and sometimes a winter crop of cabbages as well. This heavy cropping necessitated heavy manuring.[1] The sandy soils along the Fylde coast were also potato lands and at least one Fylde farmer fattened lambs for sale to the coastal villages 'during the sea-bathing season'.[2] Caird advised similar potato cultivation on the sands of South Hampshire, the towns of which were then being supplied from France.[3] By 1850 dairying was ceasing to mean solely the making of butter and cheese, for liquid milk was being sold in increasing quantities at 2d. per quart. Lavergne's opinion was that 'the consumption of milk under every form is enormous among the English',[4] and the price of liquid milk in England was twice what it was in France, indicative, so Lavergne thought, of a greater demand. Caird reprimanded the grass farmers near the rising towns of Warwickshire for keeping only young stock 'just as if such a market for dairy produce had been 100 miles distant' instead of at their own doors.[5] Cow-keeping within the towns was then the main source of milk supply for the West Midland industrial population, and such milk sold at 3d. per quart, indicative, no doubt, of the expensiveness of this form of production.[6] Urban cow-keeping has since declined greatly with the development of the liquid milk market and is now found only under special circumstances as in Liverpool. In the upland parts of eastern Lancashire and the West Riding, where the greater part of the land, always too cold and wet for successful corn-growing, was in grass, milk for urban consumption was already the chief object of agricultural production.

In 1866, largely as the result of Caird's advocacy, the first agricultural returns for England were collected. It took some years for the particulars required to be uniformly understood by all those making returns, but by 1870 many of these difficulties had disappeared.[7]

The distinction between arable and grass districts in England

---

[1] J. Caird: *English Agriculture in 1850–51*, pp. 261–2.

[2] J. Caird: *English Agriculture in 1850–51*, p. 281.

[3] J. Caird: *English Agriculture in 1850–51*, p. 94.

[4] L. de Lavergne, *op. cit.*, p. 34.

[5] J. Caird: *English Agriculture in 1850–51*, p. 227.

[6] J. Caird: *English Agriculture in 1850–51*, p. 228.

[7] In 1866, for example, permanent pasture was described as exclusive of hill pastures. Many occupiers excluded their downland accordingly. The description

and Wales or, to adopt the nomenclature of the reports on the returns for 1869–70, between corn and grazing counties, was clearly marked. In 1850–51 Caird had earlier noted the same distinction. Both Caird and the reports attempted to draw a line between them, but their lines do not everywhere coincide. They are both given in Figure 3. It was indeed impossible to draw such a line, for some of the arable counties contained grass districts and some of the grass counties arable districts, such as South-west Lancashire. The East Riding, Lincoln,

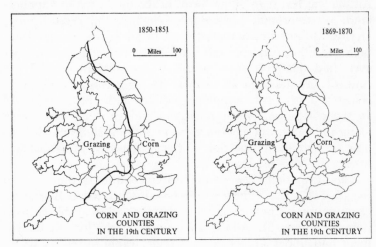

Figure 3A   Figure 3B

Corn and Grazing Counties in England and Wales in the Nineteenth Century

A is according to J. Caird: *English Agriculture in 1850–51* (1852), and B according to the *Agricultural Returns* for 1869–70. In each map the *corn* counties lie to the east and the *grazing* counties to the west of the thick line.

Norfolk, Suffolk, Essex, Huntingdon, Cambridge, Hertford, Bedford, and Berkshire, were arable counties wherever the line was drawn; they had over 70 per cent. of their total cultivated land in arable and most of them over 60 per cent. of their total area.[1] To the west of these, grass and arable districts inter-

---

was altered the following year to permanent pasture exclusive of heath or mountain land. In the early years, to give another example, some of the returns of fallow included waste and not simply bare fallow in rotation, as was intended.

[1] For the percentages, see Appendix and Figure 4.

G

digitated—grass on the deep clays of the Oxford (in their southern drift-free parts) and Lias Clay Vales, arable on the chalk and Jurassic uplands—and, as some of these counties consisted almost equally of both types of land, they could with equal justification be placed in either group. Nottingham and Oxford had 50–60 per cent. of their total area in arable and Northampton, Rutland, Warwick, Buckingham, Worcester, Gloucester, Wiltshire, Hampshire, Sussex, and Kent[1] had 40–50 per cent. In the west arable was generally subordinate to grass. Arable was less than 30 per cent. of the total area in Cumberland, Westmorland, Lancashire, Cheshire, the West Riding, Derby, Monmouth, Somerset, and in all Wales, except Denbigh and Flint, Anglesey and Pembroke. The South-west, however, had relatively more arable, Cornwall having 42·2 per cent. of its total area and Devon 38·7 per cent.—which represented a very substantial proportion of the *cultivated* land.[2] In the north-east, Northumberland and Durham had arable along the coast, but as both these counties include much Pennine upland the proportion of their total area in arable was necessarily low (see Figure 4).

The distinction between the arable counties of the east and the grass counties of the west can be substantiated further by an examination of the individual crops involved in arable cultivation (see Figure 5). All the counties east of the Jurassic escarpment had under 21 per cent. of their arable in temporary or rotation grass, except Hampshire and Dorset, whose emphasis on grass-fed as well as on root-fed sheep presented rather

---

[1] The 1870 returns do not include the acreage under orchards and small fruit. The inclusion of these in the arable would substantially increase the arable acreage of Kent.

[2] The total area includes arable, permanent grass, rough grazings, agriculturally unproductive land, and built-up areas. The cultivated land includes only arable and permanent grass.

Figure 4.—A is *Arable*, B *Permanent Grass*, C *Cows and Heifers in Milk and in Calf*, D *Sheep over one year*. A and B are expressed in number of acres, C and D in number of head, in all cases per 100 acres of total agricultural area of each county. Maps constructed from the *Agricultural Returns* for 1870. The scale of shading is identical in A and B. In C and D the scale of shading is such that, except for the lowest densities, 5 head of sheep are equivalent to 1 cow. For the validity of this ratio in a particular case see my paper ('A Live-Stock Index for the Fylde District of Lancashire', *Empire Journal of Experimental Agriculture*, Vol. 7 (1939).

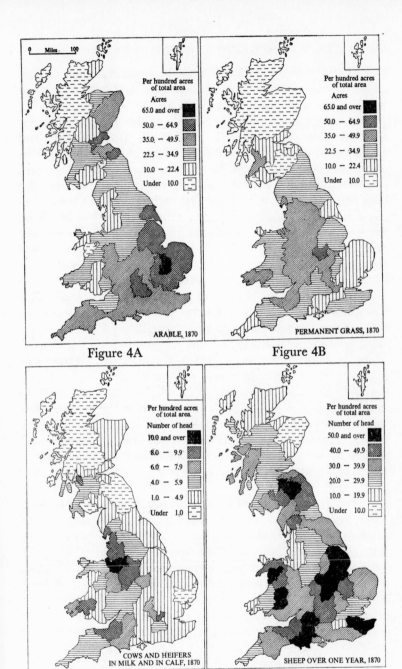

Figure 4A

Figure 4B

Figure 4C

Figure 4D

ARABLE, 1870

PERMANENT GRASS, 1870

COWS AND HEIFERS
IN MILK AND IN CALF, 1870

SHEEP OVER ONE YEAR, 1870

Agriculture in 1870 by Counties.   I.

special conditions. The same counties, with the same except-tions, had over 50 per cent. of their total arable in corn, used in its widest sense to include beans and peas. Westwards, the percentage under corn diminished and the percentage under rotation grass increased. In Cornwall, Cumberland, and Westmorland, under 40 per cent. of the total arable was in corn and over 30 per cent. in rotation grass. In these western counties the higher rainfall discouraged corn and favoured the long ley. This feature had been strongly marked at the end of the eighteenth century, and convertible husbandry, involving the long ley or else the more primitive method of allowing the land to reclothe itself with self-sown seed, had characterised these western districts earlier still. There were wide variations in the particular corn sown. Wheat was widely grown and in most counties took up 20–30 per cent. of the arable. This was prior to the collapse of corn prices owing to American competition. It was most important of all, expressed as a per-centage of the total arable, on stiff clay soils within the English Plain, in Huntingdon or Warwick, for example. Wheat was least important in northern and western districts, and in Cum-berland, Westmorland, and West Wales from Anglesey to Pembroke, it took up less than 10 per cent. of the arable. Oats showed the reverse regional emphasis. In many counties of the English Plain less than 10 per cent. of the arable was sown with oats and, with very few exceptions, those western counties which had under 20 per cent. of their arable in wheat had over 20 per cent. of their arable in oats. The influence of the cooler climate of the north and of the wetter climate of the west is clear. These northern and western districts had grown little wheat at all during the Middle Ages, but wheat, increasingly entering into the national dietary, had spread into them with the development of commercial farming. Of the roots, potatoes were relatively more important in the west, as they had been from their first introduction, and turnips relatively more important in the east, but roots were no longer limited to light soils. Mangolds, more suited to heavy land, had an acreage

Figure 5.—A is *Temporary Grass*, B *Wheat*, C *Barley*, and D *Oats*, expressed in number of acres in each crop per 100 acres of total arable area in each county. Maps constructed from the *Agricultural Returns* for 1870. The scales of shading are identical in the four maps.

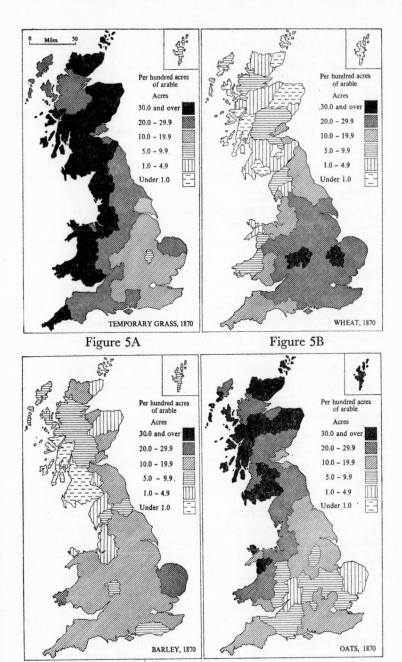

Figure 5A

Figure 5B

Figure 5C

Figure 5D

Agriculture in 1870 by Counties. II.

exceeding turnips and swedes only in Essex, though they were being grown increasingly. They were to increase much more later on in the century. Beans, though a declining crop, were still important on heavy lands within the English Plain, and they took up over 10 per cent. of the arable in Bedford and Worcester. Even in a western district such as the Fylde in West Lancashire, they were sown on 6·7 per cent. of the arable in 1870; the arable then included some of the clay loams now entirely under grass.[1]

In Scotland also there were distinctions between east and west. The eastern lowland counties of Aberdeen, Kincardine, Fife, the Lothians, and Berwick had over 40 per cent. of their total area in arable, while the Western and North-western Highlands had under 10 per cent., but the climatic contrast was here heightened by a topographical and soil contrast. In the western parts of the Central Lowlands and of Galloway the amount of arable was not inconsiderable. The proportion of the arable under corn in Scotland was usually lower than in England (40·9 per cent., as compared with 55·1 per cent.), and the proportion under rotation grass higher (38·4 per cent., as compared with 20·2 per cent.). Scotland, as a whole, was, in this respect, more comparable to western England and Wales. The percentage under corn was, however, usually lower and the percentage under rotation grass usually higher in the western Central Lowlands and in Galloway than along the east coast from Aberdeen to Berwick, but the difference was not as pronounced as between West and East England. Throughout Scotland, wheat was the least important of all corn crops (3·6 per cent. of the arable as compared with 23·7 per cent. in England), and it was really significant only in Fife and the Lothians, the most sunny parts of Scotland. In the Orkneys and Shetlands no wheat at all was grown. Everywhere the most important corn was oats, a clear reflection of the cooler and less sunny summers. Beans were unimportant except on certain carse soils. Roots were extensively grown: the yield per acre was high in the cool moist climate of Scotland, and they fitted in with the stock, always an important element in Scottish farming. The turnip acreage was greatest in the

[1] W. Smith: 'Agrarian Evolution since the Eighteenth Century', *A Scientific Survey of Blackpool and District, Brit. Assoc. Reports* (1936), p. 49.

eastern districts, but potatoes were grown alike in Highland crofting communities, in the western Central Lowlands, and in the arable Lothians and Fife.

The Shetlands presented features distinct from the rest of Scotland. Two-thirds of the arable were under corn (oats and barley), a sixth under potatoes, and over a fifth in fallow. Only 5·8 per cent. of the whole arable acreage was in turnips, rotation grass, and other crops. The turnip and clover husbandry, which had spread all over Scotland, was, even in 1870, practised on only a very limited scale in the Shetlands, the outpost. Potatoes were grown, as in all crofting communities, but more extensively here than in most. Shetland agriculture thus clearly retained many old features; the arable was concerned almost entirely with the growth of human food (oats, barley, potatoes) and still in large measure practised a rotation of several successive corn crops broken by an occasional fallow. The chief improvement introduced was the substitution of potatoes for much of the fallow. Stock food was almost entirely natural grass, but very little was made into hay and stock only survived the winter in low condition.

There were marked regional variations within Britain in stock as well as in arable farming (see Figure 4). In Hampshire, Kent, Essex, and Suffolk there were fewer head of cattle per 100 acres than elsewhere: these were arable counties which kept few cattle in summer.[1] There were over fifteen head of cattle per 100 acres in Lancashire, Cheshire, Derby, Stafford, and Salop; in Somerset and Cornwall; in Anglesey, Carmarthen, and Pembroke; in Buckingham; and in Leicester, Northampton, and Rutland. The first three groups are western counties with ample grass, a product of both soil and climate, and they include much lowland country. In the north-western group the cattle were mainly dairy cows. In Somerset, Carmarthen, and Buckingham, dairy cows were also more numerous than the other categories of cattle. But in Anglesey, Pembroke, and Cornwall, western peninsulas remote from the centres of consumption, young cattle were as numerous as dairy cows: these were rearing rather than dairying districts. The

[1] The agricultural returns refer to conditions in June and cattle-fattening in the arable counties is a winter business, lean or forward stores being bought in in autumn. In recent years the Ministry of Agriculture has occasionally taken a winter stock census to obtain this supplementary information.

western hill regions generally (the Lake District, the Northern Pennines, Wales, and the Welsh Border) were also rearing districts, but, because of the lower average quality of their land, they could carry fewer stock per 100 acres. In Leicester, Northampton, and Rutland the most important category of cattle was neither dairy cows nor young cattle under two years old, but cattle over two years old; that is, cattle fattening for the butcher. The best feeding lands in these counties were the deep clays of the Lias, which had come to be employed for this purpose, at any rate by the seventeenth century, if not in Leland's time. The only other county where cattle over two years old were more numerous than any other category was Northumberland. The distinction between rearing, feeding, and dairying districts was thus already well marked.

The regional variations in sheep density present some interesting features (see Figure 4). Density was greatest on the uplands of Central Wales. Brecon, Merioneth, and Radnor, had seventy or over adult sheep per 100 acres, but they had a comparatively low proportion of lambs even for mountain breeds. Within the English Plain there were three areas with over fifty adult sheep per 100 acres—Wiltshire and Dorset, the Western Downlands; Kent (Romney Marsh); Leicester, Northampton, Rutland, and Lincoln, the home of the long-wool Leicester and Lincoln breeds, whose wool was in demand by the worsted industry and whose large joints suited the large families of Victorian England. All of these had a higher proportion of lambs than the Welsh upland breeds. In certain western lowland districts with a high density of cattle (Lancashire, Cheshire and Flint, Anglesey and Pembroke) and in the metropolitan districts of Middlesex and Surrey, there were under twenty adult sheep per 100 acres. The arable districts had intermediate densities, thirty to fifty adult sheep per 100 acres, but this was in June, and it was a common practice in arable districts to keep only a flying flock bought in solely for the winter feeding season. Sheep were bought in autumn also in those western lowlands with a low summer sheep density.

In Scotland the density of stock was generally less than in England and Wales, but by far the greater proportion of the area of Scotland consisted of rough grazings which had necessarily a lower carrying capacity than lowland pasture. Rough grazings were not limited to the Highlands and the Southern Uplands, but were present also on the hummocky uplands within the Central Lowlands. Only the lowland counties had an appreciable cattle density. The only important dairying districts were in the western Central Lowlands—Ayr, Renfrew, and Lanark—together with Wigton in West Galloway. This was the domain of the Ayrshire cow. In the eastern arable districts young cattle under two years old outnumbered dairy cows, and in many of these districts there were also more feeding cattle over two years old than dairy cows. The dominant breed here was the beef Aberdeen-Angus. The eastern arable districts had comparatively few sheep, many fewer than the arable districts of England. Beef cattle were their chief stock. The western part of the Central Lowlands had more sheep and usually more than the western lowlands of England. But the chief sheep districts in Scotland were the Southern Uplands, with densities very similar to those of upland Wales and, to a lesser extent, the Highlands, where sheep were now more important than cattle, especially when equated with cattle as grazing units. The old cattle economy of the Highlands had largely gone and the sheep flocks, which were spreading north at the end of the eighteenth century, had by 1870 become general.[1]

H. Rider Haggard made a tour of most of the counties of the English Plain in 1901-02. The trough of corn prices had been reached in the 'nineties and everywhere he found depression among English arable farmers, great reductions in rent, and the laying down of arable to grass.[2] On strong lands, notably in Essex, there were derelict farms. These heavy soils were essentially wheat and bean land and the collapse of corn prices, greatest in wheat, affected them severely. In the grass districts agricultural depression was not so severe. In North Wiltshire the rental of the arable had fallen 50-60 per cent., but of the grass 15-20 per cent.[3] In Salop conditions were similar. The complaint in the grass districts was not of low commodity prices, but of the shortage of labour. This difficulty of obtaining

[1] There is an excellent series of essays on agriculture at the time in the *Journal of the Royal Agricultural Society* for 1878.

[2] H. Rider Haggard: *Rural England* (1906), 2 Vols.

[3] H. Rider Haggard, *op. cit.*, Vol. 1, p. 28.

agricultural labour was general in all districts, arable and grass alike. It limited, if it did not prohibit, farming 'in detail'. The tendency was more and more to 'skim over' the land, to reduce costs, and, as an inevitable consequence, to reduce yield also. In Salop the small farm, under 50 acres, small enough to be worked by family labour alone, continued to pay rent at the old level. It was the larger farm, requiring hired labour, whose rental had fallen. The shortage of labour was, of course, the result of the rural depopulation which had been proceeding since the middle of the nineteenth century. It was a product of the mobility of labour, consequential on the disappearance of the common-field system, and of the attraction of the towns, consequential on the Industrial Revolution. The workshop rather than the farm had come to dominate the British economy and to attract the British labourer.

The course of rural depopulation during the nineteenth century has been analysed by Prof. P. M. Roxby.[1] The rural population in 1851 had grown far beyond that of 1801, but it began to decline slightly after 1851 and rapidly after 1871. The decline was not arrested until the first decade of the twentieth century. This rural depopulation was not, however, uniform. It varied substantially from district to district with the type of farming, which in its turn depended on the qualities of the environment. In other words, it varied geographically. Table V abstracts some of the figures from this analysis in order to show the course of change in a number of different arable districts. Each area was purely rural and the significance of the figures is not vitiated by the inclusion of any extraneous urban population. It is clear that since 1871 the decline was substantial in districts practising 'standard' arable farming, but it was greater on the heavier than on the lighter soils. In the fruit and market gardening districts population, in contrast, either remained steady or actually increased. Evesham, which registered a progressive increase of rural population, had a favourable geographical position and tenurial conditions very favourable to the small-holder.

Although Rider Haggard demonstrated the unprofitability of 'standard' types of farming, he did not fail to visit new kinds of

[1] P. M. Roxby: 'Rural Depopulation in England during the Nineteenth Century', *The Nineteenth Century and After*, No. 419 (1912), pp. 174–90.

TABLE V

TRENDS OF RURAL POPULATION IN ENGLAND DURING THE
NINETEENTH CENTURY IN SELECTED ARABLE DISTRICTS

	1801	1851	1871	1891	1911
Kimbolton (Hunts.) Clay land arable	5,934	9,339	9,126	6,836	6,141
Bungay (Suffolk) Light land arable	4,597	6,539	6,331	5,803	5,456
Evesham (Worcs.) Fruit and vegetables	5,048	7,696	8,324	9,112	12,307
Spalding (Lincs.) Fruit and vegetables	10,751	22,388	23,184	21,733	23,497

Source: P. M. Roxby: *The Nineteenth Century and After*, No. 419 (1912), p. 177

farming enterprises. The importance of the new types of farming was underlined by E. A. Pratt in a book to which he gave
the significant title *The Transition in Agriculture*.[1] The burden of
Pratt's argument was that, as cereal-growing had proved un-
profitable owing to the competition of virgin colonial land,
British farming should devote itself increasingly to the production of the more diversified articles of food, the demand for
which was increasing with changes in diet owing to the rising
standard of living; that is, to milk, eggs, poultry, green vegetables, fruit. He drew an industrial analogy from the Birmingham
district which had turned from heavy standard iron and steel
production to the lighter metal trades.[2]

The urban demand for milk had continued to grow. Morton
had estimated in 1878 that the average *per capita* consumption
for the whole country was 0·25 pint per day.[3] A report of a
committee of the Royal Statistical Society in 1904 was to the
effect that the average consumption of whole milk in the United
Kingdom per head was 15 gallons per annum,[4] which works
out at 0·33 pint per head per day. It thus appears that the
consumption per head was increasing and, as the total population (especially the urban population) of the country was increasing also, the rise in the total requirements of milk was

[1] E. A. Pratt: *The Transition in Agriculture* (1906).

[2] E. A. Pratt, *op. cit.*, p. 323.

[3] R. H. Rew: 'Observations on the Production and Consumption of Meat and
Dairy Products', *Journal Royal Statistical Society* (1904), p. 418.

[4] 'Third Report on the Production and Consumption of Meat and Milk in the
United Kingdom', *Journal Royal Statistical Society* (1904), p. 391.

substantial. The dairy herd had increased considerably and the yield per cow had probably increased also. This increasing urban demand for milk was met by an expansion of the radius from which fresh milk was drawn. The railway carriage of whole milk was increasing on almost every railway system. On the Great Western, which handled more milk than any other company, it had doubled in a decade.[1] While almost every town obtained some of its milk by rail, the greater part of the rail-borne milk went to London, which drew in its supplies from the Home Counties, the East Midlands, the middle Trent Valley, North Wiltshire, and, in smaller quantities, even from as far afield as Cheshire and Cornwall. Many of the districts supplying milk to the towns were ancient dairying districts which were selling whole milk instead of, as formerly, making it into butter and cheese. But the Essex clays, too expensive to work for wheat at 30s. or under per quarter, had been occupied by Ayrshire dairy farmers, who were creating a new dairy district on derelict land. The London Clay did not, however, make good grassland owing to its tendency to burn up in the summer, for the effective rainfall is here the lowest in Britain and dairying, then as now, was partly on the basis of arable cropping. Dr. Willatts has demonstrated a substantial substitution of grass for arable on the London Clay in other parts of the London Basin.[2]

The increasing production of fruit and of market garden crops was equally striking. In some districts, in the Fens, the Lothians, along the Ayrshire coast,[1] or South-west Lancashire, market-garden crops were grown in the ordinary course of arable cultivation in rotation with grain and temporary grass; but in other areas, usually much smaller in extent though intensively cultivated, land was withdrawn from grass or standard arable cultivation and devoted entirely to specialist fruit and vegetable production. Such, to name a few outstanding areas, were the Vale of Evesham, the Biggleswade and

---

[1] E. A. Pratt, op. cit., p. 11.

[2] E. C. Willatts: 'Changes in Land Utilization in the South-west of the London Basin, 1840–1932', Geographical Journal, Vol. 82 (1933), pp. 515–28. His comparison is of the tithe maps of c. 1840 and the Land Utilisation Survey of 1931–32. Some of the substitution is post-1918.

[3] Some of the Ayrshire coastlands were cropped with potatoes annually when visited by Sir Daniel Hall in 1912 (A. D. Hall: A Pilgrimage of British Farming, 1910–12 (1913), p. 394).

Sandy district of Bedford, the Wisbech district of the Fens, Kent, Blairgowrie, and the Carse of Gowrie, Holt in Denbigh, Ashton Moss and Irlam Moss in Lancashire, West Cornwall. Most of these had suitable soil and, in several cases, suitable climate, particularly for early spring production. But the intensively cultivated market garden often created its own conditions of soil and climate. A market garden soil was frequently a 'made' soil by reason of the vast quantities of manure added to it, and in glass-house cultivation (which, following the Guernsey pattern, was rapidly increasing) the air temperature and the soil moisture were capable of manipulation to any requirement. The celery growers of Ashton Moss and Irlam Moss had made their own soil with town manure and the forced-rhubarb growers of the outskirts of Leeds had made their own climate in darkened and heated forcing-sheds. It was, of course, only the intensively cultivated market gardens growing high-priced crops which could afford so to transform the physical environment to specification, and not all market gardening was as intensive or as specialised as this. Market gardening and fruit growing, implying more intensive uses of the land, required special tenurial conditions (such, for example, as the Evesham Custom), and, producing perishable commodities, required easy access to large urban markets, either by physical proximity or by good railway services. Where these conditions were absent, market gardening or fruit growing (except for cider-making) did not develop on any considerable scale.

By 1913, the real economic terminus of the nineteenth century, the reactions of the changed economic conditions— the relative unprofitability of cereal-growing and the relative profitability of the newer forms of agricultural enterprise— on the agricultural geography of Britain were already considerable. It is possible to measure them statistically by a comparison of the agricultural returns for 1870 and 1913.[1] Calculated as percentages, these are set out in the Appendix. The 1913 returns have been mapped in Figures 6 and 7.

In every county of Great Britain there was a decrease in the

---

[1] These are not strictly comparable. The 1870 statistics have no return for rough grazings. In most counties the area of cultivated land (arable+permanent grass) had increased by 1913, but it cannot be determined whether this represented a real increase in the extent of the improved land or simply greater completeness in the returns.

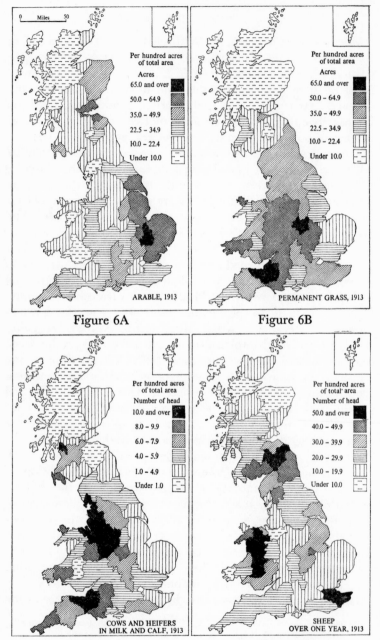

Figure 6A

Figure 6B

Figure 6C

Figure 6D

Agriculture in 1913 by Counties. I.

arable acreage. It was comparatively small in Scotland (5 per cent.), but in England it amounted to one-quarter and in Wales to over one-third. In 1870 England had had 58·6 per cent. of the total cultivated land in arable; in 1913 it had 57·5 per cent. in permanent grass. The balance of the agricultural economy had changed. Wales had been predominantly pastoral even in 1870. These averages, however, mask considerable regional differences. In the English arable districts the decline was comparatively small: this was true not only of East Anglia, but also of the intensively farmed arable district of South-west Lancashire and North Cheshire. These were mostly areas of light soil. But on the heavy soils of the east, such as Essex, and of the Midlands, such as Leicester, and in the western counties generally including Wales, the decline was substantial. In Scotland most of the eastern arable districts had an arable acreage that was stationary or had declined but little. The western parts of the Central Lowlands and the Southern Uplands showed more substantial decreases.[1] The decrease in arable was thus mainly in the non-arable districts, in western areas and, within the English Plain, on the clays. These could satisfactorily be laid down to grass. But those arable districts which were of light soil were not convertible to the same degree: they were not so suited to grass and had perforce to remain largely in arable or lapse to rough heath.

The abandonment of arable and the laying down to grass was one of the most obvious adaptations to the economic situation, but there was also a widespread substitution of crops in the arable that remained. In the light soil arable districts of the English Plain the modifications in the general character of the rotation—the proportion of the total arable in corn, in rotation or temporary grass, and in root and green crops—were at their

[1] Most of the counties north of the Highland Line (except Shetland) displayed actual increases. These same northern counties registered also increases in the acreage of permanent grass, usually greater than the increases in arable. Either rough grazings were being improved substantially or the returns were becoming more complete.

Figure 6.—A is *Arable*, B *Permanent Grass*, C *Cows and Heifers in Milk and in Calf*, D *Sheep over one year*. A and B are expressed in number of acres, C and D in number of head, in all cases per 100 acres of total agricultural area of each county. Maps constructed from the *Agricultural Statistics* for 1913. The scales of shading are identical with those in the corresponding maps in Figure 4. See notes under Figure 4.

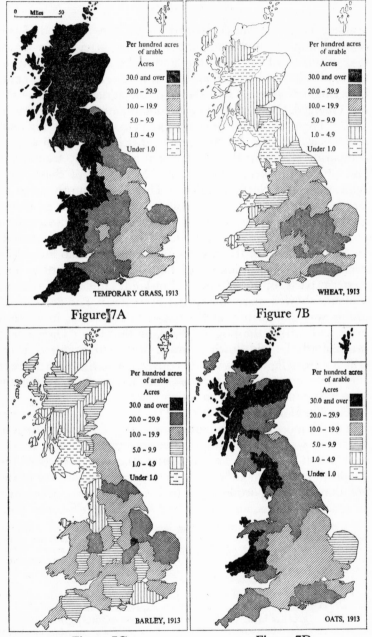

Figure 7A

Figure 7B

Figure 7C

Figure 7D

Agriculture in 1913 by Counties. II.

minimum. Changes were much more substantial on the Midland clays and in the western districts. The most general feature of change here was a decrease in the proportion of the arable in corn and an increase in the proportion in temporary grass. The long ley was no new feature of the arable rotations of Wales and of western England: it was an adaptation to the climate and it was now also an adaptation to the economic situation. It was an alternative to laying the land down to permanent grass, a movement active in these western districts as shown in the preceding paragraph, and some, in fact, returned as temporary grass ultimately became permanent grass.[1] In Cheshire, Radnor, Pembroke, and Westmorland the proportion of the arable under rotation grass was by 1913 one-third or over, and in Cornwall it was nearly one-half. In the eastern arable districts changes within the arable mainly took the form, not of alterations in the rotation, but of the substitution of one crop for another of the same kind. Although the proportion of the arable under corn remained steady, the proportion in wheat declined and in oats increased. Wheat had suffered most from the collapse of corn prices owing to foreign competition. Beans, grown extensively only on heavy land, almost everywhere declined. The proportion of the arable under root and green crops did not change substantially, but almost everywhere part of the turnip acreage was being sown with mangolds and the acreage in potatoes was increasing. The decrease in turnips and the increase in mangolds was correlated with changes in the proportion of sheep and of dairy cows, as will appear later. In Scottish arable districts a decline in the proportion under corn and an increase in the proportion under rotation grass, long a well-marked feature of Scottish arable farming, was more general. The acreage under all classes of corn declined. Scotland had never grown much wheat and by 1913 the wheat acreage had fallen to 1·7 per cent. of the total arable. Even oats also declined in some counties, though to a

[1] On the statistical basis for this, see J. A. Venn: *Foundations of Agricultural Economics* (1923), p. 366.

Figure 7.—A is *Temporary Grass*, B *Wheat*, C *Barley*, D *Oats*, expressed in number of acres of each crop per 100 acres of total arable area in each county. Maps constructed from the *Agricultural Statistics* for 1913. The scales of shading are identical in the four maps and with those of Figure 5.

H

lesser extent. Shetland had lost many of the archaic features which it had still retained in 1870: there were more turnips, seed grasses and hay, and less fallow and corn. It was concerned less exclusively with the growing of human food and more with the growing of stock food, like the neighbouring counties of North-east Scotland.

Parallel with these changes in the balance of arable and grass and of crops within the arable, there were changes in the numbers of farm stock. The New Husbandry of the eighteenth century had produced food for man and beast and the changes in the arable economy at the end of the nineteenth century, which have just been traced, were in the direction of producing less food for man and more food for beasts. The increasing proportion of the arable under rotation grass and under oats both contributed to this end. Except perhaps in some hill districts, the number of dairy cows everywhere increased, and, in an even greater proportion, the number of young cattle under two years old.[1] The increase in the number of dairy cows was greatest in the dairying districts and least, both actually and relatively, in the arable districts. The increase in the number of feeding cattle was comparatively small,[2] and in most districts their numbers were stationary or declined slightly. It was only in the arable feeding districts[3] (Norfolk, the Lothians, Aberdeen) and in the specialist grass-feeding districts (Leicester and North-ampton) that increase was encountered. There were even more striking changes in the numbers and geographical distribution of sheep. One general change was an increasing ratio of lambs to adult sheep, explicable partly by a higher lambing per-centage and partly by the slaughter of wethers at a younger age than formerly.[4] There was a marked decline in the numbers of sheep in the arable districts of eastern England and in the low-land districts of the Midlands and of the west. The eastern arable districts were substituting cattle (of all ages and classes) for sheep and were growing more mangolds and less turnips.

[1] The increase in Great Britain of dairy cattle (cows and heifers in milk and in calf) in 1913, as compared with 1870, was 24·7 per cent. and of young cattle under two years old, 50·9 per cent.

[2] Other cattle over two years old were 5·0 per cent. more than in 1870.

[3] The statistics refer to June and, as arable feeding is a winter business, these statistics do not necessarily give a correct impression.

[4] The number of sheep over a year old had increased by 15·9 per cent., but the number of lambs by 47·4 per cent.

The lowland grass districts of the Midlands and of the west were becoming more completely cattle regions, feeding and dairying in the one case, dairying and rearing in the other. But in Wales and in the Northern Pennines there was a substantial increase in the sheep population. In Scotland even the arable districts showed an increase—sheep had not hitherto been as important here as in the English arable districts—but the increase was most marked in the Southern Uplands. Only the Western Lowlands of Scotland showed a stationary or slightly declining sheep population. It was clearly on the grassy uplands of Wales, the Northern Pennines, and the Southern Uplands that sheep were increasing. The lowland arable sheep were mostly large animals, the upland hill sheep small animals. By 1913 the size of the family had already begun to decline and the smaller joint was more suited to the smaller family unit. The hill sheep also gave sweeter mutton.

Many of these changes, outlined above, contributed to an increasing regional specialisation of farming. The arable districts were remaining largely arable, the grass districts were becoming more completely under grass and devoting themselves more exclusively to *one* form of stock economy. This regional specialisation was the result of the interplay of a complex of physical and economic factors, some of which have already been indicated in general terms. It was the response, on the agricultural side, to the specialist economy which developed in Britain during the nineteenth century, in industry even more than in farming.

CHAPTER 2

Industry

I

THE MIDDLE AGES

The Middle Ages was a period of self-sufficiency in industry as well as in agriculture. Clothing and tools were manufactured, just as corn was grown, at the point of consumption, but the geographical unit of self-sufficiency was the region rather than the village. Some of these manufactures were the product of part-time household industry,[1] others the work of craftsmen. It is probable that the first preceded the second,[2] but specialist craftsmen were already established by the twelfth century,[3] though both persisted, and still persist, side by side. By the thirteenth century, the point at which this survey of the antecedents of the modern economic geography of Britain begins, the specialist crafts were to a considerable extent concentrated in the towns. This, however, implied little modification of regional self-sufficiency. The town crafts produced simply for the locality and regarded the local region as their natural area of monopoly. Most medieval master craftsmen were retail traders or shopkeepers, as well as manufacturers: they sold direct like the producer-retailer dairyman of today. There was only a limited regional specialisation of industrial production, for the same kind and range of consumption goods were produced and consumed in each region.

[1] The family system of Ashley's nomenclature (W. J. Ashley: *The Early History of the English Woollen Industry* (1887), p. 72).

[2] G. Unwin: *Industrial Organisation in the Sixteenth and Seventeenth Centuries* (1904), pp. 1–2. Household industry persisted into centuries long subsequent to the medieval. There was household brewing in the North of England in the latter half of the nineteenth century and household baking in the twentieth. But these are consumption rather than manufacturing industries, and to-day produce for a regional market.

[3] E. Lipson: *Economic History of England*, Vol. 1, pp. 365–6. Craft gilds were mentioned in a pipe roll of the reign of Henry I.

But manufacturing production was not limited to the urban centres.[1] Lipson records a Leicester gild regulation of the thirteenth century which he takes to be a measure of defence for the Leicester town craftsman against the country weaver in the villages near by.[2] There was country weaving and fulling in the West Country, though the towns probably dominated production here before the fifteenth century;[3] and Prof. Heaton[4] shows that in Yorkshire, although York and Beverley were the largest individual woollen working centres, there were thirteenth-century cloth workers throughout the present West Yorkshire textile district, in the Vale of York and in some of the Pennine dales in addition. There was thus a rural as well as an urban distribution of cloth workers,[5] but, except probably for blacksmiths and some few others, this may not have been true of other industrial crafts. Mining and smelting had, of course, entirely a rural distribution. After this general statement, the industrial geography of the Middle Ages will now be considered item by item.

The most important industry was the woollen and worsted. Sheep were kept in most vills and as wool producers, though not as producers of meat, they could be kept successfully on the commons and on the stubble, the pasture available to the medieval grazier. Wool was not only a by-product of mixed farming practice, but was also the chief object of much monastic farming. Thus extensively produced, wool was a clothing material appropriate to the climate. In the form of raw wool it was the chief export of the country and was sent across to the Low Countries, from which in the early Middle Ages some was transhipped overland to Italy. English wool was the best in Europe.[6] England was then largely contributory to more advanced industrial centres elsewhere, much as the Argentine

---

[1] E. Lipson doubts whether membership of craft gilds was in all cases strictly confined to those resident within the town.

[2] E. Lipson, op. cit., p. 444.

[3] R. H. Kinvig: 'The Historical Geography of the West Country Woollen Industry', Geographical Teacher, Nos. 44 and 45 (1916), p. 244.

[4] H. Heaton: The Yorkshire Woollen and Worsted Industries (1920), pp. 5–7.

[5] The Little Red Book of Bristol, folio 120. Such rural fulling was considered to be of inferior quality.

[6] H. Pirenne: Economic and Social History of Medieval Europe (1936), p. 37, and E. Power: 'The Wool Trade in the Fifteenth Century', Power and Postan, Studies in English Trade in the Fifteenth Century (1933), p. 39.

or Australia are today. Concurrent with wool export abroad, there was, however, woollen manufacture at home. It supplied the greater part of the consumption needs of the country and, although finer cloths were imported, they were mainly for the court, the nobility, and the wealthier merchants. There was indeed a substantial export of cloth abroad. In the early part of the Middle Ages export of wool greatly exceeded export of cloth, but by the middle of the fifteenth century the export of cloth (reckoned in terms of wool equivalents, $4\frac{1}{3}$ cloths to 1 sack of wool) had grown to exceed the export of raw wool.[1]

There is specific information on the geographical distribution of the woollen industry during the Middle Ages from the aulnage accounts. These have been printed in summary form for three periods, 1353–58, 1394–98, and 1468–73.[2] The aulnage accounts[3] were not a census of production in the modern sense; they excluded worsteds, coarse cloths, and pieces woven in the household for household use, and they registered therefore much less than the total production of the country. But they give an approximate idea of the relative magnitude of *woollen weaving* in different parts of the country. It must be noticed that they do not necessarily indicate the distribution of woollen spinning, a household craft performed largely by women and children and, though carried on mainly in the same towns and rural districts as weaving, was not necessarily confined to these. The aulnage accounts are mapped county by county for 1356–58 and 1470 in Figure 8 as actual quantities; and percentages for regional groups of counties calculated for 1356–58, 1394–98 and 1468–73 are set out in Table VI.

Though they must be accepted with some reservations because of the limitations of the accounts as a census of production and because of the untrustworthiness of some of the returns,[4] some very interesting conclusions may be drawn. In

[1] H. L. Gray: 'English Foreign Trade, 1446–82', Power and Postan, *op. cit.*, pp. 10–11 and 362.

[2] For 1353–58 and 1394–98 by H. L. Gray: 'The Production and Exportation of English Woollens in the Fourteenth Century', *English Historical Review*, Vol. 39 (1924), p. 34; for 1468–73 by H. Heaton, *op. cit.*, p. 85.

[3] The aulnager was an official appointed 'to enforce the assize of cloth as fixed by the government of the day, and to collect the subsidy levied on cloth manuactured for sale' (H. Heaton, *op. cit.*, p. 127).

[4] It has been shown that some of the fifteenth-century accounts were unquestionably 'cooked' (E. M. Carus-Wilson: 'The Aulnage Accounts: A Criticism', *Economic History Review*, Vol. 2 (1929), pp. 114–23).

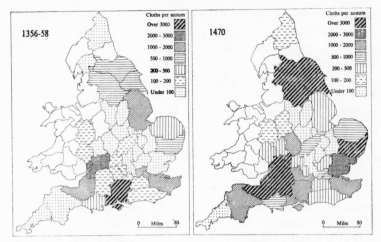

Figure 8A   Figure 8B

Production of Woollen Cloths in Each County of England in the
Fourteenth and Fifteenth Centuries

According to the Aulnage Accounts for 1356–58 (A) and 1470 (B). In
number of cloths of assize per county per annum, irrespective of size of
county. Scale identical in the two maps. Maps drawn from abstract to
Aulnage Accounts in H. L. Gray: *English Historical Review*, Vol. 39 (1924)
and H. Heaton: *Yorkshire Woollen and Worsted Industries* (1920). Where
cloths were smaller than a cloth of assize, they were reckoned in equivalents
of a cloth of assize.

the middle of the fourteenth century the urban distribution of
woollen weaving was clearly marked. The production of ten
towns, according to the generalised calculations made by Prof.
Gray,[1] amounted to approximately 9,000 cloths of a total production of 16,000. The most important towns were Salisbury,
Bristol, London, and Winchester. From Table VI it is clear
that south-east England, the metropolitan district including
London and Winchester, was the most productive single region.
The West Country (Gloucester, Somerset, Wiltshire, Dorset,
Devon, and Cornwall) was the second, and, following far
behind, were East Anglia and Yorkshire. But East Anglia
made more worsteds than woollens and, if these be added, it
was probably not far behind the West Country. By the end of
the fourteenth century the changes in distribution were considerable. The proportion of the total production which came

[1] H. L. Gray: *English Historical Reivew*, Vol. 39, p. 22.

from the ten towns had fallen to one-half.[1] The urban domination of the clothing industry was beginning to pass away. The south-east, the metropolitan region, had declined both actually and relatively. It was now surpassed by both the West Country and, if worsteds also be taken into account, by East Anglia. In the metropolitan region manufacture had been largely urban, in the West Country and East Anglia it was becoming partly rural. The country districts were outside gild control and already had numbers of capitalist clothiers.[2] By the second half of the fifteenth century these changes had proceeded further. The metropolitan district continued to decline, East Anglia and Yorkshire continued to grow, and, although the share of the West Country in the total production was less than at the end of the fourteenth century, it was greater than in the middle of that century. In Yorkshire, which offered a mirror of the local changes proceeding elsewhere, the number of cloths annually attributed by the aulnage accounts to York was approximately 3,200 in 1394–95 and 1,170 in 1473–75, and to West Yorkshire (the present-day woollen and worsted district) 290 in 1396–97 and 1,290 in 1473–75.[3] The decay of the town and the rise of the country manufacture was striking. These changes in the geographical distribution of the industry, though in progress during the fourteenth and fifteenth centuries,[4] were to become more pronounced during the sixteenth. A discussion of the causes of these changes in distribution, of the relationship of the regional manufacturing districts to their local environment, and of the differences in type of fabric woven within them, will accordingly be deferred.

There were important leather-working 'misteries' based, like clothing, on the beasts of the farm. Both issued out of the agricultural basis of medieval Britain and particularly out of the pastoralism characteristic of northern and western districts. The leather crafts were widely distributed,[5] for they served a local market: hides were worked into shoes, sheep- and

---

[1] H. L. Gray: *English Historical Review*, Vol. 39 p. 32.

[2] E. Lipson, *op. cit.*, pp. 469–70.

[3] H. Heaton, *op. cit.*, pp. 60, 70–1, 75.

[4] The beginning of rural fulling can be placed in the thirteenth century (E. M. Carus-Wilson: 'An Industrial Revolution of the XIIIth Century', *Economic History Review*, Vol. 11 (1941)).

[5] L. F. Salzman: *English Industries in the Middle Ages* (1923), p. 246.

deerskins into gloves, points or laces, and the like. A surplus of hides was available for export, especially from Wales, but, like that of wool, export diminished towards the end of the Middle Ages.[1]

TABLE VI

DISTRIBUTION OF WOOLLEN PRODUCTION BY DISTRICTS
IN THE MIDDLE AGES

	1356–58	1394–98	1468–73
Metropolitan south-east	46·6	11·1	10·7
West Country	28·3	52·8	39·4
East Anglia	5·8	11·4	22·6
Yorkshire	5·4	8·7	12·6
Others	13·9	16·0	14·7
	100·0	100·0	100·0

Source: Calculated from H. L. Gray: English Historical Review, Vol. 39 (1924), and H. Heaton: The Yorkshire Woollen and Worsted Industries (1920).

There were metal crafts in addition to those based on agricultural materials. Certain of these were inevitably localised mainly in the metropolitan centre, goldsmiths and silversmiths being examples. The pewterers, making household ware, were more widely dispersed: London was their first, York their second, centre. Bell-founders were in many towns, particularly ecclesiastical centres such as London, Gloucester, York, Canterbury, Bury St. Edmunds, Norwich; and the Middle Ages, with numerous parish churches and monastic houses, provided a large market for their wares. Cannon, employed from the early fourteenth century onwards, were made largely in the towns at first, but by the end of the fifteenth century the craft had become established, among other places, in the Weald, near the metropolitan centre, and in a smelting district.[2]

The medieval references to the use of coal are obscured by terminology: 'carbo' and 'cole' both meant charcoal, and it was only when 'cole' had a prefix (as sea-cole or pit-cole, to denote its origin, stone-coal, its appearance, or smithy-coal, its use) that the obscurity is resolved.[3] The earliest indisputable

[1] Dr. Pelham gives a map showing the relative quantities of hides exported from eastern ports, 1282–90 (R. A. Pelham: 'Medieval Foreign Trade: Eastern Ports', An Historical Geography of England before 1800, ed. by H. C. Darby (1936), p. 315).

[2] L. F. Salzman, op. cit., p. 163.

[3] J. U. Nef: The Rise of the British Coal Industry, Vol. 1 (1932), pp. 4–5; and L. F. Salzman, op. cit., p. 2.

references in Britain date to the thirteenth century, and these referred to the following fields—the Lothians, Northumberland, South Yorkshire, South Wales, and the Forest of Dean in the first half of the century; Nottinghamshire, Salop, Lancashire, Bristol, Staffordshire, Warwickshire, Derbyshire, and Fife in the second half. Almost every coalfield was involved, though it must be remembered that many of these references refer to almost infinitesimal quantities and that regular mining was not in every case implied. It was only along the Tyne that coal-working attained any substantial proportions; even here the export per annum did not exceed 7,000 tons in the most favourable year, and there is no indication that it increased between 1377 and 1514.[1] The market was small and it was not expanding. Smiths employed coal regularly in their rougher work for reheating pig and bar iron, but it was only smiths who worked on the coalfields or in London. Lime-burners also used coal occasionally. The limitations to its use were an abundance of alternative fuel, its unsuitability as a domestic fuel in the chimneyless houses of the Middle Ages, the high cost of transport for such a bulky commodity,[2] and the fact that the coalfields lay mainly in the remote and scantily peopled northern and western districts of the country. 'Except for the Tyne valley,' says Nef, 'there was no district from which, until after 1500, the new fuel was regularly carried in quantities of more than a few hundred tons per annum, for distances of more than a few miles from the outcrops.'[3] The pre-eminence of the Tyne must have been due to the cropping out of coal close to the coast and the estuary, coupled with the position of the coalfield in the eastern, and economically most developed, part of Britain.

The mining of iron, lead, and tin, though localised in fewer areas, contributed more substantially to the economic geography of the Middle Ages. Iron was in constant demand for farm implements, domestic utensils, and 'engines of war'; lead for church roofs and piping; tin for currency and metal ware. There was iron-mining in the twelfth century in West

[1] J. U. Nef, *op. cit.*, Vol. 1, pp. 9–10.
[2] 'The charge for Newcastle coal in London, even though the shipmasters took it as ballast, was rarely less than three or four times the price on the Tyne' (J. U. Nef, *op. cit.*, Vol. 1, p. 13).
[3] J. U. Nef, *op. cit.*, Vol. 1, p. 8.

Cumberland, in the dales of North-east Yorkshire, in Derbyshire, but especially in the Forest of Dean. In the thirteenth
century, Furness, Northampton, but above all the Weald, were
added, and at later times other areas in the Pennines and West
Midlands.[1] Most of the orefields of England were thus affected
whether bedded ores in the Hastings Beds, the Jurassic or the
Coal Measures, or irregular haematite ore bodies in Furness and
West Cumberland. Most, if not all, of these areas were heavily
wooded. Iron was obtained on the bloomery hearth by ham-
mering the ore (mixed with marl and lime), rendered pasty and
malleable by heating with charcoal, of which enormous
quantities were consumed. Salzman quotes a consumption in
the mid-sixteenth century of 2·7 million cubic feet of timber in
under two years by two smelting furnaces, each with a forge
attached.[2] The earliest bloomery hearths were placed on wind-
swept hills (the 'boles' of Derbyshire and Yorkshire),[3] but these
were uneconomical and left slag containing a high residue of
iron.[4] During the nineteenth century old slag from the Forest
of Dean bloomeries was resmelted at the rate of 1 ton of slag
to 1 ton of raw ore. The use of foot-bellows increased the blast,
and in the fifteenth century bellows were attached to water-
wheels. In these furnaces with a created blast the ore was
smelted and the molten iron drawn off and cast in beds of sand.
This was pig iron as distinct from bloomery iron. Forges
associated with these improved smelting furnaces sometimes
had hammers driven by water-power. The North of England
centres appear to have served mainly local markets, but the
South of England was supplied first from the Forest of Dean
and later from the Weald. The Forest of Dean had long been
worked for iron and had the institution of 'free miners' who had
their own courts. The Weald had the advantage of proximity
to London.

The chief lead-mining districts were at Alston in Cumberland, in South Derbyshire, and on the Mendips, the country

[1] L. F. Salzman, *op. cit.*, pp. 23–8.

[2] L. F. Salzman, *op. cit.*, p. 39.

[3] S. H. Beaver, Discussion on G. S. Sweeting, 'Wealden Iron Ore and the History of its Industry', *Proc. Geol. Assoc.*, Vol. 55, Pt. 1 (1944).

[4] Analysis of bloomery cinder quoted by G. S. Sweeting (*op. cit.*, p. 7) gives 53·4
per cent. FeO. This high residue of iron was inherent in the process, for the iron
did not become molten and so could not be run off. It was not necessarily an
indication of an inefficient employment of the process.

rock being Carboniferous Limestone in each case. The Cumberland and Derbyshire ores were being worked by the twelfth century, and the Mendip ores possibly also. Mining was in the hands of 'free miners', and the rules for prospecting and staking a claim were rigidly laid down. The lead veins of the Northern Pennines have their richest ores near the weathered outcrop, and in consequence the shallow mining methods of the Middle Ages presented no handicap.[1] The miners had prescriptive rights to timber for charcoal. Foot-bellows were used to provide a blast and in the fifteenth century, as in iron-smelting, bellows were driven by water-power. Tin-mining was confined to the South-west Peninsula, around the edges of Dartmoor and of the several moors of Cornwall. During the Middle Ages the greater part of the output was from alluvial deposits.[2] The institution of 'free miners' was here the most strongly entrenched of all mining districts. All smelted tin had to be sent to one of nine coinage towns, four of which were in Devon and five in Cornwall.[3] The wind-swept uplands of Cornwall were relatively bare of timber, and it appears that coal was imported coastwise from South Wales; this imported coal may have been used to supplement the limited local charcoal.[4]

Most of this mining enterprise was within or around the edges of the Palaeozoic uplands of the north and west. Apart from the Wealden iron industry, mining was almost absent from the English Plain. The industrial geography of the Middle Ages in England and Wales thus exhibited two major provinces—the English Plain, with its town crafts and its clothing industries; the uplands of the west and north, with their mining. It was a distinction between two quite different types of enterprise—extractive mining and smelting closely localised by the provenance of raw materials, and finished manufacturing relatively mobile and independent of raw materials.

---

[1] A. E. Smailes: *Geography*, Vol. 21, Pt. 2 (1936), p. 124.

[2] G. R. Lewis: *The Stannaries* (1924), p. 8.

[3] Ashburton, Plympton, Tavistock, and Chagford in Devon; Bodmin, Liskeard, Lostwithiel, Helston, and Truro in Cornwall.

[4] R. A. Pelham: 'Fourteenth-century England', *An Historical Geography of England before 1800*, ed. by H. C. Darby (1936), p. 259.

II

THE SIXTEENTH AND SEVENTEENTH CENTURIES

The regional industrial self-sufficiency of the Middle Ages, though never complete, was beginning to pass away before the end of the fifteenth century. The regional market was being replaced by the national market. The late Prof. Unwin gave a sixteenth-century illustration from the cap trade. 'The woollen caps ... which had been among the leading products of local industry in every large town, were being gradually replaced during the sixteenth century, by more fashionable headgear from beyond sea, or by the new felt hats which were beginning to be made in London.'[1] Industries were developing in particular localities beyond the capacity of the local market to absorb their production and the localities wherein they developed were those which had some special advantages. Thus in Chester the decline of the cappers was balanced by the growth of the glovers, who worked up skins imported from pastoral Ireland, and for which industry Chester, by reason of its space-relations, had a natural geographical advantage. 'The decay of crafts,' says Unwin, 'was in fact due, not only to the growth of foreign commerce, but still more perhaps to the concentration of English industries in localities specially adapted to them.'[2] The generalised manufacture of the Middle Ages, whereby each town had samples of many crafts, was beginning to be replaced by the specialised manufacture of a narrow range of commodities in harmony with the qualities of the regional geographical environment. Defoe, in the early eighteenth century, remarked upon this change which by his time had proceeded further—'some other Towns, which are lately increas'd in Trade and Navigation, Wealth, and People, while their Neighbours Decay, it is because they have some particular Trade ... inseparable to the Place, and which fixes there by the Nature of the Thing; as the Herring-Fishery to Yarmouth; the Coal Trade to New-Castle; the Leeds Cloathing-Trade; ... the Virginia and West-India Trade at Liverpool; the Irish Trade at Bristol.'[3] Specialised regional manufacture,

[1] G. Unwin: *Industrial Organisation*, p. 71.

[2] G. Unwin: *Industrial Organisation*, p. 72.

[3] D. Defoe, *op. cit.*, Vol. 1, p. 43. His examples might be open to criticism, but his point is a valid one.

thus replacing the generalised urban manufacture of the Middle Ages, was to attain its most complete expression during the nineteenth century. It was the parallel in industry to the regional specialisation of agricultural production whose progress has been traced in Chapter I.

This increasing regional specialisation of industry was bound up with a second change. Though manufacturing industry continued to persist in the towns, they were ceasing, during the sixteenth and seventeenth centuries, to dominate the industrial geography. Industry was migrating from the town to the country districts, but, judging from unemployment reported in the towns, the industrial population was not migrating with it to the same extent. The process had begun in the woollen manufacture before the close of the Middle Ages. It did not, however, proceed without opposition. Legislation endeavoured to protect the established town industries and to check the growth of rural industries by means of both local and general Acts.[1] What were the causes of this rural migration of industry? It was due, firstly, to lower manufacturing costs in the country districts. The country craftsman was outside gild control (though there were many projects to regulate rural industry)[2] and was free from gild levies; country manufacture escaped the higher rating of the towns;[3] the cost of living in the country was lower, and unemployment bore less hardly on the country worker, who in many cases had an alternative source of income from the land. These factors had been present during the Middle Ages, but the powerful gilds had kept them in check. The rural migration of industry was due, secondly, to the increasing use of water-power and of timber and coal by industrial workshops. These were post-medieval or, at earliest, late-medieval. The overshot water-wheel,[4] requiring a weir or else a mill dam and a long conduit, involved a stream-side site which, in most cases,

[1] Such a general Act was that of 1554 to remedy decay in 'Cities Borowes Townes Corporate and Market Townes'.

[2] G. Unwin: *Industrial Organisation*, p. 175; G. Unwin: *V.C.H. Suffolk*, Vol. 2 (1907), pp. 254–71; H. Heaton, *op. cit.*, Chapter 7.

[3] This was a not inconsiderable factor in the Middle Ages. In 1294 the tax was one-tenth of movables in the rural districts, but one-sixth in the towns; from 1332 it was one-fifteenth and one-tenth respectively.

[4] J. U. Nef: 'The Progress of Technology and the Growth of Large Scale Industry in Great Britain, 1540–1640', *Economic History Review*, Vol. 5, No. 1 (1934), p. 8. *The Survey of the Manor of Rochdale* of 1626 specifies 'a fulling mill . . . with damms water troughs, etc.' (Chetham Society), Vol. 71, p. 159.

necessitated a rural situation. The introduction of large-scale industrial enterprises using coal or timber in quantity also necessitated a rural situation, where alone these fuels could be obtained in sufficient bulk.[1]

There was, thirdly, a substantial change in the size of the industrial unit. In the clothing industry the productive unit, it is true, remained small. Although the commercial unit in the form of the clothier[2] who put out work to individual combers, spinners, weavers, or fullers was frequently large, the industrial processes themselves were carried on largely in the home. This was the 'domestic system', though the term is unsatisfactory, as contrasted with the medieval gild system. But even in the clothing industries there were embryo factories containing a dozen hand-looms or more, and in these cases the system was not domestic in the sense that work was carried on entirely in the home. Such a factory was rarely built for the purpose and a pre-existing building was more often employed: a monastery[3] or a disused walk-mill.[4] In other industries the industrial, as distinct from the commercial, unit was often larger. One industrialist on the Wear (County Durham) claimed to employ 300 men in salt works in 1589.[5] Alum-making near Whitby employed some 80 men in each house, a Kentish cannon foundry employed 200 men in 1613, and a paper mill at Dartford some 'scores of hands'.[6] Some of these were driven by water-power, others used coal.[7]

[1] There was a third reason, the greater fluidity of rural industry. Writing of Lancashire textile industries during the sixteenth and seventeenth centuries, Wadsworth says 'organisation was fluid and elastic . . . it was free to grow and expand on the lines best suited to its own special requirements' (A. P. Wadsworth and J. de L. Mann: *The Cotton Trade and Industrial Lancashire, 1600–1780* (1931), p. 53).

[2] Sam Hill of Soyland, in the West Riding, in the early eighteenth century could send 200 shalloons to London in one consignment and a fortnight later a further 200 (H. Heaton, *op. cit.*, p. 298). The large capitalist clothier was, however, more common in the West Country and in East Anglia.

[3] Leland: *The Itinerary, 1535–43*, Pt. 1, folios 27–8.

[4] J. Smith: *Memoirs of Wool*, Vol. 1 (1747), p. 376.

[5] J. U. Nef: *Economic History Review*, Vol. 5, No. 1, p. 19.

[6] J. U. Nef: *Economic History Review*, Vol. 5, No. 1, pp. 6–7.

[7] These examples are employed by Nef to show that industrial capitalism was well established by the sixteenth and seventeenth centuries. The effects of price movements, of changes in the incidence of labour costs, and of the progress of technique are discussed by J. U. Nef in *Economic History Review*, Vol. 5, No. 1, and in 'Prices and Industrial Capitalism, 1540–1640', *Economic History Review*, Vol. 7, No. 2 (1937), pp. 155–85.

There is not space to examine each industry in turn during the period between the Middle Ages and the Industrial Revolution. I will limit myself to samples—the wool textile and the iron, as samples of textile and metal manufacturing industries respectively.

The woollen and worsted continued to be the most important single industry in Britain. By the close of the Middle Ages three great regional centres had already emerged—the West Country, East Anglia, and, less important, West Yorkshire. The West Country area comprised Gloucester, Wiltshire, Somerset, Dorset, Devon, and Cornwall (together with the adjoining parts of Worcester and Oxford); the East Anglian comprised Norfolk, Suffolk, and Essex; and the West Yorkshire included the adjacent parts of Lancashire and the North Riding. A wool textile manufacture was not, however, confined to these districts. Several towns in the south-east were still active in the sixteenth and seventeenth centuries, but had fallen into decay by the early eighteenth. Kendal greens were well known, as were Welsh frizes and 'cottons'. In the sixteenth century East Lancashire was a woollen area, but in the seventeenth century wool was retreating eastwards to the Yorkshire border and was being replaced by fustian. One area was, however, relatively devoid of a wool manufacture. This was the East Midlands, in reference to which Fuller makes the important comment: 'Observe we here, that mid-England—Northamptonshire, Lincolnshire, and Cambridge—having most of wool, have least of clothing therein.' The three main clothing districts, though their cloths overlapped to some extent, had each their own specialities of production. Within each district, too, there were separate local varieties.

In East Anglia the sub-regions were, firstly, North-east Norfolk; secondly, South Suffolk and North Essex. In North-east Norfolk the earliest centres were Worstead and Aylsham, and they lay in that part of the county most developed agriculturally as well as industrially.[1] Norwich, close at hand, became its later and most famous centre. Though broadcloths were also made, the main output of the region was worsteds. This was especially true after the introduction in the sixteenth

[1] P. M. Roxby: 'East Anglia', *Great Britain: Essays in Regional Geography*, ed. by A. G. Ogilvie (1928), p. 156.

century of the 'new draperies', relatively fine light cloths the technique of whose manufacture was introduced from the Low Countries. The second centre was South Suffolk and North Essex, including Hadleigh, Lavenham, Waldingfield, Melford, and Sudbury, in Suffolk;[1] Colchester, Dedham, Coggeshall, Maldon, Braintree, Bocking, and Witham, in Essex. Most of these had a stream-side situation. Ipswich and Bury St. Edmunds were doing little weaving in Defoe's time, though, as in the villages, there was much spinning.[2] The standard products in this second centre until the end of the sixteenth century were woollen broadcloths made from dyed wool, but the demand for them declined and their place was taken by the says, bays, and perpetuanas of the new draperies and by the combing and spinning of long wool for weaving in the Norfolk worsted industry and elsewhere.

The relationship of this East Anglian industry to the local physical and economic environment presents an interesting study. Sheep had long been an important element in the agricultural geography of East Anglia and its ports had long been involved in the export of raw wool to the Low Countries. A wool textile industry was thus a natural result of local raw material and of space-relations alike. But the precise character of the industry was not determined by the local wool supply. The Norfolk Horn, the local breed in Norfolk, had short, relatively coarse wool; it had good felting properties but was suited only to the poorer quality broadcloths and was quite unsuited to the worsted manufacture. In the early nineteenth century it was mostly sent to Yorkshire and Lancashire for flannel-making.[3] The worsted industry of North-east Norfolk must have imported its long wools from Lincoln or the East Midlands, from the Lincoln or Leicester breeds. In Defoe's time Norwich received yarn from 'other Countries, even from as far as Yorkshire, and Westmorland'.[4] The Suffolk and Essex broadcloth manufacture could, however, have been based on local wool supplies. And these southern centres, with a stream-side situation, had some water-power (though the gradient

---

[1] G. Unwin: *V.C.H. Suffolk* (1907), Vol. 2, pp. 255–6, 269.
[2] D. Defoe, *op. cit.*, Vol. 1, pp. 45 and 52.
[3] W. Youatt: *Sheep* (1837), p. 311.
[4] D. Defoe, *op. cit.*, Vol. 1, p. 61.

G

was low and the streams in this dry eastern climate relatively uncertain and small in volume), which, since the application of the waterwheel to fulling in the fifteenth century, broadcloth manufacture required. It is not, however, certain to what extent the Suffolk cloths were fulled.

The West Country industry was widely flung, from the western scarps of the Wiltshire and Dorset chalk to the confines of Cornwall.[1] It had several local centres; first, the Stroud valley and the Cotswolds; second, the foot of the chalk scarp of the Wiltshire and Dorset Downs;[2] third, the Mendip country from Bristol and Bath to Wells and Frome; fourth, the Vale of Taunton and the margins of Dartmoor. Most of the Cotswold towns[3] were, or had been, woollen working centres, but in the seventeenth century the Stroud valley had become the most important and five hundreds in the neighbourhood had textile workers amounting to over one-third of all the names on a muster roll of 1608, a high proportion of the adult male population.[4] This was the district of superfine woollen broad-cloths. Here the clothiers had a riverine distribution. By the early eighteenth century the second and third groups were making druggets, instead of single-coloured broadcloths as formerly. Defoe described these druggets as 'Fine Medley, or mix'd Cloths' and as 'fine Spanish Cloths'.[5] The mixture was not of combed and carded yarns, but of woollen yarns dyed in different colours.[6] The designation 'Spanish Cloths' referred to the fine short wool imported from Spain, the fleece of the Spanish merino. The Vale of Taunton and the fringes of Dartmoor made serges which were mixed fabrics with a warp of combed long wool and a weft of short carded wool. Serges were fulled or milled, usually by water-power.[7]

The West Country had an abundance of local wool—in the

[1] R. H. Kinvig, *op. cit.*, pp. 243–54 and 290–306; W. G. Hoskins: *Industry, Trade, and People in Exeter, 1688–1800* (1935), map, p. 29; G. D. Ramsay: *The Wiltshire Woollen Industry* (1943).

[2] Salisbury was an outlier of this group.

[3] For the significance of Witney see A. Plummer, ed.: *The Witney Blanket Industry* (1934).

[4] A. J. and R. H. Tawney: 'An Occupational Census of the Seventeenth Century', *Economic History Review*, Vol. 5, No. 1 (1934), pp. 63–4.

[5] D. Defoe, *op. cit.*, Vol. 1, pp. 280–2.

[6] W. Youatt, *op. cit.*, p. 222.

[7] W. G. Hoskins, *op. cit.*, p. 39.

Western Downlands, in the Cotswolds, along the Welsh Border, and in the South-west Peninsula. The West Country lay within the English Plain, the most developed part of medieval England, and it had Bristol, the second port of the kingdom. A woollen industry was appropriate and was early established. It was appropriate, too, that it should be the woollen and not the worsted industry, for there was water-power in abundance for fulling the finished broadcloth,[1] by reason of both relief and rainfall in this more highly accidented western part of the English scarplands. The West Country had also the best supplies of fuller's earth, worked in the neighbourhood of Bath, and of teazles, grown in the Vale of Gloucester[2] and in Somerset north of the Mendips. These were both required in finishing the finest broadcloths. Contemporaries laid great stress on the value of fuller's earth, export of which from the country was illegal. It was thus distinguished from East Anglia. To this extent the woollen industry of the West Country and the worsted industry of East Anglia were differentiated each in accordance with the different qualities of the local physical environment. Short carding wools, which the woollen industry required, came from the short-wool down breeds of the Western Downlands,[3] and, for the finer qualities of broadcloths, from the Welsh Border. Devon had both long and short wools.[4] The Cotswold breed kept in the neighbourhood of the finest broadcloth manufacture, however, was a long wool breed, and its fleece was accordingly unsuited to carding and fulling. But with the growth of the West Country manufacture the local wools became insufficient and wool was drawn in from a wider radius. The position was aggravated by the growth of arable at the expense of down pasture on the Western Downlands, which Defoe noted, for, although sheep were folded on the arable, the head of stock declined.[5] It was aggravated, too, by an increase in the coarseness of the wool consequential upon

[1] Leland observed 'tukkynge myles', i.e. fulling-mills, in a valley bottom near Frome (op. cit., Pt. 5, folio 73b).

[2] R. H. Kinvig, op. cit., pp. 247–8.

[3] D. Defoe, op. cit., Vol. 1, pp. 282–3.

[4] Heath breeds of Dartmoor and Exmoor were short-woolled as most heath sheep of the time, and the South Hams and Bampton (the present Devon Longwool) breeds, of South Devon and Middle Devon–Vale of Taunton respectively, long-woolled.

[5] D. Defoe, op. cit., Vol. 1, p. 283.

the better feeding associated with the New Husbandry. In the sixteenth and seventeenth centuries writers had been convinced of a correlation between poor heath pasture and fine wool, and there is reason to suppose that this was true, the fine short wool being the product of a deficient diet. Wool was drawn southwards into the West Country from Leicester, Northampton, and Lincoln, but these would be mainly long and not short wools. Some Irish wools and Kentish wools, probably both long[1] and short, were imported into Devon for the serge manufacture. But, in addition, merino short wools were imported from Spain, and these became increasingly important in maintaining the quality of the finest broadcloths.[2] Colonial wools, many of them from breeds derived from the merino, did not become available from the southern hemisphere until the early years of the nineteenth century.[3]

The third of the major wool-working regions was West Yorkshire. It comprised the upper valleys of the Calder and Aire and the lower hill country of these river basins as far east as the Vale of York. There was woollen working in other Pennine dales, but not on the same scale. The histories and guides of Leeds at the end of the eighteenth century all declared that not a single manufacturer was to be found more than one mile east or two miles north of the town.[4] Leeds and Wakefield, though important market centres of the industry, lay on the eastern margins of the industrial region. Leland mentions Wakefield, Bradeforde, and Ledis as clothing towns, but he did not visit Halifax.[5] The famous Halifax Act of the reign of Philip and Mary bore witness to the importance of the industry in that district in 1555. To these Defoe added Huthersfield to make up 'the five Towns which carry on that

---

[1] During this period, before the Industrial Revolution, the export of wool was almost entirely of long wools. There was much clandestine export of wool in the late seventeenth and eighteenth centuries, and it was mainly of long wool. A pamphlet of 1694 asserted that two-thirds of the long wool grown on Romney Marsh was exported to France and the Low Countries (J. Smith, *op. cit.*, Vol. 1 (1747), p. 390); Romney Marsh was, of course, particularly well placed for this traffic. It is a striking commentary on this export of long wool that a worsted industry of any bulk was absent, as Fuller noted, from the East Midland counties, where most long wool was produced.

[2] R. H. Kinvig, *op. cit.*, p. 246.

[3] W. Youatt, *op. cit.*, pp. 183–92.

[4] H. Heaton, *op. cit.*, p. 284.

[5] Leland, *op. cit.*, Pt. 1, folio 46, and Pt. 9, folio 53.

vast Cloathing Trade'.[1] The production of West Yorkshire
was of relatively coarse cloth, as was the rule in the North of
England at this time. Leeds made broadcloths, but Halifax
the narrow coarse kerseys, three or four of which were reckoned
by the aulnager as equal to one broadcloth.[2] The Halifax
Act of 1555[3] specified the small manufacturing unit (using
one to four stones of wool per week) as the main element in the
clothing industry of that district, and Heaton concludes that one
kersey a week, requiring about two stones of wool and about
five persons (one weaver, four carders and spinners), was the
average output of such small units in the fifteenth and sixteenth
centuries. In many cases five workers could be provided by a
single family, even young children being set to carding and
spinning. But the family unit of manufacture may not have
been typical of the whole area.[4] In the eighteenth century,
towards the end of this domestic phase of the industry, considerable regional variations of production developed within
West Yorkshire. Leeds became more and more a market centre,
and with the reintroduction of worsteds at the close of the
seventeenth century (first of the half-woollen and half-worsted
bays and serges, later of the full-worsted shalloons) the western
districts turned from kerseys to worsted cloths.[5]

The localization of the wool textile industry in West Yorkshire presents somewhat different problems to those presented
by East Anglia and the West Country. West Yorkshire did not
become an important manufacturing district until the latter
part of the fifteenth century. In 1473–75 the combined output
of the whole district, according to the aulnage accounts, only
just exceeded the output of the single centre of York. East
Anglia, the West Country, and the Vale of York lay within the
English Plain, the focus of medieval life, in industry as well as

---

[1] D. Defoe, *op. cit.*, Vol. 3, p. 594.

[2] H. Heaton, *op. cit.*, p. 179, and J. Smith, *op. cit.*, Vol. 1, p. 140.

[3] An Acte for Thinhabitantes of Halyfaxe touching the Byeng of Woolles
(R. H. Tawney and E. Power: *Tudor Economic Documents*, Vol. 1 (1924), pp. 187–8).

[4] Prof. Cole doubts whether the family unit was typical even of the Halifax
district *by the early eighteenth century*, and that may well have been true (G. D. H.
Cole, Introduction to D. Defoe, *op. cit.*, pp. xiv–xv).

[5] H. Heaton, *op. cit.*, pp. 284–9. This succession is shown clearly in the *Letter
Books of Joseph Holroyd and Sam Hill*, ed. by H. Heaton (1914). Holroyd's letters of
1706–07 specify kerseys and bays, but not shalloons; Hill's letters of 1738 specify
kerseys, bays, and shalloons.

agriculture. The West Yorkshire hills, a bleaker, less fruitful environment, lay outside it. Indeed, in the upper parts of the Calder Valley during the early part of the Middle Ages there had been several vaccaries, an extensive form of land utilization. The Halifax Act of 1555 claimed privileges on account of the benefit the small clothier was bestowing on the barren hillsides of the district, for he was reclaiming the land and keeping it in cultivation, which he could not do without his subsidiary income from the making of kerseys. The agricultural poverty of the district was evident. The increase of population in Halifax parish was there placed at 500 households within forty years. It seems improbable that these smallholders kept sheep in any number, or, indeed, that they kept sheep at all; the Act related to the buying of wool through a middleman, who himself brought it from some distance. In Lancashire, in Rossendale,[1] and in the Rochdale[2] district, however, small-holders kept sheep and practised industry side by side. In West Yorkshire the domestic industry retained a semi-rural character as well as a rural distribution until the time of the Industrial Revolution. The clothiers had each a few fields with a few head of stock, though the fields were employed for tenter-frames as well as farming, and of the stock some were used for carrying wool and pieces. The whole industrial population appears to have gone into the fields at harvest.[3] In West Yorkshire manufacture was for long only of the coarser cloths, and these, cheaply produced, could often be substituted for more expensive cloths made elsewhere. It is possible, indeed, that the West Yorkshire industry grew by reason of lower production costs on account of family labour and of the combination of industry with agriculture. Although it would not be wise to push the point too far, it is possible that the small master employing family labour was relatively more prominent in the *woollen* industry of West Yorkshire than elsewhere, and that, as a productive unit, he tended to carry on more processes under one roof than the clothiers in the more sectionalised industries of the West Country and East Anglia; that is, he tended more than they in

[1] G. H. Tupling: *The Economic History of Rossendale*, pp. 165–7.

[2] A. P. Wadsworth and J. de L. Mann, *op. cit.*, p. 27.

[3] *Letter Books of Joseph Holroyd and Sam Hill.* A letter of 13 August 1706 observes: 'Now for six weeks will be little made' (p. 19).

the direction of a vertical organisation.[1] This was truer of the earlier than of the later phases of the domestic system. The West Yorkshire *worsted* industry, however, was organised from the first by big clothiers who arranged their production sectionally.[2]

The West Riding industry was not favoured by its local wools: they were not plentiful and they were coarse. It was declared in 1588 that local wool was sent to Rochdale and that Halifax drew its raw wool from Lincolnshire.[3] A few decades later wool was being imported, because it was cheaper, from Ireland and Scotland. The implication of a pamphlet printed in the *State Papers* for 1615 is that from the Midland wool districts, some qualities were sent into West Yorkshire and quite other qualities into East Anglia, the one then a woollen and the other a worsted district.[4] In the eighteenth century West Yorkshire spun a good deal of yarn for weavers in East Anglia and the West Country, but especially for East Anglia. It seems clear that local wool supply had little to do with the precise character of the industry in any of the three major centres. The trade in raw wool was well developed and it was not expensive to transport relative to its weight. West Yorkshire was as well furnished with water-power as was the West Country, and was therefore suited to the woollen manufacture, its staple industry until the eighteenth century. The localisation of worsteds during the eighteenth century in the upper Calder and Aire valleys was not due to lack of water-power, as it may have been in East Anglia, for water-power was available here to as great an extent as anywhere else in the West Yorkshire textile district. The soft water of the Pennine streams was probably better in quality than the water of the West Country and certainly better than the water of East Anglia. Defoe's description of the Halifax district shows how intensively this water was employed; a flow of water being available for every house.[5]

[1] *S.P.D. James I*, Vol. 80 (1615). Quoted by G. Unwin: *Industrial Organisation*, pp. 235–6, and by H. Heaton: *The Yorkshire Woollen and Worsted Industries*, pp. 293–4. See also Committee on Woollen Manufacture, 1806, *Report*, pp. 8–13. It is interesting to note that even at this early date the packing of cloth for export overseas seems to have been a specilised business.

[2] H. Heaton: *The Yorkshire Woollen and Worsted Industries*, pp. 296–8.

[3] H. Heaton: *The Yorkshire Woollen and Worsted Industries*, p. 118.

[4] *S.P.D. James I*, Vol. 80 (1615). Quoted by G. Unwin: *Industrial Organisation*, p. 188.

[5] D. Defoe, *op. cit.*, Vol. 2, pp. 601–2.

BROADCLOTH MILLED
IN YORKSHIRE, 1726-1810

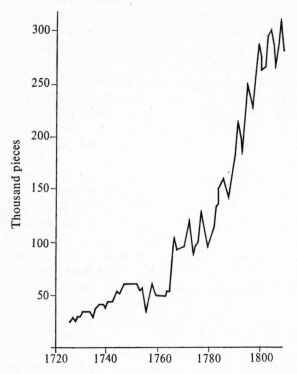

Figure 9. Broadcloth Milled in Yorkshire, 1726–1810

For the dispersed hillside settlements that is still largely true to-day.

Eastern Lancashire, adjacent to West Yorkshire and with a very similar physical environment, was also a woollen area. When West Yorkshire was weaving kerseys and broadcloths, east Lancashire was making 'cottons' and frizes, relatively light and coarse woollen goods.[1] Lancashire adopted the half-worsted bays early in the seventeenth[2] century and the full-worsted shalloons by the eighteenth. In almost every respect, the woollen area of eastern Lancashire was similar to West

[1] A. P. Wadsworth and J. de L. Mann, *op. cit.*, p. 12.
[2] A. P. Wadsworth and J. de L. Mann, *op. cit.*, p. 13.

Yorkshire—in physical environment, in the presence of water-power, in a farmer-weaver economy,[1] and, though the precise character of the fabrics differed, in a generally coarse class of woollen manufacture. But it was only the Pennine slopes which were involved in wool. There was little woollen-working in the West Lancashire Plain, or, indeed, in Manchester. Though woollen cloths were merchanted in Manchester, the place itself was concerned more with linen and with cotton smallwares. Between the woollen of upland eastern Lancashire and the linen of the West Lancashire Plain, there arose during the course of the seventeenth century an intermediate belt[2] running through Blackburn, Bolton, and what is now Oldham (but excluding Bury and Rochdale), whose staple fabric was fustian, made of a linen warp and a cotton weft. The employment of these materials provides an interesting illustration of the impossibility of ascribing the precise character of a textile industry to its local textile raw materials. Once a textile industry is established, based initially perhaps on local raw materials, it changes its character comparatively easily with changes in demand for particular fabrics. Linen-weaving in West Lancashire and Manchester, originally based on local flax, had outgrown local supplies by Leland's time, when Liverpool was importing 'moch Yrisch yarn'.[3] In the eighteenth century linen yarn was being imported also from the Continent, the shores of the North Sea and Baltic. Cotton, of course, was entirely imported: it came through London from the Levant. The weaving of fustians in Britain seems to have come in with the new draperies in the second half of the sixteenth century.[4] Its adoption in Lancashire coincided with the adoption of other new fabrics, such as bays, and marked, as A. P. Wadsworth puts it, a minor industrial revolution. It was not the only mixed cotton-linen fabric: checks,[5] which had a similar character,

[1] A. P. Wadsworth and J. de L. Mann, op. cit., pp. 25–8, and G. H. Tupling, op. cit., pp. 161–91.

[2] This represented in large measure a retreat of the woollen belt eastwards. Leland (op. cit., Pt. 9, folio 57) had described Bolton as depending mostly on 'cottons and cowrse yarne'.

[3] Leland, op. cit., Pt. 9, folio 56. This may have been woollen yarn equally as linen yarn. C. Gill: The Rise of the Irish Linen Industry (1925), assumes it to have been linen yarn, p. 6.

[4] A. P. Wadsworth and J. de L. Mann, op. cit., p. 19.

[5] Checks and fustians were not identical. See A. P. Wadsworth and J. de L. Mann, op. cit., Preface, pp. vi–vii.

were made for tropical markets.[1] When fully developed, the Lancashire fustian industry depended entirely on imported materials and the check industry largely on foreign markets as well. They were the forerunners in this respect of nine-teenth-century industrialism. As the eighteenth century wore on more cotton and less linen was put into these mixed fabrics and there were attempts at making muslins from hand-spun cotton yarn. They were not very successful and the emergence of a pure cotton manufacture on any substantial scale, for reasons which the late Prof. Daniels explained, had to await the invention of the mule.[2]

The woollen industry in Wales, as at first in the North of England, had a relatively coarse character. 'Cottons', frizes, and flannels were its staple cloths. The wool of upland Wales was coarse in character, though that of the English parts of the Welsh Border was the finest in the country. The industry was a part-time farmer's occupation and it fitted well into the pastoral character of much Welsh farming.[3] There was an abundance of water-power and, it will be noted, its fabrics were mainly woollens. In Scotland woollen and linen cloth had long been made from locally-grown wool and flax, the former largely in the form of rough plaiding for home ware, but the burghs made cloth of better quality. The Scottish woollen industry never developed to the same degree as the English and wool continued to be exported from Scotland to the Continent and, as the Yorkshire industry grew, to the West Riding. The Tweed Valley woollen industry did not develop on any considerable scale until the end of the eighteenth century.[4]

Even in the Middle Ages there had been a divorce in the iron industry between the initial reducing or smelting processes, located where ore was mined and charcoal made, and the crafts working up the malleable iron into finished consumption goods, located in the towns. The divorce was never complete, for some articles—those, no doubt, requiring less skill in

[1] A. P. Wadsworth and J. de L. Mann, *op. cit.*, p. 173.

[2] G. W. Daniels: *The Early English Cotton Industry* (1920).

[3] Much of the production, of course, was used for clothing at home, but there was an export of Welsh cloths from Bristol, at any rate as early as the first half of the fourteenth century (E. M. Carus-Wilson: *The Overseas Trade of Bristol in the later Middle Ages* (Bristol Record Society) (1937), p. 185 and elsewhere).

[4] D. Defoe noticed the export of wool from Tweeddale and the absence of a woollen manufacture.

fashioning—were made in forges attached to the bloomery hearths or smelting furnaces. In the period prior to the Industrial Revolution there was again a distinction in geographical distribution between smelting and finishing, though it was of a different nature.

Smelting was localised, as it had been previously, where there was access to both ore and charcoal.[1] Most of the ore bodies and ore deposits were known, but they were not all worked with equal intensity. Not only had ore to be available but also charcoal, and, where both were not available on the same sites, ore was carried to charcoal and charcoal to ore. According to Scrivenor, writing in the middle of the nineteenth century, one ton of pig iron required two loads of charcoal or four loads of wood.[2] Mushet, in 1840, calculated that a charcoal blast furnace with an annual production of 1,000 tons of iron required 120 acres of woodland to be cleared of timber annually in order to keep it in full operation.[3] The availability of water-power was a second factor, for the water-wheel was used for the blast and the hammers. By the time of Elizabeth timber was becoming scarce, but the technique of iron smelting remained dependent on charcoal. There ensued a centrifugal scatter of iron smelting, as Prof. Ashton has described.[4] A Wealden ironmaster migrated to the South Wales coalfield and another ironmaster from Robin Hood's Bay to the interior of Durham. The Backbarrow Company of Furness set up a furnace at Invergarry, the Newlands Company one in Argyll, and the Duddon Company one near Inveraray. In the case of these Scottish furnaces ore had to be transported from Furness or West Cumberland and the smelted iron returned for further reworking. These examples of long-distance transport refer

[1] The evidence of the Spencer papers referring to South Yorkshire is very valuable. Furnaces were invariably close to the ironstone and on water-power sites. Charcoal was made within a radius of 10–15 miles of the furnaces and it was made from coppice wood of oak and ash of 15 years' growth, and even from hedge timber. Forges were heated with small charcoal and had hammers worked by a water wheel (A. Raistrick and E. Allen: 'The South Yorkshire Ironmasters', *Economic History Review*, Vol. 9, No. 2 (1939)).

[2] H. Scrivenor: *History of the Iron Trade* (1854), p. 55. Presentments of juries in Sussex in 1548–49 printed by R. H. Tawney and E. Power (*op. cit.*, Vol. 1, pp. 233 and 236) specify three loads of wood to one load of charcoal.

[3] Charcoal was made not so much from forest timber (from branches and small logs rather than building timber), but chiefly from coppices, specially planted for the purpose.

[4] T. S. Ashton: *Iron and Steel in the Industrial Revolution* (1924), pp. 13–23.

TABLE VII

IRON FURNACES AND FORGES IN THE EARLY EIGHTEENTH CENTURY

	FURNACES			FORGES		
	No.	Total output tons	Average output per furnace in tons	No.	Total output tons	Average output per forge in tons
South-east	11	1,990	181	15	926	62
South Wales and Forest of Dean	14	5,250	375	29	2,700	93
North Wales and Cheshire	5	2,250	450	8	840	105
West Midlands	14	5,400	386	46	6,820	148
North-west	2	1,000	500	—	200	—
Yorks, Derby, Notts	9	2,300	256	16	1,690	106
North-east	—	—	—	1	120	120
Total	55	18,190	331	115	13,296	114

Source: E. W. Hulme: 'Statistical History of the Iron Trade of England and Wales, 1717–50'. *Trans. Newcomen Society,* Vol. 9 (1928–29). List A, pp. 21–2. The date is 1717. For a discussion of the West Midlands based on manuscript accounts see B. L. C. Johnson: *Birmingham and its Regional Setting* (1950), pp. 168–73, and the same author's 'The Charcoal Iron Industry in the Early Eighteenth Century' in the *Geographical Journal,* Vol. 117, Pt. 2 (1951), pp. 167–77.

Iron Furnaces and Iron Forges in 1717

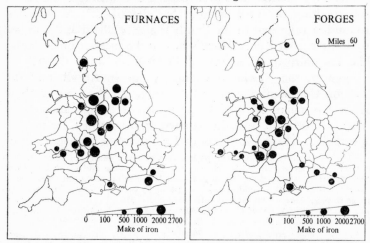

| Figure 10A | Figure 10B |

A represents Furnaces and B Forges and the symbols are in proportion to 'what Iron they are supposed to make or can make one year with another', according to the phrasing of the MSS. The scale is identical in the two maps.

to the coastwise trade: there was also a brisk trade in iron along the Severn: but land carriage was over shorter distances except for pig iron and bar iron. The distribution of furnaces and forges for 1717 is shown in Figure 10 and in Table VII. The source is the MSS. of John Fuller and Son, Gunfounders, Heathfield, Sussex. It is not a census in the modern sense and may contain omissions or errors due to incomplete knowledge. Furnaces were most numerous in the Weald,[1] in the West Midlands and the lower Severn Valley (including the Forest of Dean and the eastern end of the South Wales coalfield), and in Yorkshire and Derbyshire, but the largest furnaces were in the West Midlands and the lower Severn Valley, over half of the total production of pig iron coming from these two districts.

Although there were many forges in the charcoal-iron smelting districts, these did not monopolise the manufacture of finished iron goods. The refining and forging of pig iron required more charcoal than did smelting, about half as much again according to Scrivenor. A list of Wealden ironmasters in 1573[2] shows that approximately two-thirds of the furnaces and forges were combined in single ownership, probably, though not necessarily, on the same site. But this was in the sixteenth century, and in the Weald, which retained longest the older characteristics. Its forges, like its furnaces, were the smallest in average size of any district. The greatest number of forges in the early eighteenth century was not in the Weald but in the West Midlands. These West Midland forges used much more iron than the local West Midland furnaces produced: the West Midlands region was an importer of pig iron, unlike the South-east and North and South Wales, which were exporters of pig iron. In 1737 it was calculated that within 10 miles of Birmingham 9,000 tons of bar iron were used annually, the greater part being by nail-makers working under the domestic system.[3] The total annual production of bar iron in

[1] Furnaces in the Weald were at this time wholly valley bottom sites whose blast was provided by water-power from impounded waters. The sites were chiefly in the High Weald for reasons of power, as well as of source of ore and of charcoal. See maps in G. S. Sweeting: *Proc. Geol. Assoc.* (1944), Figs. 1 and 3, and in M. C. Delany: *The Historical Geography of the Wealden Iron Industry* (1921), maps 2 and 3.

[2] T. S. Ashton: *Iron and Steel*, p. 6.

[3] T. S. Ashton: *Iron and Steel*, p. 19.

England and Wales at this time was probably under 20,000 tons, but at least as much was imported. There were other groups of forges and smithies near Sheffield[1] and in the north-east. It will be noticed that these areas where finished iron was mainly made were coalfield sites. The import of bar iron gave rise to smithies at Newcastle, Hull, and London (importing iron from Sweden and Russia), and at Bristol and Liverpool (importing iron from America). Sweden, Russia, and North America all had timber, and therefore charcoal, in immense quantities.

During the Middle Ages coal was worked in most British coalfields, but, except in North-east England, it was on an infinitesimal scale and for strictly local use. Timber and peat were yet plentiful. But from the middle of the sixteenth century output began to increase. According to the generalised estimates made by Prof. Nef, the total production in Great Britain was 0·21 million tons in 1551–60, 2·98 in 1681–90, and 10·30 in 1781–90;[2] and, according to estimates quoted by Prof. Ashton and Prof. Sykes, it was $2\frac{1}{4}$ million tons in 1660, $2\frac{1}{2}$ in 1700, over 6 in 1770, and over 10 in 1800.[3] The increase was due to a growing shortage of timber, making imperative the use of an alternative fuel, and the growing shortage of timber was due to the increase of population with its demand for firewood; it was due to the increase in the navy and merchant shipping with their demand for oak; and it was due to the growth in industries consuming timber. Prof. Nef quotes Wiebe to the effect that the rise in the price of firewood greatly outstripped the rise in general commodity prices: in 1633–42 general prices were nearly three times as great as in 1451–1500, but firewood prices were nearly eight times as great.[4] Presentments of a Sussex jury in 1548–49 afford an interesting local example: 'within 15 years last past upon the downs a load of wood was commonly bought and sold for 14d., and now by occasion of the mills and furnaces every load is enhanced to 2s. 8d. and 3s.

---

[1] In Hallamshire D. Defoe reported, though he would pronounce no opinion on the veracity of the figure, 30,000 men employed in cutlery and hardware (*op. cit.*, Vol. 2, p. 590).

[2] J. U. Nef: *The Rise of the British Coal Industry*, Vol. 1, p. 20.

[3] T. S. Ashton and J. Sykes: *The Coal Industry of the Eighteenth Century* (1929), p. 13.

[4] J. U. Nef: *The Rise of the British Coal Industry*, Vol. 1, p. 158.

And in the Weald among the woods a load of wood was commonly bought and sold for 4d. and now by occasion of the mills every load is enhanced to the sum of 12d.'[1] The higher price on the downs than in the woods is noticeable. Although the firewood shortage was most acute in the towns and particularly in London, it was present also in most country districts. Enclosure with its hedgerow timber alleviated the position to only a very small extent. The price of coal rose much less than the price of firewood and coal was used increasingly for domestic firing. Tudor houses with their stacks of chimneys adapted for coal-burning revolutionised domestic architecture. This was an age of maritime expansion and of naval wars, and sound oak was required in quantity by the shipyards.[2] The inroads of the iron industry were very considerable and, although iron smelting may not have continued to grow in the seventeenth century, it is improbable that replanting of woodland kept pace with charcoal burning. The finishing of iron goods was becoming concentrated more and more on the coalfields, where an alternative fuel was available. Fuel was needed in increasing quantities for salt-making,[3] both inland and coastal, for glass-making, for soap-making, for alum, for copperas, and for bricks. Many of these growing industries turned over to coal. For the country as a whole, Nef estimates that in this period approximately one-third of the total output of coal was consumed for industrial and two-thirds for household purposes.

But, although the employment of coal was thus increasing steadily, there were many districts of the country where coal was not used. Nef estimates that the average distance of land carriage from pithead to point of consumption was no more than 15 miles and that the 'price of coal seems almost to have doubled with every two miles it was carried from the mines'.[4] The carriage of coal was normally only a six-months summer business, and even the coastwise colliers were laid up during the

[1] R. H. Tawney and E. Power, *op. cit.*, Vol. 1, p. 236.

[2] 'Between 1550 and 1660 the total tonnage of the Royal Navy apparently increased sixfold' (J. U. Nef: *The Rise of the British Coal Industry*, Vol. 1, p. 173).

[3] P. Pilbin: 'A Geographical Analysis of the Sea Salt Industry of North-east England', *Scottish Geographical Magazine*, Vol. 51 (1935), pp. 22–8. The Teesmouth industry, with no local coal, declined in favour of those actually on the coalfield.

[4] J. U. Nef: *The Rise of the British Coal Industry*, Vol. 1, pp. 102–3.

winter months.[1] Nef has drawn up a generalised map of the areas of coal production and consumption in the late seventeenth century. The English Plain, devoid of local supplies, consumed coal only around the coasts and along those east coast rivers which were navigable—the Ouse and Trent, the rivers of the Wash, the Thames, and, for shorter distances, the East Anglian rivers. York drew some of its coal by coastwise and river traffic from the North-east coalfield, involving a 200-mile journey, as well as from the Yorkshire coalfield, some 20 miles away.[2] The industrial parts of East Anglia are marked as coal-consuming districts, and Defoe records that many of the colliers engaged on the Newcastle–London trade were owned by Yarmouth sailing-masters who within his own recollection had largely replaced the Ipswich men.[3] The greater part of the West Country industrial district (except the Cotswold valleys) is similarly marked as receiving coal from Bristol, the Forest of Dean, and South Wales. East Anglia and the West Country, therefore, had access to coal. But there was a wide belt of agricultural land in southern England, where coal was used only by the more wealthy of the rural population, and where the labourer was reduced in the eighteenth century to burning dried dung.[4] Many of the hill districts of upland Wales and of the Northern Pennines, of the Southern Uplands and of the Highlands of Scotland were also too far removed from the coalfields to permit coal to be carried to them except at a prohibitive cost. It was only where water transport was available that coal was widely distributed and the realisation of this was the urge to many, if not most, of the canal projects of the late eighteenth and early nineteenth centuries.

The most extensively worked coalfield was that of Northumberland and Durham. It had been the most important in the Middle Ages, and it remained the most important until well on in the nineteenth century. Its early development was due to the cropping out of seams along the coast and along the River Tyne which permitted, by reason of access to the coastal trade, a wide diffusion of its products—'from whence not London only, but

---

[1] D. Defoe, *op. cit.*, Vol. 1, p. 41.
[2] J. U. Nef: *The Rise of the British Coal Industry*, Vol. 1, p. 102.
[3] D. Defoe, *op. cit.*, Vol. 1, pp. 40–1, 67–8.
[4] J. H. Clapham: *Early Railway Age*, p. 78.

all the South Part of England is continually supplied'.[1] No
other coalfield lay so close to the east coast or had such facilities
for supplying by sea that part of the country devoid of coal.
As mining proceeded larger and larger areas of the exposed
field were involved. On Tyneside the early workings were all of
surface outcrops close to the river, but the later workings lay
some distance back from the river-front—some 8–10 miles by
1700.[2] Mining at such a distance away from the river led
ultimately to the erection of wagon-ways which replaced packhorses. This method of transport may not have been first used
in the north-east, but it was adopted here extensively.[3] The
coal mined was chiefly that suitable for household use. The
pan-coal used by the salt industry was the slack inevitably produced in working for lump coal. The steam-coal district of
Northumberland, despite its coastal situation, was not worked
on a considerable scale until the end of the seventeenth century.
Nef estimates the production of the whole coalfield at the end
of the eighteenth century in round figures at 1·2 million tons, of
which 0·8 million tons was exported coastwise and abroad, the
greater part (0·7 million tons) to London and the east and
south-east coasts. Tyneside and Wearside had a monopoly
of the London market until the early nineteenth century, and
the old Tyneside pitman with relatively high wages was an
aristocrat among the artisans of his day.[4]

III

THE INDUSTRIAL REVOLUTION

The late eighteenth and early nineteenth centuries constituted a period of active technical improvement of industry
as well as of agriculture. The Agrarian Revolution was paralleled by the Industrial Revolution.[5] Both involved a more

[1] D. Defoe, *op. cit.*, Vol. 2, p. 659.

[2] J. U. Nef: *The Rise of the British Coal Industry*, Vol. 1, p. 28.

[3] The first reference that T. S. Ashton and J. Sykes give us near Nottingham in
1610 (T. S. Ashton and J. Sykes, *op cit.*, p. 63).

[4] E. Welbourne: *The Miners' Unions of Northumberland and Durham* (1923).

[5] The term 'Industrial Revolution' is, of course, only a label of convenience.
It includes a complex of changes—technical, economic, social, and political—and
when described as referring to the period 1750–1850 it is limited arbitrarily to a
time when change was most rapid. The period prior to 1850 represents, in fact,
the first phase of the Industrial Revolution, and the second phase, after 1850,
presented rather different qualities.

efficient use of material, the former of soil and climate, the latter of raw materials and power. Both involved particularly a much more efficient use of labour. Both resulted in marked changes in geographical distribution, and in an accentuated regional specialisation of production. Individual districts devoted themselves wholly to one form of enterprise, and particular industries (but not yet particular forms of agricultural production to the same extent) tended to become concentrated in a single or in a relatively restricted number of localities.

What were the characteristics of the new industrial economy? Its first characteristic was that it was a machine industry as distinct from a handicraft industry. It was not that machinery was new to industry: the hand-loom was a machine equally with the power-loom. But the new machines, when set in motion, themselves performed the industrial process and the operative became a minder of machines making the fabric instead of the creator of the fabric himself. This implied, what Ruskin deplored, that the workman ceased to be a craftsman, but it also implied a much greater uniformity of products and it enabled a manufacturer to supply an article more exactly according to specification. The mechanisation of industry, however, proceded irregularly and at an uneven pace. It came much earlier in the cotton, for example, than in the woollen, and in the cotton and worsted industries it came earlier in spinning than in weaving.[1] Some industries, or at least some processes within those industries, remain in a handicraft phase even today. Industries manufacturing a standard product on a large scale are obviously more suited to mechanisation than industries making individualised articles for a restricted market. Clearly, at any one moment during the course of the Industrial Revolution, the pattern of industry was a mosaic of old and new, of handicraft and of machine manufacture. The substitution of factory for handicraft manufacture implied that materials contributed an increased and labour a

[1] For example, in 1833, out of 74 worsted factories in Yorkshire, 66 were for spinning only, 7 both spun and wove, and only 1 was for weaving only. (Calculated from the returns of the Children's Employment Commission (1834) by H. D. Fong: *Triumph of Factory System in England* (1930), p. 86.) The saving from machine-spinning was self-evident, but the saving from power-loom weaving was for a time problematical, for the cost of operating the machines and keeping them in repair had to be set against the saving of labour at the loom (J. Bischoff: *A Comprehensive History of the Woollen and Worsted Manufactures*, Vol. 2 (1842), p. 273).

decreased share of total costs of manufacture, and, as a corollary, that industry became more closely located by its materials than hitherto.[1]

The second characteristic of the new industrial economy was that its machines were driven by power. Some early models may have been worked by hand or by animal labour, but most machines were too heavy to be so driven. Machines driven by power were employed long before the Industrial Revolution, wind and falling water being harnessed even during the Middle Ages, but only on a very restricted scale. From the fifteenth century onwards water-power was used more extensively. Wind and water-power are intermittent and unreliable, and in Great Britain, with its variable winds and its small streams and rivers, were adequate for only small industrial units. A single mountain stream could provide a sufficient gradient for many water-wheels in turn, but each water-wheel was large enough to drive only a limited number of machines. Before the Industrial Revolution and during its early phases water-power drove cutlery grindstones, forge hammers, mine pumps, spinning-frames, fulling-mills, and corn-mills. The use of water-power meant geographically a dispersed and rural industrial distribution. But the intermittency of working and the distribution in small units were both unsatisfactory. It was the lack of water during 'the thirsty season' that first interested Matthew Boulton in a steam-engine. The steam-engine erected at the Soho Manufactory in Birmingham was engaged in pumping water to drive the water-wheel, which in turn drove the machines for polishing and turning the buttons and inlaid goods, metal wares in whose manufacture Boulton was engaged.[2] The same volume of water could thus be used time and time again and a constantly renewed supply was unnecessary. The Boulton and Watt engine was a great improvement on the Newcomen, which had preceded it, in respect of fuel efficiency,

---

[1] W. Smith: 'Mobility in the Location of Industry in Great Britain', *The Advancement of Science*, Vol. 6, No. 22 (1949), pp. 115–17.

[2] J. Lord: *Capital and Steam Power* (1923), pp. 95–7 and 153. T. S. Ashton states that it was as a substitute for horse-power that attracted Boulton to the steam-engine (T. S. Ashton: *Iron and Steel*, p. 62). The water-wheel interpretation is adopted also by D. Brownlie: 'Steam Power in Evolution', *Journal Textile Institute* (1927). The earliest Watt engines had a horse-power of 15–20, about the horse-power of the larger water-wheels. But they soon increased and, being thus able to drive more and more machines, permitted larger factory premises.

and the annual payment due to Boulton and Watt was at first calculated on the difference in coal consumption between the two.[1] This greater fuel efficiency was of considerable significance, for it permitted the Boulton and Watt engine to be used in industries other than coal-mining. Over half the Newcomen engines in 1769, but little more than one-tenth of the Boulton and Watt engines erected between 1775 and 1800, were installed at collieries. There were only six Boulton and Watt engines at collieries on the Northumberland-Durham coalfield between 1775 and 1800: the same field had had fifty-seven Newcomen engines in 1769. The saving of coal was of little advantage to colliery owners. Just over one-quarter of the Boulton and Watt engines, but 85 per cent. of the Newcomen engines, were devoted to pumping water—in coal and ore-mines, or for canals and waterworks. Between 1775 and 1800 the Boulton and Watt partnership had a monopoly of steam-engine manufacture on the Watt principle and, as full records of the firm's trading have been preserved, it is possible to draw up a table of the geographical distribution of Boulton and Watt steam-engines in the last quarter of the eighteenth century, and of the industries for which they provided power. These particulars, summarised from Lord's tables, are set out in Tables VIII and IX.

Most of the industries of the country had steam-engines to a greater or less extent. Cotton-mills, woollen- and worsted-mills, flax-mills, textile finishing works, forges and foundries, metal workshops; pot-banks and glassworks, corn-mills, breweries and distilleries, and many miscellaneous industries all had some establishments driven by steam. Even at this early date, steam-power was widely diffused among industries of very different type. It was also widely diffused geographically. The greatest number in a single industry was in cotton—92 out of a total of 318. It will be noticed that the steam-using cotton industry, though concentrated in Lancashire together with North-east Cheshire and West Yorkshire, was not confined to it. There were many in Nottinghamshire (together with Leicester and Northampton), several in the West of Scotland

---

[1] J. Lord, *op. cit.*, p. 109. According to one of Watt's letters, the efficiency per bushel of coal was almost four times as great. The Newcomen was the first successful 'fire-engine'. For the history of the steam-engine see H. W. Dickinson: *A Short History of the Steam Engine* (1939).

Table VIII

DISTRIBUTION OF BOULTON AND WATT STEAM-ENGINES, 1775–1800 (A)

	Textiles	Collieries	Ore-mines	Iron Works	Pottery and Glass	Canals	Water Works	Corn Mills, Breweries, Distilleries	Others	Total
Cheshire	9	—	—	—	—	—	—	1	2	12
Cornwall	—	—	21	—	—	—	—	—	—	21
Cumberland	—	3	—	—	—	—	—	—	—	3
Derby	1	1	1	—	—	—	—	1	—	4
Durham	4	—	—	—	—	—	—	—	2	6
Essex	—	—	—	—	—	—	1	—	1	2
Gloucester	1	—	—	—	—	3	—	1	1	6
Kent	—	—	—	—	—	—	—	3	—	3
Lancashire	47	—	—	—	2	3	—	1	2	55
Leicester	2	—	—	—	—	—	—	—	1	3
Lincoln	—	—	—	—	—	—	—	—	1	1
Middlesex	5	—	—	—	—	1	10	15	10	41
Northampton	1	—	—	—	—	—	—	—	—	1
Northumberland	1	6	—	—	—	—	—	—	2	9
Nottingham	15	—	—	—	—	—	—	1	1	17
Oxford	—	—	—	—	—	1	—	2	—	3
Salop	1	13	—	11	—	—	—	—	—	25
Stafford	1	4	—	11	4	9	—	—	2	31
Surrey	3	—	—	3	—	—	1	4	5	16
Warwick	1	3	—	1	—	—	—	1	—	6
Wiltshire	—	—	—	—	—	1	—	—	—	1
Worcester	—	—	—	1	—	—	—	—	—	1
Yorkshire	12	—	—	4	—	—	1	2	3	22
Anglesey	—	—	1	—	—	—	—	—	—	1
Flint	—	—	—	1	—	—	—	—	—	1
Glamorgan	—	2	—	3	—	—	—	—	—	5
Monmouth	—	—	—	1	—	—	—	—	—	1
Argyll	—	—	—	—	—	1	—	—	—	1
Clackmannan	—	—	—	—	—	—	—	2	—	2
Edinburgh	—	1	—	—	1	—	—	1	—	3
Falkirk	—	—	—	—	—	—	—	1	—	1
Fife	1	—	—	—	—	—	—	—	—	1
Forfar	1	—	—	—	—	—	—	—	—	1
Haddington	—	—	—	—	—	—	—	1	—	1
Lanark	3	—	—	1	—	—	—	2	—	6
Perth	1	—	—	—	—	—	—	—	—	1
Renfrew	4	—	—	—	—	—	—	—	—	4
Total	114	33	23	37	7	19	13	39	33	318

Source: J. Lord: *Capital and Steam Power* (1923).

TABLE IX

DISTRIBUTION OF BOULTON AND WATT STEAM-ENGINES,
1775–1800 (B)

	Cotton	Woollen and Worsted	Rope and Flax	Textile	Total
Cheshire	9	—	—	—	9
Derby	1	—	—	—	1
Durham	3	—	1	—	4
Gloucester	—	1	—	—	1
Lancashire	42	2	—	3	47
Leicester	2	—	—	—	2
Middlesex	4	—	—	1	5
Northampton	1	—	—	—	1
Northumberland	—	—	1	—	1
Nottingham	15	—	—	—	15
Salop	—	—	1	—	1
Stafford	1	—	—	—	1
Surrey	—	—	—	3	3
Warwick	1	—	—	—	1
Yorkshire	5	6	1	—	12
Fife	1	—	—	—	1
Forfar	—	—	1	—	1
Lanark	2	—	1	—	3
Perth	1	—	—	—	1
Renfrew	4	—	—	—	4
Total	92	9	6	7	114

Source: J. Lord: *Capital and Steam Power* (1923).

(Lanark and Renfrew), Durham and London and individual mills elsewhere. The woollen and worsted industries had comparatively few steam-engines. Yorkshire and Lancashire had eight, the West Country one, and East Anglia none. Textile finishing works using steam-power were entirely in Lancashire and London. The use of the Boulton and Watt steam-engine for colliery work was chiefly in the West Midland fields— Salop, Stafford, and Warwick—and to a lesser extent in the North-east, Cumberland, and South Wales. The employment of steam-power in forges and foundaries was greatest again in the West Midlands, where there were twenty-four out of thirty-seven, but they were to be found to a lesser extent in Yorkshire, South Wales, and London. Pumps worked by steam were widely distributed when used for canals, but practically confined to London when used for waterworks. Corn-mills, breweries, and distilleries worked by steam were widely diffused, mainly in non-industrial districts, but the largest single group was in London and the Home Counties. It will be clear from this bare catalogue that 'steam-industrialism' was most highly developed in Lancashire, Cheshire, and Yorkshire, in the West Midlands, and in London; and to a lesser degree in Nottingham, the North-east coalfield, South Wales, Cornwall, and the West of Scotland. It is not without significance that with the exception of London and Cornwall, these were all coalfields. London and Cornwall, indeed, were special cases. Though the steam-engines associated with transport and public services and with food and some miscellaneous industries were remote from the coalfields, those attached to textile mills, forges and foundries, pot-banks and glassworks were with few exceptions directly on the coalfields. 'Every traveller in Britain', remarked Prof. J. H. Clapham, 'noticed the extraordinary way in which industry and population were being concentrated on or near the coal measures.'[1] The new industrial economy, based on steam-driven machines, was bound up essentially with the coalfields.[2]

The third characteristic of the new industrial economy, consequential in fact on those just considered, was that it consisted of relatively large operating units. Machines and steam-engines both required capital, and for it to be run economically a steam-engine needed to operate not one but many machines. A water-wheel or a steam-engine harnessed to drive a single loom could be a wasteful and expensive use of resources and equipment. The factory became the typical industrial unit and the large capitalist or the joint-stock company the typical business unit. Neither originated with the Industrial Revolution. Though rare in the textile industries, there had been 'factories' in the sense of large groups of workers collected together on one site, in the sixteenth century. There had long been large capitalists, though in the textile industries they tended to employ their capital in stocks of materials rather than

[1] J. H. Clapham: *Early Railway Age*, p. 42.

[2] Steam-engines increased steadily and before 1838 steam-power had outpaced water-power in textile factories. The following table has been constructed from Fong's abstracts of Factory Inspectors' Returns for 1838:

	Cotton h.p.	Woollen h.p.	Worsted h.p.	Silk h.p.	Flax h.p.
Steam-power	40,589	10,847	5,863	2,309	3,134
Water-power	9,478	6,844	1,313	928	1,131

in buildings and machines. There had long been joint-stock companies, but they tended to be in banking and public works rather than in manufacture. In the early eighteenth century, even in the textile industries organised mainly on the domestic or putting-out system, 'factories' were becoming more numerous, and they became still more numerous after the middle of the century. Even before the adoption of water-power or steam-power hand-looms were gathered in groups up to 100 in loom-shops under one roof. Gott's Bean Ing Mill in Leeds employed 744 persons wholly on the premises in 1813, all except some 200 scribblers, etc., still on hand-operated processes. With the installation of power to drive the machines, the factory tended to get larger. As early as 1815–16 there were two spinning-mills in Manchester, each of which had an average employment of over 1,000.[1] But the growth in the size of the manufacturing unit was irregular and spasmodic and small establishments existed side by side with the large. It depended not only on the progress of technique, but also on the nature of the industry. There is a wide variety in the size of the firm and of the factory in the cotton industry, for example, even today and the variety is certain to persist. In the Birmingham metal trades, to give another modern example, the number of workshops is legion. The large industrial unit led to a growth in the size of the settlement unit. The farmer and the manufacturer were ceasing to be one person before the Industrial Revolution and, with the establishment of power-driven factories, the factory-worker became a full-time operative. The rural character of industry became less and less pronounced and the urban character more and more pronounced. It is not that there was migration of industry from the country to the towns, but that as factories grew settlements grew with them. Former villages became towns and towns grew into cities, and some of these acquired legal urban status.

There is not space, of course, to deal with the geographical consequences of this first phase of the Industrial Revolution over the full and complete range of British industry. A sample only will be given, for the cotton, the woollen and worsted, and the iron and steel industries.

The antecedents, both in mechanical devices and in economic

[1] J. H. Clapham: *Early Railway Age*, p. 184.

organisation, of the Industrial Revolution in the textile industries date back to the seventeenth century. For an account of these the reader is referred to *The Cotton Trade and Industrial Lancashire*, by A. P. Wadsworth and Miss J. de L. Mann. We are concerned here only with their geographical consequences. Hargreaves, Arkwright, and Crompton, the inventors of spinning frames, were all Lancashire men. Hargreaves's spinning jenny (the first) varied greatly in size; smaller models with twenty-four spindles or less did not require power and were widely adopted by cottage spinners organised on the domestic system. Before he had invented his mule, Samuel Crompton had used a jenny of eight spindles. Larger models were collected into factories and some were driven by power. They were often made by mechanics on the spot where they were to be used, and there was little standardisation. Arkwright's famous mill at Cromford on the Derwent was started in 1771 and was driven by water-power; his machine came to be known as the water-frame in contrast to Hargreaves's jenny, the smaller models of which were worked by hand. By 1780 there were in operation some fifteen to twenty factories employing Arkwright's water-frames, comprising 30,000 spindles in all and distributed in Lancashire, Derbyshire, Yorkshire, Nottingham, Cheshire, and Denbigh. They were invariably in factories. The water-power factories, whether using the jenny or the water-frame,[1] spun chiefly cotton twist or warp, weft being spun by hand, either on the wheel or on a small jenny in the cottages on the domestic system. In 1780 (he had begun to work on it in 1774) Crompton's mule was made public.[2] The mule spun much finer cotton yarns than either the jenny or the water-frame.[3] If Arkwright had made calicoes possible, Crompton made possible the much finer muslins. The mule

[1] A. P. Wadsworth and J. de L. Mann regard the jenny as spinning warp as well as weft, but Unwin states categorically that the jenny could spin only weft (G. Unwin, A. Hulme, and G. Taylor: *Samuel Oldknow and the Arkwrights* (1924), p. 69).

[2] This is the date as given by G. W. Daniels: 'Industrial Lancashire prior and subsequent to the Invention of the Mule', *Journal Textile Institute* (1927). Special issue in association with the Samuel Crompton Centenary Celebrations. The date of the invention is usually stated as 1779. The first mule had 48 spindles; by 1786 there were mules of 100 spindles, and before the end of the century mules or 400 spindles and over.

[3] The significance of the mule is discussed in detail by G. W. Daniels: *The Early English Cotton Industry* (1920), and by T. Midgley: *Samuel Crompton and the Spinning Mule* (1927).

was first known, in fact, as the muslin wheel.[1] At first, the mule, like the jenny, was a hand-machine, but water-power and the steam-engine were soon in turn applied to it. These machines were set up not only in Lancashire, Cheshire, and the Southern Pennines generally, but also in the West of Scotland, which had been making attempts at muslin manufacture since 1780. The spate of spinning-mill building along the streams and rivers of the West of Scotland was between 1785 and 1795.[2]

There was thus a phase in the development of cotton-spinning when hand-spinning and water-power spinning existed side by side. Hand-spinning was still organised on the domestic system, though jennies and mules, especially when driven by power, were being collected into factories; and cotton-spinning in its total sense had a widely dispersed geographical distribution. Water-power spinning, necessarily in factories, had a linear distribution along the rivers, whether in the towns[3] or in the country. But the water-power sites in the towns were limited: Arkwright built his mill at Cromford in Derbyshire, Smalley at Holywell in Flintshire, and Oldknow moved from the town of Stockport to the village of Mellor. Cotton-spinning mills driven by water were being set up in Rossendale in 1790,[4] and Samuel Greg built his water-mill at Styal in Cheshire in 1784.[5] The distribution of the water-power factories was probably mainly a rural one.

This water-power phase with its dispersed rural distribution was gradually replaced by a steam-power phase. Coal could be transported, and the site of industry was no longer tied to remote valleys. But many water-power mills installed steam-engines and remained on their old sites. The date of the first application of steam to the cotton industry is uncertain. The late Prof. Unwin placed it at 1789,[6] but Lord's tables show two

---

[1] G. Unwin, A. Hulme and G. Taylor: *Samuel Oldknow*, p. 3.

[2] H. Hamilton: *The Industrial Revolution in Scotland*, pp. 123 *et seq.*

[3] See map of water-power mills in Stockport, 1790–91, in G. Unwin, A. Hulme and G. Taylor: *Samuel Oldknow*, p. 120.

[4] G. H. Tupling, *op. cit.*, p. 204.

[5] F. Collier: 'An Early Factory Community', *Economic History*, No. 5 (1930), p. 117.

[6] G. Unwin, A. Hulme and G. Taylor: *Samuel Oldknow*, p. 119.

Boulton and Watt steam-engines at cotton-mills in Nottingham-shire before 1786.[1] Arkwright's water-frame was driven by water-power, the jenny was largely a hand and small factory machine, and it was to the mule that the steam-engine was mainly applied: Watt declared in 1812 that two-thirds of the steam-engines he had erected in cotton-spinning mills were for mules.[2] Mules increased rapidly, owing partly to the much finer yarn which they could spin and owing possibly to this more intimate association with steam-power. In preparation for a petition presented to Parliament in 1812, Crompton investi-gated the number of spindles in existence in 1811. Including Scotland, the total number of mule spindles was 4,209,570, of water-frame spindles 310,516, and of jenny spindles 155,880. Mules thus constituted 90 per cent of the total spindleage.[3] Baines quotes the returns of a sample of 225 mills for 1833 which employed 20,784 persons on mule-spinning and 2,457 on throstle-spinning (Arkwright's frame when driven by steam), that is, mule-spinners constituted 89·4 per cent. of all spinners in this sample.[4] These figures are not intrinsically unlikely for as late as 1907–08 83·6 per cent. of the total spindleage of Great Britain was of mules.[5]

Crompton's census was admittedly more complete 'within 60 miles of Bolton' than for other districts of Great Britain. All but 20 per cent of the spindles he enumerated were in Lan-cashire, Cheshire, and West Yorkshire. Of the Boulton and Watt steam-engines in cotton-mills erected between 1775 and 1800, Lancashire, Cheshire, and West Yorkshire had fifty-six out of ninety-two; that is, 61 per cent. Nottingham, Leicester, and Northampton, the hosiery centres, had 20 per cent., and Scotland had 9 per cent. These figures for 1775–1800 of steam-engines in cotton-mills show a lesser concentration into Lan-cashire, Cheshire, and West Yorkshire as the primary and into the West of Scotland as the secondary region of the cotton

[1] J. Lord, *op. cit.*, Table I, p. 167.

[2] C. R. Fay: *Great Britain from Adam Smith to the Present Day* (1924), p. 294.

[3] G. W. Daniels: 'Samuel Crompton's Census of the Cotton Industry in 1811', *Economic History*, No. 5 (1930), p. 108.

[4] E. Baines: *History of the Cotton Manufacture in Great Britain* (1835), p. 374.

[5] Returns of the International Federation of Master Cotton Spinners Associa-tions.

industry than Crompton's census of cotton-spinning in 1811. Most, if not all, of the Boulton and Watt engines in the cotton industry were in cotton-spinning, so there is little likelihood of discrepancy between the two sets of figures on that account. Some allowance must be made for the incompleteness of Crompton's figures for the minor cotton-spinning districts, but even after this is made, it is possible that there was by 1811 a greater concentration of cotton-spinning into Lancashire, Cheshire, and West Yorkshire and into the West of Scotland than there had been in 1775–1800. The steam-engines erected in cotton-mills outside these two regions were mainly in the earlier years of the 1775–1800 period, and of the forty-three installed in the years 1796–1800 all but three were in these two regions. It thus seems clear that, while in the earlier stages cotton-spinning was widely diffused, it rapidly became concentrated in the later stages, particularly after 1795, into Lancashire (with the adjacent parts of Cheshire and West Yorkshire) as the primary and into the West of Scotland as the secondary region.

Of the summary list calculated by Daniels from Crompton's figures, all the spindles in the Lancashire, Cheshire, and West Yorkshire district were in those areas which today practise cotton-spinning (see Figure 11). No spindles are noted north of Rossendale. Cotton-spinning was limited to South-east Lancashire, North-east Cheshire, and, in Yorkshire, the Calder Valley. The distribution within the present-day spinning district showed, as compared with today, a much greater emphasis on Manchester, which had nearly one-quarter of the whole, and a much lesser emphasis on Oldham and Rochdale. These last still had their woollen industry. The firms were mostly small, operating on the average 8,161 spindles apiece, but they varied greatly, being of a greater average size in Manchester (15,759 spindles apiece), where there were two

Figure 11.—The scale of the symbols is identical in the two maps, the size of the symbol varying in proportion to the number of spindles in each district. The evidence refers to districts and not to towns: the symbol is placed on the site of the town which gives its name to the district. Map constructed from Samuel Crompton's lists as printed by G. W. Daniels: *Economic History*, Vol. 2, No. 5 (1930).

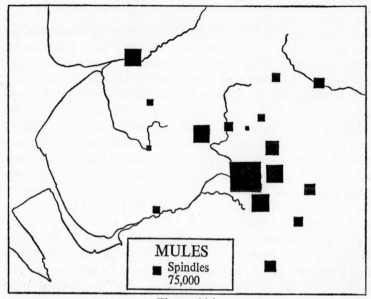

Figure 11A

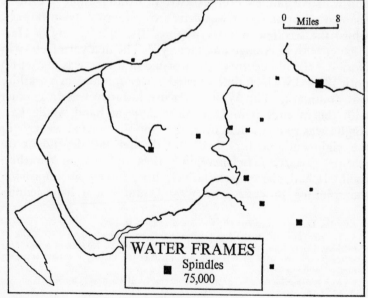

Figure 11B

Mule and Water-Frame Spindles in the Cotton Industry
of Lancashire and Parts of Bordering Counties in 1811

firms with over 80,000 spindles each, and being smallest in the Yorkshire districts, Halifax and Todmorden.[1] The average cotton-spinning mill to-day is approximately ten times the size, reckoned in spindleage, of the average in 1811.

The revolution in woollen- and worsted-spinning came later than in cotton.[2] Cotton was a new industry and it more easily adopted a new technique. It was the worsted industry, which as a considerable manufacture in West Yorkshire was relatively new and which was organised on a more capitalist basis than the West Yorkshire woollen, that earlier adopted power-spinning. There were water-frames spinning worsted yarn at Dolphinholme in Wyresdale in North Lancashire in 1784, at Addingham in Wharfedale in 1787, and at Bradford in 1794. By 1800 there were ten worsted-spinning mills in Bradford. It will be noticed that the earlier mills using the water-frame had a remote rural situation. 'Throughout the early nineteenth century,' W. B. Crump has declared, 'the West Riding could show side by side cotton mills spinning with Crompton's mule, and worsted-spinners using Arkwright's water-frame or throstle (named according as it was driven by water or steam power), whilst the woollen industry retained the hand jenny of Hargreaves both in cottage and factory.'[3] The first yarn factory in Norfolk,[4] the old centre of the worsted industry, was not set up until 1834,[5] by which time worsted power-spinning in Yorkshire was dominant. The West Yorkshire industry was in contact with the inventions in Lancashire close at hand, while East Anglia was remote; moreover, the Norfolk worsted weavers in the eighteenth century had already become dependent on worsted yarn spun elsewhere, in Suffolk and in West Yorkshire itself. It had, therefore, relatively little interest in improving the spinning process. The West Country had hand-jennies

[1] G. W. Daniels: *Economic History*, No. 5 (1930), p. 109.

[2] The first 'factory' in the Leeds district was established about 1789 (*Minutes of Evidence*, Committee on Woollen Manufacture, 1806, p. 76), but it is not clear whether power was used at this date nor whether the factory included spinning frames or looms or both.

[3] *The Leeds Woollen Industry, 1780–1820*, ed. by W. B. Crump (Thoresby Society), Voll. 32₁(1929), p. 25.

[4] E. Lipson: *The History of the English Woollen and Worsted Industries* (1921), p. 184.

[5] J. H. Clapham: 'The Transference of the Worsted Industry from Norfolk to the West Riding', *Economic Journal*, Vol. 20 (1910), pp. 197–8, dates it at 1838.

possibly earlier than Yorkshire and they appear to have superseded the wheel by 1803. But the adaptation of the power-
driven mule to woollen-spinning seems to have taken place
earlier in Yorkshire. There was little mule-spinning in the
West of England before 1828.[1] The Yorkshire industry adopted
power much the more readily.

The transformation of weaving came rather later than that of
spinning. It is true that there was the important invention of
the wheel shuttle or fly shuttle by John Kay in 1733, but this
was an invention somewhat comparable to that of the Dutch
smallwares loom in that it speeded up production on the hand-
loom. It permitted broadcloth weaving by one weaver instead
of the two required hitherto, and it increased the speed of
weaving on the narrow loom. The earliest districts to adopt it
were Rossendale and Rochdale, which spun wool rather than
cotton, and the fly-shuttle was being adopted in West Yorkshire
itself by 1763 for certain worsted and half-worsted cloths,
though not for all. At the same time that it was being introduced into the woollen and worsted manufacture, it was being
adopted extensively in Lancashire in weaving cotton or part-
cotton goods. So extensively was it employed in the Lancashire
cotton trade that it upset the balance of output between spinner
and weaver, the weaver finding it difficult to obtain sufficient
yarn for his needs. Machine-spinning was hastened accordingly. The fly-shuttle was not adopted in the West Country
woollen industry until the 'nineties, but it had long been used
at Colchester in East Anglia, where Kay had settled shortly
after his invention in 1733, though it was not adopted in

TABLE X

NUMBER OF POWER LOOMS, 1813–33

	1813	1820	1829	1833
England	} 2,400	12,150	45,500	85,000
Scotland		2,000	10,000	15,000
Great Britain	2,400	14,150	55,500	100,000

Source: Reports of Assistant Hand Loom Weavers' Commissioners (1839–40), p. 591, and
   Baines' History of the Cotton Manufacture in Great Britain, pp. 235 and 237.
   Whether the figures refer to all power-looms, weaving all textile materials, or
   simply to looms weaving cotton alone, is uncertain. Compare with Table XI.

[1] L. C. A. Knowles: The Industrial and Commercial Revolutions (1927), p. 52.

Norwich, a more important weaving centre than Colchester, until after 1800.[1]

The power-loom was a much later invention. Cartwright's loom was patented in 1785[2] and, after improvement, it was in work at Doncaster, driven by a steam-engine, and by 1791 in Manchester. But in neither place was it used for long, and Salte, the London merchant associated with Oldknow in his muslin manufacture at Stockport, wrote in 1787: 'Mr. Arkwright was a happy Mechanic. In his Life time he has received the reward of his Ingenuity—It does not happen so in general. We think Mr. Cartwright will not be equally fortunate.'[3] A really successful loom, by Horrocks of Stockport, was not introduced until 1803, and this was improved by successive patents in 1805, 1813, and 1821.[4] From this date, power-looms rapidly increased in number in the cotton industry (see Table X), and in Baine's day the Horrocks loom was the one in general use. Power-looms were mostly set up by power-spinners who already had the power and the premises and the experience in managing a power-driven industry. Spinning and weaving were then in the hands of the same firm under the same roof. Table XI gives the number of power-looms in England and Scotland by counties in 1835 in each textile industry. The concentration of power-spinning into the two chief districts, Lancashire and the West of Scotland, has already been noticed as pronounced by 1811, and these particulars of power-looms in cotton-weaving show that it was true of the whole industry. The once extensive hand-loom cotton weaving in the Ipswich district, for example, had only six looms remaining in 1840.[5] But considerable numbers of hand-looms weaving cotton did remain in the two chief districts; they were estimated at 220,000 for 1830 and 60,000 for 1844–46. If it be assumed that four hand-looms had an output equal to that of one power-loom,[6] the number of hand-looms in power-loom equivalents

[1] J. H. Clapham: Economic Journal, Vol. 20 (1910), p. 207.

[2] E. Lipson: Woollen and Worsted Industries, p. 165. There were subsequent patents in 1786, 1787, 1788, and 1792 (W. Wilkinson: 'Power Loom Developments', Journal Textile Institute (1927), Special Issue).

[3] G. Unwin, A. Hulme and G. Taylor: Samuel Oldknow, p. 99.

[4] E. Baines, op. cit., p. 234, and W. Wilkinson: Journal Textile Institute (1927).

[5] Reports of Assistant Hand Loom Weavers' Commissioners (1839–40), pp. 350–6.

[6] In weaving shirtings, the output of the power-loom weaver was placed as high as six to seven and a half times that of the hand-loom weaver. Reports of Assistant

TABLE XI

DISTRIBUTION OF POWER LOOMS IN 1835

	Cotton	Woollen and Worsted	Silk	Flax	Total
Lancashire	61,176	1,142	366	—	62,684
Westmorland	—	8	—	—	8
Cheshire	22,491	8	414	—	22,913
Derby	2,403	—	166	—	2,569
Yorkshire	4,039	3,770	—	—	7,809
Stafford	336	—	119	—	455
Devon	—	—	80	—	80
Essex	—	—	106	—	106
Kent	—	—	—	12	12
Leicester	40	89	—	—	129
Middlesex	8	—	—	—	8
Norfolk	—	—	300	—	300
Somerset	—	74	156	—	230
Warwick	—	—	—	—	25
Worcester	—	—	7	—	7
Gloucester	—	4	—	—	4
Montgomery	—	4	—	—	4
Cumberland	186	—	—	—	186
Durham	—	—	—	29	29
Northumberland	—	6	—	—	6
Lanark	14,069	—	—	—	14,069
Renfrew	1,339	—	—	26	1,365
Dumbarton	534	—	—	—	534
Bute	94	—	—	—	94
Ayr	736	—	—	—	736
Kirkcudbright	90	—	—	—	90
Perth	421	—	—	—	421
Aberdeen	248	—	—	142	390
Roxburgh	—	22	—	—	22
Total:					
England & Wales	90,679	5,105	1,714	41	97,574
Scotland	17,531	22	—	168	17,721
Total:					
Great Britain	108,210	5,127	1,714	209	115,285

Source: G. R. Porter: Progress of the Nation (1847), p. 204.

would be 55,000 in 1830 and 15,000 in 1844–46.[1] By 1830, then, the power-loom was dominant in the cotton industry and the

Hand Loom Weavers' Commissioners, p. 438. W. Wilkinson, op. cit., states that the earliest power-looms had an efficiency three and a half times that of contemporary hand-looms, and that by 1835 relative efficiency was ten times as great.

[1] Power-looms at first wove chiefly the coarser fabrics. By 1840 power-weaving had entirely superseded hand-loom weaving of calicoes and fustians at Eccles.

hand-loom was recessive. The number of handlooms in the cotton trade had become insignificant by 1856.[1]

The distribution of power-loom weaving in 1841 within Lancashire, already the focus of the industry, presents some interesting features which are set out in Table XII. It is clear that the association of power-spinning and power-weaving in the combined firm was dominant both in South-east and in North-east Lancashire, and that there were more power-looms in South-east than in North-east Lancashire. Only 23·6 per

TABLE XII

DISTRIBUTION OF OPERATIVES IN POWER-SPINNING AND POWER-WEAVING IN LANCASHIRE IN 1841

	South-east Lancs.	North-east Lancs and Preston	Unspec.	Total
A. *Actual Numbers*				
Spinning only	53,257	8,411	7,579	69,247
Combined spinning and weaving	65,324	32,654	11,521	109,499
Weaving only	3,794	3,007	1,492	8,293
Total	122,375	44,072	20,592	187,039
B. *Percentages*				
Spinning only	43·5	19·1	—	37·0
Combined spinning and weaving	53·4	74·1	—	58·5
Weaving only	3·1	6·8	—	4·5
Total	100·0	100·0	—	100·0

Source: J. Jewkes: 'The Localisation of the Cotton Industry'. *Economic History*, No. 5 (1930). Calculated from *Factoty Inspectors' Reports* (1841).

cent. of the factory operatives in the cotton industry were in North-east Lancashire and Preston, but, expressed as a percentage of the total factory employment in the district, weaving was already *relatively* more important in North-east than in South-east Lancashire. The weaving district of to-day, though it adopted the cotton industry later than South-east Lancashire, and though in 1841 it may have had more power-spinners than power-weavers, was, therefore, just beginning to emerge. Advance figures supplied to Baines by the Factory Inspectors for 1835, though they do not distinguish between spinning-mills

[1] J. Jewkes: 'The Localisation of the Cotton Industry', *Economic History*, No. 5 (1930), p. 92.

and weaving-sheds, show a similar regional distribution of the factory cotton industry. Of 657 mills in Lancashire, 23·0 per cent. were in North-east Lancashire, Rossendale, and Preston, and of 137,352 factory operatives 17·4 per cent. were in this district.[1] The particulars given by Baines for districts of the number of mills, the number of persons employed, and the steam-power and water-power employed, are sufficiently detailed to permit mapping.[2] Figure 12 registers the predominant importance of Manchester as in Crompton's census, but Oldham, Bolton, Rochdale, and Bury were rapidly growing. The North-east Lancashire centres had relatively few mills. Some of these northern districts, where the factory cotton industry was not yet established on a large scale, had more water-power than steam-power. This was even truer of the Yorkshire mills, the cotton-mills of Yorkshire having 1,429 h.p. water-power and 956 h.p. steam-power. The Yorkshire mills, as to-day, were much smaller in average size.

The power-loom, like power-spinning, was introduced into the woollen and worsted industries later than in cotton. In 1835 there were in Great Britain, according to Table XI, only 5,127 powerlooms weaving wool as compared with 108,210 weaving cotton. Of those, approximately 73·5 per cent. were in Yorkshire, 22·3 per cent. in Lancashire, 1·4 per cent. in Gloucester and Somerset, 1·5 per cent. in Leicester, 0·4 per cent. in Scotland, 0·9 per cent. elsewhere, and none in East Anglia. Over half—58·5 per cent.—were in worsted factories, all in Yorkshire. Power-weaving, like power-spinning, was adopted more extensively at this date in worsted than in woollen. A Halifax merchant-manufacturer wrote in 1830: 'With regard to power-looms, . . . Their introduction into the woollen manufacture, (with the exception of worsted stuff goods) has been . . . recent.'[3] The Gott woollen factory in Leeds had power applied to spinning after 1820, but the loom shops still had hand-looms only in 1830. There was a factory and a Boulton and Watt steam-engine in 1792, but power was used only in scribbling,

[1] E. Baines, op. cit., p. 386.

[2] The returns are for districts and the symbols refer to districts and not to places. Mills were, in fact, more dispersed than the maps would appear to indicate. Thus, Halifax parish had forty-three mills, but many of these were strung along the valleys of the Calder and its tributaries and were not all in Halifax town.

[3] J. Bischoff, op. cit., Vol. 2, p. 269.

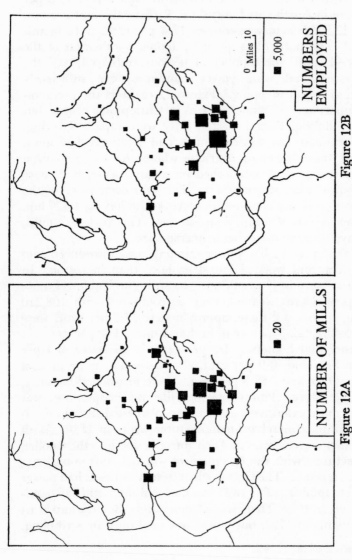

Figure 12A

NUMBER OF MILLS

■ 20

Figure 12B

0 Miles 10

■ 5,000

NUMBERS EMPLOYED

Cotton Mills in Lancashire and Parts of Bordering Counties in 1835. I.

A shows the *number of mills* and B the *numbers employed* in each district, the size of the symbol varying in proportion to the numbers in each case. Maps drawn from returns of Factory Inspectors as listed by E. Baines: *History of the Cotton Manufacture* (1835). These are incomplete for some districts in respect of numbers employed. Evidence refers to districts and not carding, and fulling.[1] Even in the worsted industry the power-loom was not introduced until 1822; this was at Shipley, near Bradford.[2] According to the *Reports of the Assistant Hand-loom Weavers' Commissioners*, the first power-loom in Gloucester-shire dated from 1836, but Lipson and Porter give four in Gloucestershire for 1835. But, although the power-loom was introduced later in the West Country than in Yorkshire, the collection of hand-looms into loom-shops or factories had long been in progress. In 1840 Gloucestershire had 32 loom-shops with an average of 33 hand-looms apiece. The power-factories, at this date, had few looms unemployed, the loom-shops had more and the cottage hand-loom weavers more still. These relative frequencies are obviously significant. In the same year, Norwich had 656 hand-looms in 'factories' and 3,398 cottage hand-looms. Contemporaries were aware of the more rapid growth of power-weaving in Yorkshire than in the West Country or East Anglia. But, even in West Yorkshire, power-looms did not entirely supersede hand-looms until the middle of the nineteenth century, and the small domestic clothier persisted till this time. There was a great spate of mill building about 1850 in Halifax and Bradford on sites removed from river, canal, and railway.[3] It indicated an urbanised industry, with a nuclear and not a linear distribution.

The adoption of power-weaving registered the final stage in the supremacy of the West Yorkshire industry over the West Country and East Anglia, but it was only the final stage for the decline of the older centres had begun long before this time. Fig. 10 gives the number of pieces of woollen cloth stamped at fulling-mills in Yorkshire from 1726 to 1810. It was admitted by the West Country witnesses to the Select Committee of the House of Lords of 1828 that much of their cloth trade had gone to the North of England.[4] What was equally indicative of the rise of the West Riding industry was the transfer which was taking place from London to Yorkshire as the main site for the organization of the cloth export trade.[5] All this was in 1828

[1] W. B. Crump, *op. cit.*, pp. 1–58.
[2] E. Lipson: *Woollen and Worsted Industries*, p. 187.
[3] On the evidence of dated stones built into factory walls.
[4] *Report*, Select Committee, p. 116.
[5] *Report*, Select Committee, p. 305.

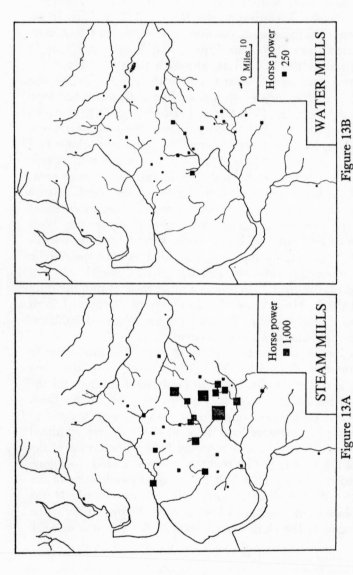

Figure 13A

Figure 13B

Cotton Mills in Lancashire and Parts of Bordering Counties in 1835. II.

A shows horse-power in *steam mills* and B horse-power in *water mills* in each district, the size of the symbol varying in proportion to the numbers in each case. Maps drawn from returns of Factory Inspectors as listed by E. Baines: *History of the Cotton Manufacture* (1835). Evidence refers to districts and not to individual places.

when the power-loom had only just been introduced into the
woollen and worsted industries in West Yorkshire.[1] It is clear
from some cost of production figures of West Country superfine broadcloth that, while the costs of weaving had remained
practically unchanged from 1781–96 until 1828, the costs of
spinning had declined from £3 1s. 10d. in 1781–96 to 1s. 9d.
in 1828 in those cases where the mule was being employed.[2]
Power-spinning, adopted earlier in the north, gave Yorkshire
an earlier advantage. But it was not machinery alone, whether
in spinning or in weaving, which was responsible for the change.

'There is not, I believe,' says Clapham, 'any reason to seek
novel causes explanatory of the first rise of Yorkshire. It is the
ordinary case of a pushing, hard-working locality, with certain
slight advantages, attacking the lower grades of an expanding
industry.'[3] It may be argued that the 'pushing, hard-working'
qualities were rooted in the poverty of the West Riding environment. Whether wages in Yorkshire were lower, as has often
been asserted, is uncertain.[4] Indeed, Miss Gilboy finds that
wages of labourers and craftsmen other than industrial workers
rose substantially during the eighteenth century, and that,
though lower than those of the West Country at the beginning
of the century, were higher at its close.[5] By 1850–51, Caird
found that agricultural wages in the North of England were
higher than in the South.[6] Miss Gilboy argues that 'It is not
merely coincidence that Yorkshire and Lancashire, which were
the centre of industrial expansion in eighteenth century
England, were characterised by a laboring class with steadily
increasing real wages and economic and social ambition; nor
that the western counties, from which the once-important
woollen trade was fast disappearing to the north, should possess

[1] The West Country had lost trade to West Yorkshire before this. See *Minutes
of Committee on Woollen Manufacture* (1806), p. 29. 'Do you not know that
Yorkshire has gained a great deal of the West of England trade? . . . Do you not
conceive that the Factory system operates to preserve to Yorkshire that trade
drawn from those counties where the trade is not carried on in the same way?'

[2] These figures require some adjustment before they can be taken to refer to
strictly the same work, but the difference remains enormous. The figures are
abstracted from the *Reports of Assistant Hand-Loom Weavers' Commissioners.*

[3] J. H. Clapham: *Economic Journal*, Vol. 20 (1910), p. 201.

[4] The evidence taken by the Hand-Loom Weavers' Commissioners was not
clear on this point.

[5] E. W. Gilboy: *Wages in Eighteenth-century England* (1934).

[6] J. Caird: *English Agriculture in 1850–51*, p. 480.

a poor and unambitious working class. . . . The goad of an expanding standard of life is necessary before labor can be induced to undergo disciplined factory labor'.[1] But, even if wages were no lower in Yorkshire, its cloths were cheaper, although less well-made. West Yorkshire had a more fluid economic and social organisation than the West Country or East Anglia. The Yorkshire workman was more ambitious and he oftener rose to fortune. The small clothier organisation which persisted beyond the middle of the nineteenth century in the Yorkshire woollen industry was a training ground for advancement.

In addition to these technical, economic, and social factors the West Riding had a number of material advantages for a power-using industry. Coal could be mined at the point of manufacture, and the four main manufacturing towns—Halifax, Leeds, Bradford, and Huddersfield, in the order of their manufacturing population in 1831—all lay at the contact of Coal Measures and Millstone Grit, where both soft water and coal were available. Moreover, there was fruitful experimental contact between manufacturer and machine-maker, both in the same town.[2] Iron ore was mined from the Lower Coal Measures and iron-working and engineering industries came to be second in importance only to the textile. These advantages in materials must not be overrated. Much of the Newcastle to London coasting trade was in the hands first of Ipswich and later of Yarmouth ship-masters, and Norwich imported coal. Nor was coal far away from the West Country industry. In the early years of the nineteenth century it was, however, still expensive to transport coal, except by water, and the price of coal away from the Norfolk coast and away from the banks of the Severn would be higher than in the West Yorkshire manufacturing district.[3] The factories used slack, relatively expensive to transport in proportion to its value. By the time the railways were built and inland coal distribution facilitated, the West Yorkshire industry had triumphed: it had an advantage not only in resources, but also in timing. The West Country

[1] E. W. Gilboy, *op. cit.*, pp. 242–3.

[2] J. H. Clapham: *Economic Journal*, Vol. 20 (1910), p. 203.

[3] J. U. Nef reports very low prices for coal on the banks of the Severn in the seventeenth century—at Tewkesbury in 1678 only one-third of the price in London (J. U. Nef: *The Rise of the British Coal Industry*, Vol. 1, p. 96).

retained only its superfine woollen broadcloths, in which quality of workmanship rather than cost of production was the chief factor, and East Anglia retained some of its mixed worsted-silk fabrics until they too disappeared. In 1850, West Yorkshire had 87 per cent. of the worsted spindles and 95 per cent. of the worsted looms, while Norfolk had only 2·3 per cent. of the spindles and 1·3 per cent. of the looms. Leicester, with its local demand for hosiery yarns, had more worsted spindles than Norfolk, and Lancashire had more worsted looms.[1] By 1850 also, Yorkshire and Lancashire together had 87·4 per cent. of the woollen spindles of England and 94·8 per cent. of the looms, the West Country 10·2 per cent. of the spindles and 4·7 per cent. of the looms.[2] The statistics refer in each case to factories alone.[3] Coal did not create the transference to the West Riding, but, applied to machine-power, it confirmed it and stabilised it.

The rise of the Tweed Valley woollen manufacturing district coincided with the Industrial Revolution. In the eighteenth century woollen cloths were made, but in no greater quantities than at Kilmarnock or Stirling, Edinburgh or Aberdeen. Galashiels made kerseys, 'Galashiels greys', an inferior imitation of Yorkshire kerseys. They were from local wool, the Southern Uplands being already a great wool-producing region. Machinery was introduced fairly early: the hand-worked jenny in 1791, the mule in 1814, and the power-loom at Hawick in 1830. By 1840 the hand-loom weavers were mostly in factories, and the transition to power-weaving was thereby facilitated. The geographical advantages which the Tweed Valley possessed for a woollen industry were local wool and water-power. But the first was unsuitable for tweed-making and it was on tweeds that the industry grew. Water-power was employed during the early years of the machine industry, but the Tweed Valley possessed no monopoly of

---

[1] J. H. Clapham: *Economic Journal*, Vol. 20 (1910), p. 210.

[2] Calculated from H. D. Fong's abstract of Reports of Factory Inspectors (H. D. Fong, *op. cit.*, pp. 64–5).

[3] Woollen manufacture in North Wales also suffered. During the domestic phase it had been widely diffused. The dispersion persisted during the early factory phase when spinning frames and carding engines were driven by water-power. It was only with the rise of steam-power factories that the dispersed distribution gradually disappeared, but not entirely (A. H. Dodd: *The Industrial Revolution in North Wales* (1933), pp. 229–81).

water-power in Scotland. When steam-power was adopted coal had to be imported. Both local wool and water-power were therefore of only temporary importance. Other possible sites for a woollen industry in Scotland on a substantial scale, however, were devoting themselves to cotton or to linen or to iron and steel. Regional specialisation in a single textile material was characteristic of the nineteenth century.

The inventions which transformed the iron industry involved two sets of conditions—first, the substitution of coal for charcoal, and, second, the improvement of the technique of smelting and finishing the iron. It has been pointed out above that raw coal had long been employed to reheat bar iron to render it malleable and capable of being hammered by the smith into goods ready for use. But smelting, the initial separation of the metal from the ore, remained dependent on charcoal despite the experiments of the seventeenth-century ironmasters, of whom the best-known was Dud Dudley. These experimenters possibly did produce iron of some sort with coal, presumably raw coal, but it was probably too brittle for the forge hammer.[1] The use of coal in smelting was first successfully established by Abraham Darby at Coalbrookdale. He was using coke by 1709, as Ashton shows from the entries in *Darby's Journal*.[2] Coke is a purer fuel than coal, just as charcoal is than wood, but its use in the furnace required higher temperatures than charcoal and needed therefore a more powerful blast. It was the provision of more powerful bellows than those in general use that constituted, so Prof. Ashton thinks, the reason of Darby's success. The Coalbrookdale site not only had ore, coal, and limestone in close proximity, but also water transport along the Severn waterway and water-power from tributary streams tumbling into the river at the point of the Coalbrookdale gorge, a deepened glacial overflow channel.[3] Despite the known shortage of charcoal, the use of coke from smelting did not spread rapidly. The early coke iron was suited more to castings than to wrought iron: the greater heat of the coke furnace allowed the metal to run more freely and made possible lighter castings than the fire-backs which was the type of cast iron

[1] T. S. Ashton: *Iron and Steel*, p. 12.
[2] T. S. Ashton: *Iron and Steel*, pp. 28–31.
[3] L. J. Wills: *Physiographical Evolution of Britain* (1929), pp. 226–8.

article produced from the charcoal furnace,[1] but it was unsuited, being too brittle, for working into ploughshares and
tools. Darby produced cast wares such as pots, pipes, and
kettles, and he was substituting cast iron for brass wherever he
found it possible to do so. So difficult was the early coke iron
to work by the methods then available to the smith that smiths
demanded higher rate of pay in compensation.[2] Until about
1750 coke iron was made only in the Coalbrookdale district
and at Bersham, near Wrexham. Both sites retain to-day the
semi-ruralism typical of industry at that time. After 1750 it
was adopted in Worcestershire, in South Wales (Dowlais), in
West Cumberland (Seaton), in Scotland (Carron), and later in
South Yorkshire, Northumberland, and elsewhere.[3] Other
improvements were one by one introduced—the making of coke
in ovens instead of in the open, the substitution of cylinders
instead of bellows to give a more continuous blast,[4] the use of
the Newcomen engine to assist the water-wheel at times of low
water and, in the last quarter of the century, the employment
of the Boulton and Watt steam-engine. Cast iron was used for
steam-engine parts, and in 1779 the famous Severn bridge at
Coalbrookdale, the monument of the early coke iron industry,
was completed. In its turn, the steam-engine was applied to
the iron industry, first for producing the blast for smelting and
later for working the forge hammer.

The second set of improvements, those involving the technique of smelting and finishing, proceeded contemporaneously.
The improvements in cast iron consequential upon the employment of coke have already been indicated. Cast steel refined
in crucibles was being made at Sheffield after 1742. Although
coal had long been employed in smithies and, since 1709, as
coke in blast-furnace work, it had not been used in refining
pig iron into bar iron; that is, in the refinery between the blast
furnace and the smithy. The refinery process was particularly
extravagant in charcoal. Coal or coke was used in the refinery
by the Cranages in Shropshire in 1766, by Cort at Fontley in
Hampshire in 1783–84, and by Onions at Merthyr Tydfil in

---

[1] Cast iron had been made in England from the sixteenth century.
[2] T. S. Ashton: *Iron and Steel*, p. 35.
[3] T. S. Ashton: *Iron and Steel*, pp. 36–7.
[4] H. Scrivenor, *op. cit.*, pp. 84–6.

South Wales. The product was puddled iron. Cort then passed his puddled iron through rollers instead of putting it under the hammer, and greatly increased the volume of production. The amount of work which a hammer driven by water-power could do was limited, but the rollers could deal with fifteen times more iron in the same time. Bar iron suitable for the smithy could now be made entirely by coal or coke, first in the blast furnace and then in a refinery.[1] In 1788, according to a table given by Mushet, there were 208 refineries making bar iron by 'the old method', and these had a total output of 16,400 tons, that is, 79 tons apiece; but there were also 60 melting refineries using coke with a total output of 15,600 tons, that is, 260 tons apiece. These 'old method' refineries were most numerous in the West Midlands, South Wales, and Yorkshire, Derby and Nottingham.[2] By 1791 the production of puddled and rolled iron alone reached 50,000 tons, a threefold increase in as many years. Puddling and rolling spread northwards from South Wales and the West Midlands to Yorkshire by 1790, to the North-east some years later,[3] and to Scotland perhaps a little earlier.[4]

By the end of the eighteenth century the main outlines of the technical revolution in the iron industry were completed: the industry was freed from dependence on the limited woods and coppices, dependence on which had hampered its growth, and came to be dependent instead on the coalfields, whose resources were ample for an immense multiplication of production. There was, in fact, an immense increase in iron output, as Table XIII shows. The 18,190 tons of 1717, when output was entirely of charcoal iron, became 63,300 tons in 1798, of which 14,500 tons were of charcoal iron and 53,800 tons of coke iron. The production of charcoal iron, though still considerable, was declining.[5] The total output doubled between 1786 and 1796 and doubled again by 1806, by 1839 it was five times the level of 1806 and by 1847 had practically reached two million tons, over one hundred times the output of 1717. This multiplication

[1] T. S. Ashton: *Iron and Steel*, p. 93.

[2] D. Mushet: *Papers on Iron and Steel* (1840), p. 44.

[3] T. S. Ashton: *Iron and Steel*, p. 97.

[4] H. Hamilton, *op. cit.*, pp. 165–8.

[5] It was 7,800 tons in 1806 and 800 tons in 1839.

of production entirely reversed the external trade in iron. At the beginning of the eighteenth century Britain had been importing about two-thirds of the bar iron used in the smithies; but by about 1805 exports of British iron equalled imports of foreign iron, and from that time onwards imports declined and exports increased. Instead of being an importer, Britain became an exporter of iron. The inventions in the technique of iron smelting were paralleled by new uses for iron —as machines for industry, as power-plant for driving industrial machines, as metal fittings for innumerable household purposes, as pipes and standards for urban sanitation and lighting, as railway equipment, and as iron steamships. Iron replaced wood and, to a lesser degree, copper and brass. During the Revolutionary and Napoleonic Wars iron for armaments provided the largest single market and there was depression in the industry when the wars ceased.

TABLE XIII

DISTRIBUTION OF PIG IRON PRODUCTION, 1717–1847

	1717	1788	1796	1806	1839	1847
A. *Quantities* (in tons)						
South-east	1,990	300	173	—	—	—
South Wales and Forest of Dean	5,250	15,500	37,300	79,674	472,080	706,680
North Wales and Cheshire	2,250	600	3,252	2,075	33,800	16,120
West Midlands	5,400	31,800	46,180	104,426	445,353	474,240
North-west	1,000	3,500	2,034	3,991	800	—
Yorks, Derby, Notts	2,300	9,600	20,054	37,000	86,788	162,760
North-east	—	—	—	—	13,000	99,840
Scotland	—	7,000	16,086	23,240	196,960	539,968
Great Britain	18,190	68,300	125,079	258,206	1,248,781	1,999,608
Average each furnace	331	804	1,034	1,493	3,310	4,618
B. *Percentages*						
South-east	10·9	0·4	0·2	—	—	—
South Wales and Forest of Dean	28·9	22·7	29·8	31·8	37·8	35·4
North Wales and Cheshire	12·4	0·9	2·6	0·8	2·7	0·8
West Midlands	29·7	46·6	36·9	41·7	35·7	23·7
North-west	5·5	5·1	1·6	1·6	—	—
Yorks, Derby, Notts	12·6	14·1	16·0	14·8	7·0	8·1
North-east	—	—	—	—	1·0	5·0
Scotland	—	10·2	12·9	9·3	15·8	27·0
Great Britain	100·0	100·0	100·0	100·0	100·0	100·0

Calculated from Table VII and from T. S. Ashton: *Iron and Steel in the Industrial Revolution* (1924), pp. 98, 235–7; H. Scrivenor: *History of the Iron Trade* (1854), pp. 57, 87–8, 95–7, 99, 256, and 295; and 1871 *Coal Report*, Vol. 3, p. 59. The total production for 1806 includes the output of eleven charcoal furnaces omitted from the regional grouping. The table includes both charcoal and coke pig iron. See also notes under Table XIV.

But it was not only a technical revolution; it was a geographical revolution as well. The general regional distribution of iron furnaces at several dates is set out in Tables XIII and XIV and of iron forges in Table XV.

These tables permit the distributional changes to be traced with as much precision as the material will allow. In 1717 the county with the greatest number of furnaces was still Sussex, though they were smaller in size than elsewhere. The south-east had a fifth of the furnaces, but only 10·9 per cent. of the output. South Wales, and the Forest of Dean had one-quarter of the furnaces, but 28·9 per cent. of the output. The furnaces were here chiefly around the edges of the Forest of Dean, and although some were on the coalfield it was the ore and the surface timber and not the coal of the Coal Measures which was responsible. In the West Midlands, it was Salop and not Staffordshire which had the greatest number. By 1788 there was a marked change. The production of the south-east had become negligible, though it was to persist a little longer.[1] Though producing more than in 1717, the percentage share of South Wales and the Forest of Dean had fallen, but that of the West Midlands had increased enormously. In 1788 the West Midlands were producing nearly half the total pig iron output and over half (30,000 tons out of 53,800 tons) of coke iron output; of this five-sixths was from Salop. The Forest of Dean still retained a considerable charcoal iron production and its coke iron industry was as yet only beginning. During the next twenty years output increased almost everywhere except in the charcoal iron districts of the south-east and of the north-west. The percentage share of the West Midlands fell slightly from the high level of 1788, but it continued to have the greatest output into the 'thirties, despite the restricted size of its resources. Within the West Midlands, however, the balance of output was changing. Although it was growing continually in Salop in actual quantities, it was growing very much faster in Staffordshire as Table XVI shows. By the middle of the nineteenth century output was coming to bear a closer relationship to bulk of resources than at the end of the eighteenth century.

[1] The Ashburnham furnace closed down in 1828. The extinction of the Weald industry was due to the employment of coke in place of charcoal and not to the extinction of the charcoal resources for charcoal has been made for hop-drying in this century. There were other reasons as well.

TABLE XIV

NUMBER AND SIZE OF IRON FURNACES IN DISTRICTS, 1717–1847

| | 1717 | | 1788 | | 1796 | | 1806 | | 1839 | | 1847 | |
	No.	Size	No.	Size	No.	Size	No.	Size	No.	Size	No.	Size
South-east	11	181	2	150	1	173	—	—	—	—	—	—
South Wales and Forest of Dean	14	375	20	775	32	1,166	53	1,943	127	3,717	196	4,680
North Wales and Cheshire	5	450	1	600	5	650	4	692	13	2,600	11	3,204
West Midlands	14	386	33	964	37	1,248	84	1,770	142	3,136	192	3,919
North-west	2	500	6	583	4	509	8	665	—	—	—	—
Yorks, Derby, Notts	9	256	15	640	25	802	46	1,057	36	2,411	58	3,785
North-east	—	—	—	—	—	—	—	—	5	2,600	36	4,160
Scotland	—	—	8	875	17	946	27	1,291	54	3,648	130	6,067
	55	331	85	804	121	1,034	233	1,594	377	3,310	623	4,618

Size is expressed in terms of average actual output per furnace in tons of pig iron. In 1806 and 1847 the statistics distinguish between furnaces in blast and furnaces not in blast: the total number in blast was 162 and 433 respectively. The calculations of average size for these two years refer only to those actually in blast. In other years the calculations refer to all furnaces, for the returns do not distinguish between those in blast and those not in blast. Calculated from statistics printed by T. S. Ashton and H. Scrivenor as for Table XIII and from Table VII. The figures for 1806 include eleven charcoal furnaces omitted from the regional grouping.

TABLE XV

DISTRIBUTION OF IRON FORGES IN DISTRICTS, 1717–88

| | 1717 | | 1788 | |
	No.	Per cent of total	No.	Per cent of total
South-east	15	13·0	4	3·8
South Wales and Forest of Dean	29	25·2	28	26·6
North Wales and Cheshire	8	7·0	7	6·7
West Midlands	46	40·0	32	30·5
North-west	—	—	13	12·4
Yorks, Derby, Notts	16	13·9	20	19·0
North-east	1	0·9	—	—
Scotland	—	—	1	1·0
Total	115	100·0	105	100·0

Source: Table VII, and D. Mushet: *Papers on Iron and Steel* (1840).

TABLE XVI

PIG IRON OUTPUT IN THE WEST MIDLANDS, 1717–1847

	1717	1788	1796	1806	1839	1847
Salop	2,600	24,900	32,969	54,966	80,940	88,400
Stafford	1,450	6,900	13,211	49,460	364,413	385,840

Before the middle of the nineteenth century the West Midlands had been surpassed first by South Wales and then by Scotland. By 1847 these three districts combined were responsible for no less than 86 per cent of the total pig iron output of Great Britain. The supremacy of the coalfields, and of particular coalfields, was clearly accomplished. These were coalfields with a long tradition of metal working, such as the West Midlands, or coalfields where the textile tradition was either weak or relatively fluid, such as South Wales and Scotland respectively. The coalfields of Lancashire and Yorkshire were dominated by their textile manufacture and had no labour to spare. The North-east field was late in the race, partly because of its well-established coasting trade in coal and partly because of the paucity of its resources in Coal Measures ores.

During the first phase of the coke iron industry, then, smelting furnaces were concentrated on the coalfields, where coal and iron ore could both be obtained, often from the same mine. Much of the coal production was from the Lower Coal Measures, where iron-stones are intercalated with coal seams. Iron smelting was localised where ore and fuel could both be obtained on the same site, but the fuel was now coal instead of charcoal. Of the iron ore mined about 1850, perhaps 95 per cent. was of Coal Measure ores.[1] The vertically organised coal and iron company was common. Charcoal iron had required for its production great quantities of charcoal and the early coke iron required similarly great quantities of coal. In 1829 at the Clyde Ironworks the weekly average of fuel consumed for 111 tons of iron was 403 tons of coke (from 888 tons of coal), that is, 8 tons of coal for 1 ton of iron.[2] Although the consumption of coal was not as high in England[3] as in Scotland, smelting was obviously localised on the coalfields. But, with Neilson's invention of the hot blast, the amount of coal required for smelting was greatly reduced. In 1830, when the blast was heated to 300°F., the coal consumed was 901 tons for 126 tons of iron as a weekly average, that is, $5\frac{1}{2}$ tons of coal for 1 ton of iron; while in 1833, when the blast was heated to 600°F., 652 tons of coal were consumed weekly for 245 tons of iron, that

---

[1] Ll. Rodwell Jones: *North England* (1926), p. 246.

[2] H. Scrivenor, *op. cit.*, p. 260.

[3] D. Mushet placed it at 5 tons of coal to 1 ton of iron in Staffordshire in 1810.

is $2\frac{2}{3}$ tons of coal for 1 ton of iron. The rapid increase of Scottish pig iron production after 1830 is to be attributed partly, at any rate, to the more extended use of the hot blast and to the saving in coal consumption that it made possible.[1] The way was being prepared, through economy in fuel, for changes in the localisation of iron smelting later on in the nineteenth century, but as yet smelting was still tied to the coalfields.

There was no such striking revolution in the geographical distribution of forges and refineries. The forges had long tended to be situated in part on the coalfields, where most of the smithying was concentrated even before the beginnings of coke iron manufacture. Even in 1721 the West Midlands had the largest group of forges, and within the West Midlands there were more in Stafford than in Salop, the reverse of the distribution of smelting furnaces. By 1788 the charcoal iron districts had fewer forges than in 1721, but forges were retained more easily than furnaces.

At a later date Ruskin described the iron industry as having 'changed our Merry England into the Man in the Iron Mask', but it was not accomplished immediately, and it had to await the development of an engineering technique. The earliest textile machines were of wood, constructed by carpenters, and even when, as later, they came to be made of iron, each part had to be forged separately; after the machine had been assembled it was often some time before it could be got to work. It was the same with other machines as well as the textile. In the second quarter of the nineteenth century methods for exact measurement of machine parts and the elaboration of machines 'to make machines' were gradually worked out,[2] but machine tools did not become part of the standard equipment of engineering firms until about 1850. What may be termed the handicraft phase of British engineering was passing away and the engineering firm was growing rapidly in size.[3] It was now possible for machines each exactly alike to be made in indefinite numbers, and it was possible to produce them much

---

[1] H. Scrivenor, *op. cit.*, pp. 259–61. Also J. H. Clapham: *Early Railway Age*, pp. 425–6. The use of blackband ores in Scotland was another factor: they contained so much 'coaly' material that the consumption of coal was greatly lessened.

[2] J. H. Clapham: *Early Railway Age*, pp. 446–9. Also H. Hamilton, *op. cit.*, pp. 207–10.

[3] J. H. Clapham: *Early Railway Age*, pp. 448–9.

more cheaply and expeditiously than hitherto. The stage was set for the mechanical age.

The technical revolution in the methods and the geographical revolution in the site of industrial production proceeding throughout the range of British industry, though the treatment above has been limited to samples, were dependent on three sets of conditons:

(a) The provision of sufficient quantities of coal. If the new age was an iron age, it was also a coal age. The domestic fire and oven, the manufacture of iron, engines, and machines, the driving of machines in industry and of transport on land and sea—all were dependent on coal, whether directly or indirectly in the form of steam or gas. The rapidly multiplying consumption of coal gave rise to fears of the adequacy of supplies for the future, fears later crystallised by Jevons in his famous analysis of 1865. Contemporaries were all aware of the influence of coal on industrial localisation. 'The seat of various manufactures,' writes Porter, 'having in great part been determined by the presence, in certain districts, of cheap fuel, and the growth of population having by that means been greatest in or near to some of our principal coal-fields . . .'[1]

(b) The provision of an adequate labour force. The population of Britain was increasing during the period of the Industrial Revolution, but the rate of population growth and the rate of growth of demand for labour did not always coincide. There was, as Prof. T. H. Marshall puts it, 'a failure of economic progress and the increase of numbers to keep step together'.[2] Perhaps for the country as a whole population growth outpaced 'economic progress',[3] but in particular districts population was insufficient to meet the demand for labour. Most of the rising industrial districts, where the demand for labour was greatest, were in those parts of the country which had been scantily peopled during the Middle Ages. The

[1] G. R. Porter: *The Progress of the Nation* (1847), p. 281.

[2] T. H. Marshall: 'The Population Problem during the Industrial Revolution', *Economic History*, No. 4 (1929), p. 438.

[3] T. H. Marshall, *op. cit.*, pp. 436–8.

relative shortage of labour in these districts may have been responsible for high wage rates and for an early introduction of machinery to increase production per unit of labour in order to offset the labour shortage and so to intensify and accelerate the progress of the Industrial Revolution. Whether this was so or not, the regional variation of labour demand was a factor of great importance.

(c) The improvement of transport. The Industrial Revolution coincided with, indeed called forth, a revolution in the means of transport. Road surfaces were improved, canals were dug and railways were built. It may be argued with some truth that transport improvement in Britain lagged behind the need of it. Improvement was indeed always due to the efforts of local men anxious to solve a local problem, whether the improvement was a turnpike road, a canal, or a railway. Josiah Wedgwood, for example, was one of the chief promoters of the Trent and Mersey Canal. The rising industrial districts, drawing in raw material from outside and sending finished manufacturers back into the outside world, could breathe only if their channels of communication were kept clear.

The growth of coal production and the growth of population will be considered further in this chapter, but the improvement of transport will be treated in the next.

The revolution in coal-mining began early in the eighteenth century. Before this time the bell-pit and the adit had been the common methods of working coal, though shafts had been sunk in the North-east field to 400 feet.[1] The average number employed even in this field, however, may have been no more than forty per pit, and in most districts six to twelve or less was more usual. The small-scale working was due to difficulties of drainage and ventilation. A hillside position permitted natural drainage, of which the collier took full advantage, but a low-lying pit was dependent upon mechanical drainage. Water-wheels were used in the North of England particularly, and from 1711 to 1717 onwards the Newcomen engine, and from

[1] T. S. Ashton and J. Sykes, *op. cit.*, p. 10.

1776 the Boulton and Watt engine, were applied to supply the water-wheel with water or to work the pumps direct. By the beginning of the nineteenth century mining, in consequence, had reached a depth of 993 feet in West Cumberland, and by 1838–40 of 1,392 feet in South Lancashire and 2,100 feet in North Staffordshire.[1] There were systems of ventilation during the eighteenth century, but the solution of the problem of

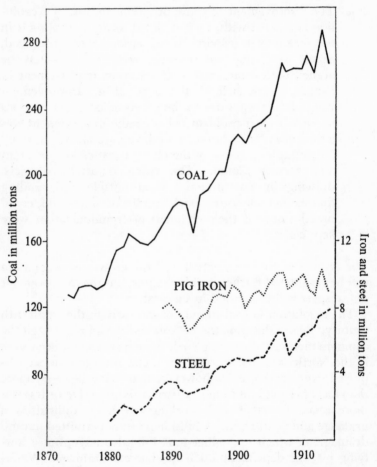

Figure 14. Output of Coal, Pig Iron and Steel in Great Britain to 1914

[1] J. H. Clapham: *Early Railway Age*, p. 435.

fire-damp was not in sight until 1816, when the safety-lamp first came into use.[1] But the problem of fire-damp was not solved, for the safety-lamp was used to permit the mining of seams hitherto considered too dangerous to work. These advances in the technique of coal-mining made possible the greatly increased output which the Industrial Revolution demanded.[2] The Royal Commission on Coal which reported in 1871 estimated production in 1770 at over 6 million tons and in 1800–01 at over 10 million tons. It rose rapidly during the first half of the nineteenth century as the demands of industry, transport, and domestic consumption increased, and by 1854, the date of the first statistical returns, it had reached 65 million tons. Jevons assumed on the basis of the 1854–64 decade a rate of increase of $3\frac{1}{2}$ per cent. annually,[3] and Clapham attempts a reconstruction of the course of coal production in 1770–1856 as a steepening curve.[4] Jevons insisted 'both from principle and fact, that a nation tends to develop itself by multiplication rather than addition—in a geometrical rather than an arithmetical series. And though such continuous multiplication is seldom long possible, owing to the material limits of subsistence... up to the present time (1865) our growth is unchecked.... Now while the iron, cotton, mercantile, and other chief branches of our industry thus progress, it is obvious that our consumption of coal must similarly progress in a geometrical series. This, however, is matter of inference only'.[5] His worst fears were not realised.

It is not possible to state with any exactitude the precise share of each coalfield in this expansion of production. The first statistics were not collected until 1854.[6] Output in 1855 is set

[1] T. S. Ashton and J. Sykes, *op. cit.*, pp. 52–3.

[2] The long wall system of coal-getting gradually spread during the eighteenth century from Salop, where it originated early in the seventeenth, to other fields in the West Midlands (in the early eighteenth) and to Derbyshire, Lancashire, and Scotland (in the late eighteenth). Where surface and roof conditions permitted its employment, the long wall was the most economical method and permitted the extraction of the maximum quantity of coal (T. S. Ashton and J. Sykes, *op. cit.*, pp. 14–32).

[3] W. S. Jevons: *The Coal Question* (1865), 3rd edition, ed. by A. W. Flux (1906), p. 269.

[4] J. H. Clapham: *Early Railway Age*, p. 431.

[5] W. S. Jevons, *op. cit.*, p. 261. He contended that this geometrical increase would, in fact, not persist, and that the curve would, at some time in the future, flatten itself out.

[6] R. Hunt: *Mineral Statistics of the United Kingdom for 1854*.

TABLE XVII

REGIONAL COAL PRODUCTION IN GREAT BRITAIN IN 1855

	No. of collieries	Output Tons	Output per colliery Tons
Northumberland and Durham	272	15,431,400	56,733
Cumberland	23	809,546	35,198
Yorkshire	333	7,747,470	23,266
Derby	171	2,256,000	13,193
Nottingham	20	809,400	40,470
Warwick	17	262,000	15,412
Leicester	11	425,000	38,636
Stafford	500	7,323,000	14,646
Lancashire	357	8,950,000	25,070
Cheshire	32	755,500	23,609
Salop	56	1,105,250	19,558
Gloucester and Somerset	86	1,430,620	16,633
North Wales	65	1,125,000	17,308
South Wales	245	8,550,270	34,899
Scotland	403	7,325,000	18,172
Great Britain	2,591	64,305,456	24,820

Source: R. Hunt: *Mineral Statistics of the United Kingdom for 1855* (1856).

out field by field in Table XVII. The Northumberland and Durham field had then still the largest production of any single British coalfield. The factors which promoted its development before the Industrial Revolution still continued to operate. The vend of coal from the north-east ports, of which a record exists, for it was subject to dues, was 2½ million tons in 1800. The import of London alone was 1 million tons in 1800 and over 3½ million tons in 1850. The regional markets served by British fields were delimited in the *Report* of the Select Committee on the State of the Coal Trade in 1830. The North-east coalfield had a virtual monopoly of the coal trade along the whole of the east coast and along the south coast as far west as Plymouth. There was some competition with Yorkshire coal from the Humber and with West Midland coal brought by the Grand Junction Canal into London,[1] but neither was substantial. Parts of North England and of the East Midlands formerly supplied by sea from the North-east field were being furnished from inland fields along canals by 1816.[2] Not only had the North-east field the largest share of the coastwise trade,

[1] Canal-borne coal was only 1,484 tons in 1826.
[2] G. R. Porter, *op. cit.*, p. 282.

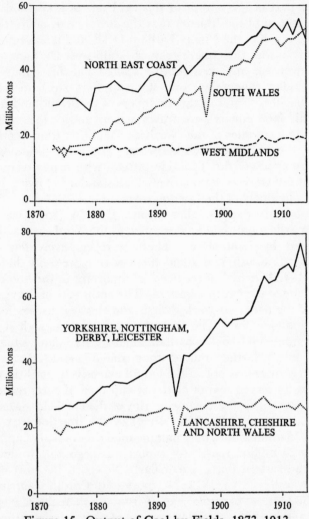

Figure 15. Output of Coal by Fields, 1873–1913

but it also contributed the largest proportion to the export trade. Export in 1850 has been estimated at 3·8 million tons, and the share of the North-east ports at 63·6 per cent.[1] The

---

[1] D. A. Thomas: 'The Growth and Direction of our Foreign Trade in Coal', *Journal Royal Statistical Society* (1903), pp. 440 and 498. The export from this field had been only 260,314 tons in 1821 (W. S. Jevons, *op. cit.*, p. 313).

greater part of the output of this field was of household coal. It was not until the 'thirties that the steam coals of Northumberland north of the Ninety Fathom Dyke, and it was not until the 'forties that the coking coals of South-west Durham, came to be won on any considerable scale. The first shaft sunk through the Magnesian Limestone in East Durham was in 1821, but the output of this shaft was of household and not of gas coal. New miners were drawn in from outside the coalfield, from the lead-dales of the Northern Pennines, from Scotland, Wales, the Midlands, and elsewhere, and these swamped the old aristocracy of the Tyneside pitman with a relatively high standard of work and a relatively high standard of living based on the monopoly of the London market.[1]

South Wales had a smaller output. Even by 1855 it was producing little more than half as much as the North-east and was surpassed by Lancashire. There were relatively few deep workings in South Wales and there were more adits than pits in 1841–42.[2] It had never been as important in the household coal trade as the North-east field. The anthracite of the western part of the field was worked first, and this was useless for the then domestic fire. The bituminous district, though it produced household coal, was hampered by its inland situation, being much farther inland than the Tyneside pits. This eastern district was not worked at all extensively until the ironmasters, in search first of charcoal and then of coke, settled in the valleys along the north-east rim of the coalfield—Merthyr Tydfil, Aberdare, Dowlais. In 1828 the iron industry consumed 1½ million tons, over half the total production of approximately 2¾ million tons.[3] An export was beginning to develop from the eastern ports, particularly Newport, the port of the eastern valleys. In 1828 Newport and Cardiff contributed 459,986 tons out of a total export from South Wales of 904,896 tons,[4] and in 1855, 1,869,948 tons out of a total shipment (coastwise and foreign) of 2,897,579 tons. The centre of gravity was shifting from the western to the eastern ports of the South Wales littoral. Nevertheless, this export was much less than that of the

---

[1] E. Welbourne, *op. cit.*, pp. 46–9.

[2] J. H. Clapham: *Early Railway Age*, p. 433.

[3] E. J. Jones: *Economic History of Wales* (1928), p. 67.

[4] *Report of the Commissioners . . . Coal in the United Kingdom*, Vol. 3 (1871), p. 50.

North-east field: the Bristol Channel ports in 1850 contributed 13·3 per cent. of the total coal export of Britain, while the North-east coast contributed 63·6 per cent.[1] It was not until 1880 that the South Wales export equalled that from Northumberland and Durham, a growth based on steam coal, mined in the central part of the field and exported from Cardiff.

The Lancashire field ranked third in output. Cotton-mills and coal-pits lay close together, and coal was used in quantity by numerous textile and general engineering shops and by the thickly spread industrial population, as well as by the cotton-mills themselves. By the middle of the nineteenth century the cotton industry had become wholly a machine industry and wholly dependent on coal. The Liverpool bunker market and export to Ireland also took coal from the western end of the field. Of the West Midland fields the most important were in South Stafford, North Stafford, and at Coalbrookdale. South Stafford and Coalbrookdale were associated with the rapidly developing metal industries: one-third of the Salop and one-third of the Stafford output was consumed in blast furnaces. Coalbrookdale still retained some of its shipment along the Severn, its most important market prior to the Industrial Revolution, but Staffordshire coal was all consumed in the district, and some special qualities were drawn in from other fields; for example, gas coals from North Wales. The Warwickshire and Charnwood Forest fields were worked to a much lesser extent, but their coals were distributed southwards and eastwards by canal as far as Oxford and Reading.

The Yorkshire, Derby, and Nottingham field produced over 10 million tons, and was the second field in the country on the basis of output. Its northern, or Yorkshire, part was the more important. This was the most industrialised district, with woollen and worsted industries, textile and general engineering, cutlery and hardware. It had also the largest domestic consumption. The Derbyshire part of the field had ironworks, then as now, and Nottingham had an industrial demand from textile industries. There was also a not inconsiderable quantity distributed by rail away from the coalfield. The 1830 map shows the regional market of the York–Derby–Nottingham

[1] D. A. Thomas, *op. cit.*, p. 498.

field as extending from Nidderdale and the Vale of Pickering to Northampton and Boston. In addition, some coal was sent to London from the Yorkshire field, but the Nottingham field, despite attempts from the late sixteenth century onwards, did not send coal regularly.[1] This mining before 1850 was entirely in the exposed coalfield, and in Nottingham the first shaft through the Permian and Trias cover into the concealed field was not sunk until 1854. The 'inland coal' of this field, particularly of the Yorkshire portion, was pushing back towards the coast the market supplied by sea from the North-east coalfield. At Wisbech the depth of country supplied by the coasting trade had been reduced from 60 miles to 40.[2]

Coal-mining in Scotland increased parallel with the growth of Scottish industries and of the Scottish industrial population. Coal superseded peat as a domestic fuel except in the Highlands, and it was used for the usual range of industrial purposes. The consumption of coal in ironworks had been estimated to be approximately 250,000 tons in 1812,[3] but 2½ million tons in 1855 in the West of Scotland alone;[4] there had been an immense increase in iron production in the interval. The domestic, manufacturing, and bunker consumption in the West of Scotland in 1855 was placed at nearly 3 million tons. The shipment of coal, coastwise and abroad, had also increased. By 1855 it had reached nearly a million tons. From the Firth of Forth ports shipment coastwise was mainly to other parts of eastern Scotland, but more was sent abroad, to Baltic and North Sea markets. From the Clyde and Ayrshire coasts shipment coastwise was mainly to Northern Ireland, and export abroad (a minor feature of its shipment trade) was mainly across the Atlantic. The difference in space-relations between east and west coast ports is clear. Up to the Industrial Revolution the greater bulk of the production was close to the coast, but with the growth of an internal domestic and industrial market and with the improvement of internal communications,

---

[1] H. Green: 'The Nottinghamshire and Derbyshire Coalfields before 1850', *Journal Derbyshire Archaeological and Natural History Society*, No. 56, p. 60.

[2] *Report and Minutes of Evidence*, Select Committee of the House of Lords on the State of the Coal Trade (1830), p. 98.

[3] H. Hamilton, *op. cit.*, p. 172.

[4] *Mineral Statistics for 1855*.

mining spread into interior districts.[1] There was also a change in the balance of development between the eastern and the western fields. Hitherto output had been greatest in the eastern districts, prior to the Industrial Revolution economically the most important part of Scotland. But with the growth of the textile and of the iron industries of the West of Scotland and with the development of the Lanarkshire field, the largest of all Scottish coalfields, the balance of output changed. In 1855 the West of Scotland had two-thirds of the collieries of Scotland[2] and nearly three-quarters of the output of coal.[3]

The second conditioning factor in the progress of the Industrial Revolution was the labour force. Not only was coal required to drive the machines, but labour also to man them. The opinion was widely held in the late eighteenth century that the population of the country was declining.[4] There seemed some doubt whether the demand for labour would be met adequately by the supply. The early census returns refuted this contention and proved that the total population of the country was not declining, nor even stationary, but was rapidly increasing. It is probable that the period of rapid increase was mainly during the hundred years, 1750–1850, and that it coincided in fact with the Agrarian and Industrial Revolutions. Although all figures of population prior to 1801 are uncertain estimates, the following, extracted from the *Report* on the Census of 1851, summarise the position. For *Great Britain* the total population was estimated at 6,378,000 in 1651, 7,392,000 in 1751, and 21,185,000 in 1851;[5] that is, an annual increase (if the figures will bear the calculation) of 0·16 per cent. in the 100 years 1651–1751 and of 2·87 per cent. in the 100 years 1751–1851. The most rapid rate of increase was subsequent to 1775,[6] culminating in the decade 1811–21. In general terms it may be

[1] For this movement in the Ayrshire field see maps for 1793 and 1840 in J. H. G. Lebon: 'The Development of the Ayrshire Coalfield', *Scottish Geographical Magazine*, Vol. 49 (1933).

[2] H. Hamilton, *op. cit.*, p. 191.

[3] *Mineral Statistics for 1855.*

[4] J. H. Clapham: *Early Railway Age*, pp. 53–4 for a summary.

[5] *Census of 1851. Population Tables II. Ages, Civil Condition, Occupations, and Birth-Place of the People, Report*, Vol. 1 (1854), p. li. For the eighteenth-century population of England, see E. C. K. Gonner: 'The Population of England in the Eighteenth Century', *Journal Royal Statistical Society*, Vol. 76 (1913).

[6] E. C. K. Gonner, *op. cit.*, p. 285.

said that this threefold increase of population was a response to the multiplication of the wealth of Britain, agricultural and industrial, made available by the Agrarian and Industrial Revolutions. Improved agricultural and industrial technique set free resources inherent in the physical environment, but hitherto unutilised or only partially utilised.

This much can be said with some confidence. But, when the attempt is made to analyse the mechanics of this increase, to express the relative share of the birth-rate, the death-rate, and the migration-rate, and to trace the relationship between increase on the one hand and economic and non-economic motives on the other hand, the position is much more uncertain. Some attention has been directed to this problem.[1] There was an increase in the crude birth-rate and in the corrected birth-rate: the increase began after 1780, but it was beginning to die away after 1821. There was a decrease in the death-rate which was progressive until 1821, after which it appears to have increased again slightly. Prof. Marshall accepts this increase as real,[2] but Mrs. Hammond shows that in the particular case of Manchester the apparent increase was due to defective statistics of the census years prior to 1831, when many burials were not registered.[3] The death-rate was greatest among infants and in the towns, and the decline in the crude death-rate was largely due to decreased mortality among newly-born infants and to improved sanitation and cleanliness in the towns. There is no exact correspondence between the decennial trends in birth-rates on the one hand and prices, wages, and prosperity on the other.[4] Changes in birth-rates and death-rates seem to be more clearly related to social changes, which were themselves, however, often indirectly related to the economic. The decline in handicraft industry, for example, reduced the incidence of apprenticeship and of living-in: the average age of

---

[1] See G. T. Griffith: *Population Problems of the Age of Malthus* (1926); T. H. Marshall: 'The Population Problem during the Industrial Revolution', *Economic History*, No. 4 (1929); T. H. Marshall: 'The Population of England and Wales from the Industrial Revolution to the World War', *Economic History Reivew*, Vol. 5, No. 2 (1935).

[2] T. H. Marshall: *Economic History*, No. 4 (1929), p. 454.

[3] B. Hammond: 'Urban Death-Rates in the Early Nineteenth Century', *Economic History*, No. 3 (1928).

[4] T. H. Marshall: *Economic History Review*, Vol. 5, No. 2 (1935).

marriage was reduced and the effective child-bearing years of the mother increased.[1]

This is a general statement for the country as a whole, but there was considerable regional variation. The increase in the total population was not evenly distributed. It was least in East Anglia, the West Country, and the rural counties of the East Midlands. The former were losing their industrial pre-eminence to the North of England, and the latter, which included much clay land, were changing from arable to grass or, where arable remained, were economising in labour. Increase was greatest in the industrial districts of the North of England, the West Midlands, and South Wales. Arranged according to density of population, the first five counties in 1700 were Worcester, Somerset, Devon, Lancashire, and Gloucester, but in 1801 Lancashire, Warwick, the West Riding, Stafford, and Gloucester.[2] The scatter of counties in 1801 was between a much wider range of densities than in 1700: in 1700 the county with the lowest density had 54 per square mile and the county with the highest density 141, but in 1801 the highest and lowest densities were 353 and 55 respectively. The lowest densities had not changed, but the highest had grown two and a half fold. There were regional differences, too, in birth-rates and death-rates, as might be expected from these differing rates of increase. Porter gives tables showing the proportion to the total population of births and deaths for the individual years, 1839–42, for each county of England.[3] The crude birth-rate was above the average for England as a whole in Lancashire, the West Riding, Northumberland, Durham, Monmouth, Bedford, Berkshire, Cambridge, Hertford, Leicester, Northampton, Nottingham, Worcester, and Cornwall. The list includes the most rapidly developing manufacturing districts and the most rapidly developing coalfields, but it also includes enigmatically a group of Midland counties in the very heart of the district latest to be enclosed. The counties with crude birth-rates well below the average for the country as a whole included most of the West Country, East Anglia, the Welsh Border, and

---

[1] T. H. Marshall: *Economic History Review*, Vol. 5, No. 2 (1925), p. 69.
On the assumption that the wife was of approximately the same age as the husband.
[2] E. C. K. Gonner, *op. cit.*, p. 287.
[3] G. R. Porter, *op. cit.*, p. 34.

some hill counties in the North of England. These were areas of declining industry or areas of hilly land from whence population was migrating, attracted by industrialism near by, and where, it may be presumed, population had a relatively small proportion of young married couples. The death-rate was above the average for England in Lancashire, Durham, Monmouth, Middlesex, Surrey, and Worcester. It was, therefore, in rapidly developing urban and mining districts that the death-rate was greatest. The rural areas had a death-rate below the average. They were regarded as the healthy reservoirs from whence the ravages amongst the town population were repaired. Regional variations in birth-rates and death-rates alone do not explain regional changes in population density. A vast amount of internal migration was in progress in response to changes in the distribution of economic opportunity.

Internal migration within England during the period of the Industrial Revolution has been examined by Prof. Redford.[1] The first detailed statistical record is in the birthplace tables of the 1851 census, but Redford uses also scattered references in earlier census reports and in contemporary literature. The *Report* on the Census of 1851 stressed the volume of this internal migration and calculated that 'of the 6,589,048 inhabitants of London and of sixty-one English and ten Scotch towns, 3,598,891 are natives and 2,990,157 are settlers who were born in other parts. But of the 3,767,626 persons of the age of 20 and upwards, only 1,477,949 were born in the towns, while 2,289,677 were born in other parts'.[2] These figures are eloquent. Of the population of these towns, only 54·6 per cent. were born there, and of those aged over twenty only 39·2 per cent. were born there. It was, of course, the towns which were the chief recipients of the flow of population. Prof. Redford has affirmed that internal migration was essentially of a short-distance character.[3] 'The majority of the migrants to the town

---

[1] A. Redford: *Labour Migration in England, 1800–50* (1926). For movement from and into a particular county see H. C. Darby: 'The Movement of Population to and from Cambridgeshire between 1851 and 1861', *Geographical Journal*, Vol. 101 (1943).

[2] *Census of 1851. Population Tables II, Report*, Vol. 1 (1854), pp. cv–cvi.

[3] This was more nearly true of the period prior to 1850, of the time when movement was primarily from country to town: but the greater mobility given by the railway and the increasing movement between town and town permitted longer distance migration which became increasingly significant after 1850. These are the conclusions arrived at by R. Lawton from an analysis of the census data.

came from the immediately surrounding counties, their places in turn being taken by migrants from places further away.'[1] In respect of the population aged over twenty, of the immigrants into Lancashire over two-thirds came from adjacent counties and from Ireland; of the immigrants into London, few came from beyond the English Plain, and it was from the Home Counties that most were drawn.[2] There was comparatively little transference of population from south to north, from the declining to the rising industrial districts. A few migrated from East Anglia and the West Country into the West Riding (chiefly from East Anglia), but the hand-loom weavers displaced from the declining centres in the English Plain were not needed in Yorkshire, which had its own unemployed hand-loom weavers to absorb. Emigrants from East Anglia and the West Country went mainly to London and South Wales respectively and were recruited into occupations other than the textile. There was rather more migration of miners and of metal-workers, whose skill could be utilised in other districts. North Pennine lead-miners entered the coal-pits of Durham, Cornish tin-miners those of South Wales, Derbyshire lead-miners those of the Midlands; ironmasters and iron-workers dispersed from Shropshire to the Black Country and South Wales. But the greater part of migration was not of skilled men continuing to practise their craft in a new region, but of young men and women largely untrained in industry. They either entered the mill or workshop or undertook carting, building, or domestic service, ancillary occupations, associated with the growing industries, and the growing urban population. Their children were absorbed into industry more readily. But while there was little long-distance migration from south to north, the counties of the English Plain exported much of their population. The *Report* on the Census of 1851 lists the following counties as having a substantial excess of emigrants over immigrants: Norfolk, Suffolk, and Essex; Wiltshire, Somerset, Dorset, Devon, and Cornwall; Hereford and Shropshire; Berkshire, Oxford, Buckingham, Hertford, Northampton, Leicester, Lincoln, Derby, and Kent.[3]

[1] A. Redford, *op. cit.*, pp. 158 and 160.
[2] *Census of 1851. Population Tables II*, Vol. 1 (1854), Summary Tables, Table XXXIX. See also A. Redford, *op. cit.*, Maps D and E.
[3] Extra-metropolitan Kent.

The result of these movements on occupational distributions is summarised by the occupation tables of the census returns. Already in 1811 there were more families in trade and manufacture than in agriculture in England and Scotland, though not in Wales. There were, of course, regional differences within each country and within each county. On this classification, the English industrial counties were Northumberland and Durham; Lancashire, Cheshire, and the West Riding; Stafford and Warwick; Nottingham, Leicester, and Gloucester; Middlesex and Surrey. Lancashire and the West Riding headed the list in the proportion that families engaged in trade and manufacture bore to the total number of families.[1] From 1831 the occupational classification was more detailed, and by 1851 an elaborate classification had been adopted. Some of these 1851 categories, calculated as percentages of the total male population of twenty years and over, have been mapped (see Figure 16). Of the male population of Great Britain in 1851 of twenty years and over, 27·2 per cent. were engaged in agriculture or stock-keeping.[2] In the greater part of the country this formed the largest single occupational group, but in Lancashire there were more cotton workers than farmers and agricultural labourers, in the West Riding more woollen and worsted workers, in Durham (but not in Northumberland) more coal-miners, in Staffordshire more coal-miners and iron-workers. Large regional concentrations of population following single industrial occupations had thus clearly taken shape by 1851. This specialist regional industrialism was becoming increasingly urban: villages were growing into towns and

[1] G. R. Porter, *op. cit.*, table p. 58.

[2] Categories IX and X of Table VIII, less fishermen and plus cowkeepers of category XII (1).

Figure 16.—As percentages for each registration county of England and Scotland of males aged 20 years and upwards.

The textile, coal and metal maps have identical keys and are exactly comparable. Owing to greater percentage densities it was not possible to have an identical key for agriculture. Wales is omitted.

The maps display clearly marked regional economic specialisms, even on a county basis—textile manufacture in Lancashire and Yorkshire, Selkirk, Renfrew, Fife and Forfar; metal working in the West Midlands, West Riding, South Wales and Lanark; agriculture in the English Plain, Welsh Border, the Scottish Border and the Scottish Highlands.

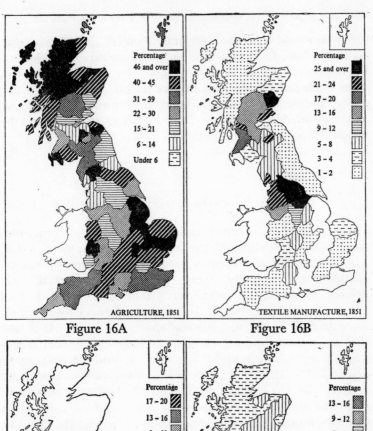

Figure 16A   Figure 16B

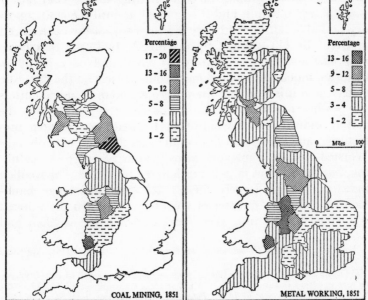

Figure 16C   Figure 16D

Agriculture, Textile Manufacture, Coal Mining and Metal Working
in 1851

towns into cities. The agglomeration of population was facilitated and the progress of this agglomeration accelerated by improvements in transport, both on land and on sea. They made possible the bulk import of food from abroad which a large industrial population divorced from the land required, and they made possible the bulk export of manufactures by which the industrial population lived.

IV

THE LATE NINETEENTH CENTURY

The middle of the nineteenth century marks an important stage in the modelling of the industrial geography of today. The mechanisation of the processes of manufacture was not yet complete, mechanically created power was not yet the sole driving force of the industrial machine, and the factory system was not yet universal, but these changes were largely accomplished in the major *manufacturing* industries. It is true that the actual winning of coal—hewing at the coal face— was still a handicraft, and it remained so until the contemporary period: even in 1913 only 8·5 per cent. of the coal output of Great Britain was cut by machine.[1] It is true that boot- and shoe-making was entirely by hand and only partly in factories, much still being done by out-workers on the domestic system, and it is true that there were yet no mechanical cutters nor sewing machines in the Leeds clothing trade. But the cotton industry was wholly mechanised, congregated into factories, and focused on Lancashire and the West of Scotland.[2] Worsted also was a machine factory industry, except for combing, but this too was largely mechanised by 1857.[3] The woollen industry, though largely mechanised, still had some hand- looms for another quarter of a century. By 1850 the worsted was concentrated into West Yorkshire and the woollen had

[1] *Report of the Royal Commission on the Coal Industry*, Vol. 3 (1925), Appendix No. 8, Table XXXI, p. 48.

[2] Of the 292,340 adults over twenty years returned as engaged in cotton manu- facture in Great Britain in 1851, 176,155 were in Lancashire and 55,037 in the West of Scotland (*Census of 1851. Population Tables II*, Vol. 1 (1854), Summary Tables, Tables XXVIII and XXIX).

[3] J. H. Clapham: *Free Trade and Steel*, pp. 30–2.

there its largest single centre.[1] The present-day regional distributions had already taken shape. In the iron industry, the few remaining charcoal iron furnaces could be counted on the fingers, and they were individually tiny compared with the coke iron plants. The iron industry was focused on the coalfields and was no longer scattered in remote woodlands. Engineering was closely associated with it. The railway had established itself as the chief means of internal communication, but the iron steamship, though growing fast in numbers and tonnage, was still completely subordinate to the wooden sailing ship. Lloyd's *Register* did not issue satisfactory rules for a classification of iron vessels until 1855.[2] In the 'fifties the Liverpool steamship owners disassociated themselves from the sailing masters and formed an organisation of their own. The Thames was still one of the major areas of shipbuilding and had not yet been superseded by the Tyne and the Clyde. Thus, although the shift of industry from the English Plain to the coalfields of the North of England, West Midlands, Scotland, and South Wales, was not complete by 1850, the main movement had already taken place and only remnants or outliers remained behind.

Changes in the geographical distribution of industry since 1850 have not been general. There have been changes of some magnitude in the regional distribution of iron smelting and, to a lesser extent, of iron and steel working and some industries, such as the cotton manufacture of the West of Scotland, have almost died away. But the major interest of the years 1850–1913 with regard to most industries is of trends in the balance of output as between different regional centres and of changes in the detailed distribution of industries within regions already roughly defined by the middle of the nineteenth century. There were substantial changes in the order of the several coalfields in bulk of output, as Figure 17 shows, and by 1913 relative output had come to accord much more closely with relative size and reserve. Within Lancashire there developed a marked regional segregation of cotton-spinning and of cotton-weaving into

[1] Of the 93,082 adults over twenty years returned as engaged in woollen cloth manufacture in Great Britain in 1851, 51,854 were in the West Riding and of 59,123 in worsted manufacture, 54,459 were in the West Riding (*Census of 1851. Population Tables II*, Vol. 1 (1854), Summary Tables, Tables XXVIII).

[2] J. H. Clapham: *Free Trade and Steel*, p. 68.

separate parts of the manufacturing region, a progressive segregation whose momentum has scarcely yet died away. Trends such as these, however, can most conveniently be examined in the chapters on specific industries in Part II.

CHAPTER 3

Trade and Transport

I

THE MIDDLE AGES

The self-sufficiency of the Middle Ages, relative and not absolute though it may have been, implied a restricted volume of trade. It was at first in such articles as salt and iron, which were in general demand, but which not every locality could itself produce. Later, there arose a trade in corn and wool which, though produced in most parts of the country, were required at some points in quantities in excess of the local production. Parallel to this there developed a trade in finished manufactures, but it was not until towards the close of the Middle Ages that regional specialisation in manufacturing production began to arise on any considerable scale. This was the internal trade. Foreign trade consisted of an export of corn and raw materials, such as wool and metals, and an import of wine, spices, and special manufactures. Though not negligible, trade was not as fundamental to the economy of the country as it is today. Its practice was not infrequently a part-time occupation, the cloth merchant, for example, being a cloth manufacturer as well, and it was largely carried on in periodic fairs and markets.[1] Transport was not dissimilar: it was irregular and spasmodic, it involved only small loads, and it frequently followed very circuitous routes.

The commodities involved in internal trade gradually increased in quantity and in range as local or regional self-sufficiency became modified and as the towns grew in size. The growth of the towns involved the development of a local trade in corn to feed the urban population which, from the twelfth century onwards, was devoting itself more and more to

[1] 'They represent in fact a phase of commerce which can best be described as periodic' (E. Lipson: *Economic History of England*, Vol. 1, p. 221).

manufacture and was ceasing to grow sufficient corn for its own requirements. Trade in corn did not necessarily involve transport over more than a few miles, from the village to the local town, but to a minor extent there was also an inter-regional trade; for example, a coast trade from Lynn to Newcastle and a river trade from the upper Thames Valley to London.[1] Trade in wool also was considerable, not only the local trade from farm to town, but also an inter-regional trade, which was probably greater in wool than in corn and was facilitated by the relatively high value of wool in proportion to its weight. Even in the Middle Ages the major clothing districts were probably not self-supporting in wool. They were certainly not self-supporting in later centuries. Traffic in heavy low-grade commodities was, however, very restricted in bulk and in range. Nef asserts that, except where river or coastwise navigation was available, coal was never transported more than a few miles from the point of mining.[2]

Trade was focused on periodic markets held once a week (or oftener) and fairs held once a year (or oftener). Markets were distributed quite thickly. It was laid down by a thirteenth-century lawyer that markets should be not less than $6\frac{2}{3}$ miles apart, that is, one-third of a day's journey of 20 miles.[3] In Lancashire this was the approximate spacing, except in the hill districts of north and east, and except in the unreclaimed mosslands of the west, where they were spaced more widely apart, and except in certain well-drained parts of the plain, where they were congregated more closely together.[4] In East Anglia, with a medieval population greater than that of Lancashire, there were relatively more markets and an average spacing of 4 miles apart would probably be more correct. But here again markets

[1] N. S. B. Gras: *The Evolution of the Corn Market* (1926), pp. 35–64. The Oxford Clay Vale probably had an excess of production over local consumption requirements, London and Tyneside probably a deficit.

[2] J. U. Nef: *The Rise of the British Coal Industry*, Vol. 1, p. 8.

[3] F. M. Stenton quotes the daily itinerary of Robert of Nottingham on a journey from Nottingham to York and back to Lincoln in 1324–25 and the average daily ride works out at just over 20 miles, but this was a passenger journey and not the transport of goods. He also quotes a journey of twenty-one carts loaded with treasure from Westminster to Norwich in 1294; these averaged 12 miles a day (F. M. Stenton: 'The Road System of Medieval England', *Economic History Review*, Vol. 7, No. 1 (1936), pp. 13–14 and 19).

[4] G. H. Tupling: 'Markets and Fairs in Medieval Lancashire', *Essays in Honour of James Tait*, Map opposite p. 346.

were unevenly distributed.[1] Not all markets and not all boroughs had a gild merchant. Figure 17, showing the distribution of gilds merchant from Gross's list,[2] might be expected to give some indication of the relative regional density of trading centres, though not necessarily of the relative regional volume of trade. It is, however, inexact even for this purpose for important trading towns, as London, Norwich, and the Cinque Ports have no records of having possessed a gild merchant. 'Indeed', says Gross, 'we are struck with the prominence . . . of the Gild Merchant in many small boroughs. . . . The Gild Merchant did not necessarily imply considerable commercial prosperity or great industrial resources.'[3] The most important of the English fairs were Winchester, St. Ives, Stourbridge (near Cambridge), Bartholomew in London, Boston, Westminster, Northampton, and Bristol.[4] These were large general fairs and their sites lay significantly in the English Plain, half of them in or close to the Oxford Clay Vale. There were many other smaller fairs, some of them for a particular commodity, such as the herring fair of Yarmouth or the cheese fair of Weyhill. At the close of the Middle Ages the annual or bi-annual fair was declining in relative importance, but it has even yet not died away. The decline of the fair in relative importance may be taken, however, to indicate the multiplication and regularisation of trade, which itinerant merchants attending occasional fairs were no longer able to satisfy.

The transport of goods was partly by river and coastal navigation and partly by road. Goods were carried by water wherever possible,[5] and the employment of the waterways was facilitated by the riverine and valley bottom distribution of the medieval population. The small boats then in use, large enough for the small unit cargoes requiring transport, permitted navigation far upstream and allowed a maximum navigable mileage. Even so late as the seventeenth century 'it would appear that boats on rivers, other than the Thames and

[1] R. E. Dickinson: 'The Distribution and Functions of the Smaller Urban Settlements of East Anglia', *Geography*, Vol. 17 (1932), Fig. 2, p. 28.

[2] C. Gross: *The Gild Merchant*, Vol. 1 (1890), pp. 9–18.

[3] C. Gross, *op. cit.*, Vol. 1, pp. 90 and 92.

[4] E. Lipson, *op. cit.*, pp. 229–32.

[5] F. M. Stenton, *op. cit.*, p. 19.

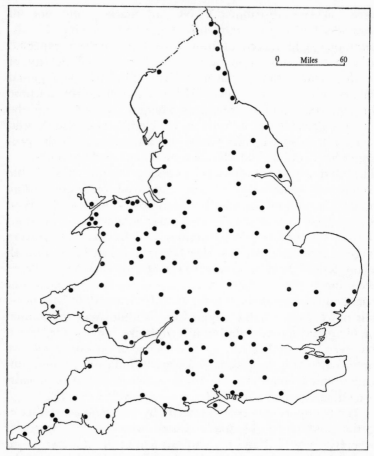

Figure 17. Boroughs in England and Wales with a Gild Merchant

Map drawn from list in C. Gross: The Gild Merchant, Vol. 1 (1890).

Severn, had usually a burden of between 20 and 40 tons'.[1] It is probable that the medieval boat was smaller still. The rate payable for water-carriage was lower than for land-carriage— 'about one-sixth', according to Thorold Rogers.[2] River transport was probably of more importance for heavy commodities

[1] T. S. Wilan: *River Navigation in England, 1600–1750* (1936), p. 99.
[2] J. E. Thorold Rogers: *A History of Agriculture and Prices in England*, Vol. 1 (1866), p. 663.

than for passengers. For personal travel[1] it was slower to travel
in a boat, unless wind and current were both favourable, than
to ride on horseback, and Prof. Stenton's view is that for the
passenger 'the waterways of England were never more than an
occasional supplement to a road-system which on the whole was
sufficient to his needs'.[2] Many transport routes, both for goods
and for passengers, were composite, being in part by river and
in part by road.[3]

The road plan involved in the aggregate a much greater
mileage. It was a mosaic of long-distance routes, the straight
Roman roads and the gently curving hill-top and hill-side
trackways, and of local lanes, leading from village to common
field and to common pasture. The Roman road system had not
remained intact during the long centuries after the withdrawal
of the Roman legionaries. Much of it stood in any case without
repair, but where the road was carried over a stream it commonly tumbled down; where it passed through a stone-built
country its shaped stones were frequently used for house or wall
building; where it was adjacent to arable it was frequently
broken up and ploughed. The Gough map of the early fourteenth century showed a plan, probably incomplete, of the
major roads of the country, and, although it included stretches
of Roman road, it did not consist entirely of them.[4] According
to the road plan of the Gough map, London was the chief focus
of the system, as it had been of the Roman roads and as it is of
the railways to-day. But there were roads running athwart
or at an angle to the pattern radial from London, and some
regional centres, as Bristol, York, and Chester, had each their
own radial road system. The dominance of London over other
regional centres of English life was not yet complete.[5]

The medieval road, except the relics of the Roman system,
had simply an earth surface, hard and dusty in summer, soft
and miry in winter. It was understood in law not as limited

[1] Personal wayfaring was of considerable volume—the king and his court, the
lord and his household, ecclesiastics, pilgrims, and merchants.

[2] F. M. Stenton, op. cit., p. 20.

[3] See examples given by R. A. Pelham: 'Fourteenth-Century England', An
Historical Geography of England before 1800, ed. by H. C. Darby (1936), pp. 262–5.

[4] F. M. Stenton, op. cit., pp. 7–13. Also Pelham in An Historical Geography of
England, p. 260.

[5] F. M. Stenton, op. cit., pp. 4–5.

between boundary walls or hedges, but as a right of way, and the medieval traveller had no hesitation, if the customary track were foundrous, in leaving it and riding on the stubble or common.[1] It is possible, as indeed it is likely owing to the difference in the condition of the road surface at the two seasons, that the cost of road carriage was higher in winter than in summer.[2] Road transport was by packhorse and by cart. Probably carts were used, except for carting between field and stackyard, to a lesser extent than in later centuries when the road surface was cut up by wagon wheels into the condition described by Arthur Young. But perhaps Arthur Young had a higher standard than the medieval traveller of what a road should be. It is possible, as Pelham argues, that there was some regional differentiation between packhorse and cart even in medieval times, the packhorse prevailing in rough hilly ground, the cart in the smoother country of the English Plain.[3] It fits in with what is known of later centuries and with what might be described as geographical probabilities.

The growth of internal and of foreign trade went on hand in hand. The commodities involved in foreign trade were chiefly wool and cloth, which were exported, and wine, which was imported. Of the trade handled by denizens[4] during the years 1446–48, out of a total export valued at £108,900 wool contributed £44,800 and cloth £60,100, and of a total import of £85,800, wine contributed £32,700.[5] The trade was a reciprocal one, the import being of commodities which England could not produce and the export being of commodities of which England produced an excess. These figures show a favourable balance of trade, which was true of that handled by aliens as well as by denizens; it was proper to a country in the stage of economic development in which England then was, but the favourable balance may have been due to political and not

[1] S. and B. Webb: *The Story of the King's Highway* (1913), pp. 5–7.

[2] J. E. Thorold Rogers (Vol. 1, pp. 659–60) gives particulars of the cost of carriage of wine from which Jackman draws this inference, but the winter and summer journeys were not between the same places in each case and the assumption that there was everywhere the same mileage rate cannot be accepted.

[3] R. A. Pelham in *An Historical Geography of England*, Maps 44–6.

[4] i.e. merchants of English nationality, the converse of aliens.

[5] H. L. Gray: 'English Foreign Trade, 1446–82', in Power and Postan: *Studies in English Trade in the Fifteenth Century* (1933), pp. 18–20.

to economic causes.[1] During the early part of the Middle Ages the export of wool exceeded the export of cloth, but by the middle of the fifteenth century the export of cloth(reckoned in wool equivalents) had come to exceed the export of raw wool. By this time the customs accounts enumerated up to two dozen different varieties of English cloth and record the import, in small quantities, of dyes and of Spanish and German wool. During the early part of the Middle Ages the foreign trade of England was mainly in the hands of alien merchants and shipped in foreign bottoms, but by its close English merchants and English ships were handling the greater part of the foreign trade of the country.[2] The share of the wool trade handled by denizens increased from 35 per cent. in 1273 to 75 per cent. in 1333–36, 80 per cent. in 1446–48, and 85 per cent. in 1479–82.

By far the greater part of this foreign trade was handled by ports along the east and south coasts stretching from Hull to Bristol. These lay in and served the English Plain, the focus of medieval England. The ports of Wales and of North-west England were of but minor importance. The largest single port was London, not so clearly in the early part of the Middle Ages, but by the end of the fourteenth century its supremacy was clearly established. At the end of the thirteenth century London exported less raw wool than Boston,[3] and in the middle of the fourteenth century less cloth than either Bristol or Southampton;[4] but by the end of the fourteenth century and the beginning of the fifteenth century it was the premier port for the export of both raw wool and finished cloth. This growth was partly at the expense of other ports and bore witness to the development of the metropolitan at the expense of the local regional centres of English life. It was the east coast ports whose trade declined during the course of the fifteenth century: their decline was due partly to the competition of London, but also to the decline in the export of raw wool, one of their export staples. The western ports, in contrast, increased their trade, and in some respects the trade of Southampton and of Sandwich

[1] H. L. Gray, *op. cit.*, pp. 20 and 37–8.

[2] N. S. B. Gras: *The Early English Customs System* (1918), p. 111.

[3] R. A. Pelham: 'Medieval Foreign Trade: Eastern Ports', *An Historical Geography of England before 1800*, ed. by H. C. Darby (1936), Fig. 49.

[4] H. L. Gray: *English Historical Review*, Vol. 39, Appendix I.

increased also.[1] The eastern and the western ports had each different overseas space-relations: the eastern were bound up with the North Sea and the Baltic, with Flanders and the Hanseatic League, while the western traded chiefly with Gascony, with Spain, and with the Mediterranean.[2] The increased trade of the western ports bore witness to the growing importance of the West Country within Britain, to their physical removal from London, and to the growing significance of the Atlantic frontage in Europe. The stage was set for the geographical discoveries of the fifteenth and sixteenth centuries.

II

THE SIXTEENTH AND SEVENTEENTH CENTURIES

By the end of the fifteenth century the localism of the Middle Ages was breaking down, a change expressed politically in the emergence of the Tudor nation-state and economically in the development of regional specialisation of agricultural and industrial production, and, consequential upon this, in an increased volume of internal trade. In the phraseology of Prof. Gras, the metropolitan market was superseding the local market. Trade was still handled in part by periodic fairs and markets, but the growing bulk of trade was becoming too large to be limited to these periodic occasions. It came to acquire more regularised channels, and the mercantile function became a full-time occupation. But, although the volume of trade increased, there was, prior to the Industrial Revolution, a quickened flow of traffic to only a limited extent. River barge, small coaster, packhorse and wagon continued as previously to carry the goods traffic of the country. Speedier transport required better roads and improved waterways, and it required mechanical means of haulage. It had to await the Industrial Revolution.

The rivers continued to handle a substantial proportion of the goods traffic, for a boat could carry a greater quantity of goods

---

[1] Tables of Enrolled Customs. Power and Postan, *op. cit.*, pp. 330–60. These conclusions are drawn from a study of the average annual figures for each port for the decades 1408–18 and 1470–80.

[2] E. M. Carus-Wilson: 'The Overseas Trade of Bristol', Power and Postan, *op. cit.*, pp. 183–246, and E. M. Carus-Wilson: *The Overseas Trade of Bristol in the later Middle Ages* (Bristol Record Society) (1936).

than a packhorse or a wagon for a given amount of horse-power. A seventeenth-century writer estimated that a 30-ton boat could carry as much as 100 packhorses.[1] The waterways, however, did not appear to carry many passengers, and travellers mostly went by road. Leland, Celia Fiennes, Defoe, and Cobbett all took to the road and rode on horseback. Leland, in the early sixteenth century, listed bridges and ferries innumerable, but his interest was focused on means to cross a river and not on means to navigate it. Celia Fiennes, when in Bristol, noted 'Little boates w[ch] are Call'd Wherryes such as we use on the Thames . . . to Convey persons from place to place', but this was purely local travel within the town.[2] The wherries plying on the Cam between Cambridge and Stourbridge Fair were similarly for local traffic.[3] The goods traffic on the rivers was chiefly of heavy low-grade commodities—coal, corn, timber, bricks—but was not confined to them, for there are records of wool, butter, bacon, wine, and cloth.[4] Concerning Leeds and Wakefield, Defoe wrote, 'I need not add, that by the same Navigation they receive all their heavy Goods, as well such as are Imported at Hull, as such as come from London, and such as other Counties supply, as Butter, Cheese, Lead, Iron, Salt; all sorts of Grocery . . . and every Sort of heavy or bulky Goods'.[5] Coal was shipped along the Severn from the Salop fields upstream to Shrewsbury and downstream to Gloucester and Bristol. It was distributed from the Port of London along the Thames upstream at least as far as Abingdon.[6] Celia Fiennes noted that the Thames between Oxford and Abingdon 'was full of Barges and Lighters'.[7] From Guildford, the head of navigation of the Wey, timber (brought on carts in summer from the Weald) and meal (ground in local river-side mills) were shipped downstream to London.[8]

These river barges were sailing vessels, and when the wind

[1] F. Mathew: *A Mediterranean Passage by Water from London to Bristol* (1670). Quoted by T. S. Willan: *The English Coasting Trade, 1600–1750* (1938), p. 190.

[2] Fiennes: *Through England on a Side Saddle in the Time of William and Mary* (ed. of 1888), p. 200.

[3] D. Defoe: *Tour*, Vol. 1, p. 84.

[4] T. S. Willan: *River Navigation*, pp. 123–7.

[5] D. Defoe, *op. cit.*, Vol. 2, p. 615.

[6] T. S. Willan: *River Navigation*, p. 125.

[7] Fiennes, *op. cit.*, p. 29.

[8] D. Defoe, *op. cit.*, Vol. 1, p. 145.

was light or in the wrong direction they were hauled by man or beast. Celia Fiennes saw on the Severn 'many Barges that were tow'd up by strength of men 6 or 8 at a tyme'.[1] Horses required towing paths to give them a foothold, but some Navigation Acts prohibited their employment in order to meet the objections of river-side landowners. River transport, as in the Middle Ages, was cheaper than land transport. It was, at the dearest, about half the rate by road and, at the cheapest, was estimated at one-twelfth, but it varied greatly locally.[2] Freight rates were often greater upstream against the current than downstream with the current.[3]

The geographical distribution of this river trade was naturally dictated by topography. Dr. Willan has drawn maps of the distribution of navigable waterways in the seventeenth century and has marked on them those parts of the country more than 15 miles from a navigable river, a distance which represented approximately the average length of haul for timber by land possible in the course of a working day.[4] These maps show that the greater part of the English Plain, together with the Vale of York and the Midland Gate, was accessible to river transport. Navigation was interrupted, however, by many of the works of man. The water-wheel, in use in the Middle Ages, became widespread in the fifteenth century for fulling, corn-grinding, and forge-work, but subsequently for many other industrial uses. The overshot water-wheel was usually associated with a weir and a mill race, and these commonly obstructed the river and prevented navigation altogether. Leland reported of 'Foderingey' in Northamptonshire that Edward IV 'had thought to have privelegid it with a market, and with putting down weres and mills, to have causid that smaul lightters might cum thither'.[5]

During this period between the Middle Ages and the Industrial Revolution there were many schemes for river

---

[1] Fiennes, *op. cit.*, p. 196.

[2] T. S. Willan: *River Navigation*, pp. 119–21.

[3] W. T. Jackman: *The Development of Transportation in Modern England*, Vol. 1 (1916), p. 208. An Act of 1774 authorised tolls on lime of ¾d. upstream and ½d. downstream on the Aire and Calder. An Act of 1699 also for the Aire and Calder, fixed maximum tolls at 10s. in summer and 16s. in winter (J. Priestley: *Historical Account of the Navigable Rivers, Canals, and Railways of Great Britain* (1831)).

[4] See estimates of length of a day's journey in the Middle Ages, above.

[5] Leland, *Itinerary*, Pt. 1, folio 4.

improvement. In the seventeenth century the Commissions of Sewers occasionally intervened to remove obstructions and so restore navigability, and in the late seventeenth and early eighteenth centuries Parliament passed some two dozen Acts to improve navigation on specified rivers. Of these Acts most referred to rivers within the English Plain, but by the end of the seventeenth century several northern rivers had become involved, and by the early eighteenth century more northern than southern rivers were affected. The rivers to which the Acts referred were mainly in one or other of the following regions: East Anglia, the lower Thames Valley, the West Country, the West Midlands, the Vales of York and Trent, and the Lancashire–Cheshire Plain.[1] These were the industrial districts of the time and the association of transport improvement with industry was not fortuitous.[2] The object of these schemes was to reduce traffic congestion: ... 'it easeth,' said the Speaker of the House of Commons, 'the People of the great Charge of Land Carriages; preserves the Highways, which are daily worn out with Waggons carrying excessive Burdens'.[3] The river improvements which these Acts specified were the extension of navigability to rivers, or parts of rivers, not previously possessing it. Work was put in hand for the improvement of the Soar up to Leicester and of the Avon up to Coventry; in neither case had the river been navigable hitherto so far upstream.[4] But there were more far-reaching schemes than these. York took out an Act to straighten the meanders of the lower Ouse so that the Humber tide could reach the city's walls, and Chester experimented with the New Cut in the Dee estuary.[5] This was another kind of improvement, the digging of straight new channels, though these were still associated with existing waterways. They heralded the canal proper, dug independently of any river course. The lock, whereby a canal could surmount a gradient, was first used early in the seventeenth century on existing river navigations, but it did not

---

[1] The list is given by T. S. Willan: *River Navigation*, pp. 28–30. See also map on p. 90.

[2] W. T. Jackman also remarks on the correlation.

[3] *Journal of the House of Lords*, XI, 675.

[4] W. T. Jackman, *op. cit.*, Vol. 1, p. 181.

[5] W. T. Jackman, *op. cit.*, Vol. 1, pp. 197–206.

become common until the canal era.[1] 'The invention of the poundlock was almost as important as the discovery of steampower. Without it the canal-building of the Industrial Revolution would have been impossible'.[2] These were the successive phases in what may be called the typology of river improvement.

The coasting trade was an important adjunct to the system of internal communications for the whole period prior to the railway era. Coal was carried in quantity coastwise, especially from the North-east coast to London, but the coast-wise coal trade involved also the South Wales, the North Wales, and the West Cumberland fields.[3] Corn was shipped from east coast ports to London, and there was also a trade in wool, in butter and cheese, and in other farm produce. Nor was traffic limited to bulky commodities. Manufactures were transported as well in small parcels in the form of miscellaneous cargoes, and many of the exports from London, the first port of the realm, had first been collected by the coasting trade.

In the aggregate road traffic was almost certainly greater than river traffic and road mileage was, of course, very much greater than the mileage of navigable waterway. By far the greater number of passengers went by road, whether on horseback or by coach. Coaches were first employed about the middle of the sixteenth century, apparently at first for town street work.[4] By the middle of the seventeenth century, stage-coaches were running from town to town on the main highways of the country. In 1658 stage-coaches were advertised to leave London on stated days for Exeter, a four-days' journey, for York, also a four-days' journey, for Newcastle, for Edinburgh, for Chester, and for Kendal, as well as intermediate destinations. These, however, ran on the average at no more than 30 miles per day, though greater distances were covered in summer, and their speed in miles per hour was very low.[5]

Goods traffic on the roads was by packhorse and by wagon. The packhorse was the earlier and more general mode of

---

[1] T. S. Willan: *River Navigation*, pp. 88–94.
[2] T. S. Willan: *River Navigation*, p. 94.
[3] T. S. Willan: *Coasting Trade*, pp. 64–9.
[4] W. T. Jackman, *op. cit.*, Vol. 1, pp. 111–18.
[5] W. T. Jackman, *op. cit.*, Vol. 1, p. 134.

conveyance, and in hilly districts it was the only one. The single animal carrying farmers' produce or clothiers' pieces to market was supplemented by the train of packhorses, twenty or so in number, run by public carriers on stated routes and on stated days. Celia Fiennes remarked on the prevalence of packhorses and the relative absence of wagons in the hilly districts of the North of England, for example, near Kendal. In such districts horse panniers were employed not only for transporting relatively valuable commodities as raw wool or finished pieces, but also relatively bulky low-grade commodities: 'They also use horses on which they have a sort of Pannyers some Close, some open, that they strewe full of hay turff and Lime and Dung'.[1] In order to facilitate packhorse traffic narrow flagged causeways were frequently built, especially in hilly regions, and these were often raised above the general level of the road. Traces of these causeways remain today. High narrow bridges with a width sufficient only for the passage of one train of animals at a time and quite insufficient for the passage of a wagon, were built also primarily for packhorse traffic. Wagons were more common in the English Plain, with its lesser gradients. There had always been carts carrying between the field and the stack-yard, but wagons carrying goods for long distances gradually became more and more numerous during the last decades of the sixteenth, but particularly during the seventeenth and early eighteenth centuries, though until 1650 or thereabouts they were virtually confined to the main roads.[2] The wagon increased the weight of goods which a single animal could effectively move. Carriers' wagons, like carriers' packhorse trains, ran on regular routes and on stated days advertised beforehand.[3] In addition to packhorses and wagons, the roads were used by stock, being driven not only over short distances between farm and market within a region, but also from region to region, from Scotland to Norfolk, from Wales and the South-west Peninsula to London. It was a product partly of the growing urbanism of England, but more of the needs of the New Husbandry for stock for winter feeding. Drove roads used by travelling stock

[1] Fiennes, *op. cit.*, p. 160.
[2] S. and B. Webb, *op. cit.*, p. 69.
[3] W. T. Jackman, *op. cit.*, Vol. 1, pp. 122–3.

were unusually wide, partly to facilitate movement, but also to provide some wayside grazing. Packhorse causeway and drove road each contributed a distinctive feature to the landscape and short stretches still remain here and there today.

The cost of road carriage was high, considerably more than the cost of water carriage. Jackman prints rates for Somerset, Lincoln, Derbyshire, and Northampton, which work out at 10d. to 1s. 3d. per ton per mile, the lower figure being frequently the summer rate and the higher the winter rate. These were for the late seventeenth and early eighteenth centuries.[1] All kinds of commodities were carried by road, but the high cost of transport implied that bulky low-grade commodities were carried for only short distances, long-distance traffic in these being possible only where river or coastal navigation was available. In that sense long-distance road traffic was selective and the packhorses and stage wagons working the long-distance routes carried mainly what the transport classifications would now describe as general merchandise.

This increasing volume of road traffic led to a deterioration in road surfaces. The endless procession of packhorses and of stock churned up the earth roads, muddy in winter and dusty in summer; and waggons, cutting deeply into the soft surfaces, wore deep ruts which further impeded traffic. Some Roman road surfaces were still used.[2] Only a small proportion of the road mileage of the country, however, was surfaced after the Roman fashion. The packhorse causeways eased the position to some extent, but many roads, even main roads, were almost impassable in winter.[3] The problem of road maintenance and improvement had become acute. The position was complicated by the character of the increased road traffic. The increase was not of local but of through traffic, the product of

[1] W. T. Jackman, op. cit., Vol. 1, pp. 140–1.

[2] Leland, op. cit., Pt. 1, folio 11. He reported of Weedon in Northamptonshire that it was 'a praty thorough fare . . . much celebratid by cariars bycause it stondith hard by the famose way . . . Watheling Strete.' (Leland, op. cit., Pt. 1, folios 42–6.) Elsewhere he wrote of 'the rigge' and 'the large high crest' of Watling Street, but whether as an antiquarian or as one interested in roads as a means of contemporary travel is not certain.

[3] D. Defoe records that the passage of geese from East Anglia to London was entirely an autumn traffic, partly because they could then feed on wayside stubbles 'as they go', but partly also because by the end of October the roads became 'too stiff and deep'. In his day geese had just begun to be carried in four-storied carts (D. Defoe, op. cit., Vol. 1, p. 59).

the regional agricultural and industrial specialisation that was gradually taking shape in this period. 'On all the main lines of communication, what may be called the local use of the roads, by the farmers and cottagers who had to maintain them, became a steadily diminishing fraction of the total traffic.' The 'new users' of the road, in fact, were not those who were legally responsible for its maintenance, for the upkeep of the road was the responsibility of the local authority.[1] Road maintenance, however, even when performed as the law required, consisted merely in scouring the ditches, in keeping hedges cut closely to prevent overhanging branches shading the road, and in filling up the holes and ruts in the road surface with whatever stones or gravel were locally available.[2] No improvement in road surfaces was contemplated and, as wagons cut up the road, statutory limits were set to the number of horses which might be harnessed (which restricted the size of the wagon and therefore its capacity for damage), and later to the width of the wheel tyre.

The turnpike system arose to tackle this problem. It was but a piecemeal and local effort. An Act was taken out for a particular stretch of road by local men who formed themselves into a trust for the purpose. The Act empowered them to erect barriers at either end and to charge tolls from traffic passing through these barriers in order to accumulate funds for the improvement of the road surface. It was necessary to have Parliament's approval for this limitation of the freedom of the King's Highway. In 1663 Parliament authorised the erection of gates and the levying of tolls at three points on the Great North Road and the devotion of the moneys thus collected to road repair.[3] Before the end of the seventeenth century other roads were involved, all, except those of Cheshire, in the English Plain. This was still, economically, the most important region of the country. Most of them were along routes leading to London or else were in East Anglia or the West Country. But the chief spate of Acts setting up turnpike trusts was,

[1] S. and B. Webb, *op. cit.*, pp. 14–18.

[2] The village of Radwell in Hertfordshire complained of 'the nature of the soil being such as the winter devours whatsoever they are able to lay on in the summer'. Quoted by S. and B. Webb, *op. cit.*, p. 115.

[3] Wadesmill (Herts), Caxton (Cambs), Stilton (Hunts). In these cases the Justices were the authorities.

significantly enough, after 1750, and it was not until the end of the eighteenth century that the more important roads of the country were continuously under turnpike administration.[1] The turnpike age did not begin in Scotland until after 1750. Jackman has classified road Acts subsequent to 1701 into regional groups. During the period 1701–50 road Acts were most numerous in the Home Counties and along the routes leading to London, in Yorkshire, Lancashire, and Cheshire, and in the West and East Midlands.[2] From this evidence it would appear that road Acts were becoming relatively more prominent in the rising industrial districts after 1700 than they had been before, though they were not yet as prominent as they were to become later. But, although so many roads had passed under turnpike administration, permanent improvement of their surface was not universal. Defoe expatiated on the benefits of turnpiking. Some improvement was unquestionably effected—roads were widened and graded and rivers bridged,[3] and, where these improvements were effective, travel was speeded and carriers' charges reduced. He admitted, however, that improvement was expensive and that where good hard material was not close at hand, as in stiff clay lands, no real improvement resulted.[4] In Bedfordshire the passage of fat bullocks to London 'often worked through in the Winter what the Commissioners have mended in the Summer'.[5] Permanent improvement had to await the road engineers, of whom Telford and Macadam were the chief. Their work was contemporary with the Industrial Revolution.

During this period, subsequent to the Middle Ages and prior to the Industrial Revolution, there was not only an increased volume of internal trade, but also an increased volume of overseas trade. It was part and parcel of the regional specialisation of production within Britain and of an improving standard of living requiring products from overseas.[6] Sir William Petty,

[1] S. and B. Webb, *op. cit.*, p. 125.

[2] W. T. Jackman, *op. cit.*, Vol. 2, Appendix 13. His table relates to all road Acts and not only to turnpike Acts.

[3] D. Defoe, *op. cit.*, Vol. 2, p. 525.

[4] D. Defoe, *op. cit.*, Vol. 2, p. 522.

[5] D. Defoe, *op. cit.*, Vol. 2, p. 523.

[6] '. . . we know that our own natural wares doe not yield us so much profit as our industry.' (T. Mun: *England's Treasure by Foreign Trade*. Reprint of ed. of 1664 (1933), p. 13).

in the seventies of the seventeenth century, asserted in his *Political Arithmetick* that Britain possessed 'Two parts of Nine of the Trade of the whole Commercial World; and about Two parts in Seven of all the Shipping'.[1] Not only was the volume of trade greater than hitherto, but its geographical range was very much wider. During the Middle Ages British foreign trade had been limited to Europe and the Mediterranean, and it was focused chiefly on the nearby ports of the North Sea and the Atlantic coast. The geographical discoveries of the late fifteenth and sixteenth centuries threw open the whole world and British ships were to be found in every sea from Hudson's Bay to Nan Hai or the South China Sea. This widely flung trade was closely associated with the Colonial Empire which arose out of trade and which, indeed, itself stabilised it. During the Middle Ages there had been two companies—the Merchant Staplers and the Merchant Adventurers—engaged in foreign trade, but by the close of the sixteenth century six more companies had been added,[2] and it is significant that the new companies—the East India, the Eastland,[3] the Levant, for example—had each a regional rather than a general sphere of operations.

The largest single element in Britain's foreign trade was unquestionably woollen and worsted manufactures. Petty estimated these at £5·0 millions out of a total trade of £10·2 million (visible trade and shipping earnings),[4] but these figures cannot be regarded with any exactitude.[5] The export of lead, tin, and coal was estimated at £0·5 million and of Scottish and Irish produce at £1¼ million. Manufactures of wool, fish, and minerals were Britain's staple exports. Her imports were iron and flax to remedy the deficiencies of home production of industrial raw materials, special manufactures from abroad

[1] *The Economic Writings of Sir William Petty*, ed. by C. H. Hull, Vol. 1 (1899), p. 297.

[2] E. Lipson, *op. cit.*, Vol. 2 (1931), p. 186.

[3] The Eastland claimed an antiquity greater than its charter of 1579. C. P. Lucas: *The Beginnings of English Overseas Enterprise* (1917), pp. 156–60.

[4] *The Economic Writings of Sir William Petty*, Vol. 1, p. 296.

[5] The import and export values in a long series of returns from 1696 to 1853 are of little use as they stand, for the values were official and not real values. In 1853 *official* values showed an excess of exports over imports; in 1854 *real* values showed an excess of imports over exports. The returns of quantities at present remain in MSS. See G. N. Clark: *Guide to English Commercial Statistics, 1696–1782* (1938).

such as brassware and calico, and a variety of warm temperate and tropical produce—wines, oranges, spices, and sugar. Trade in corn was spasmodic and depended on the state of harvest: there was an export in times of plenty, import in years of low yield. The commodities[1] involved in this foreign trade issued out of the geographical constitution of the country and of the stage in economic development which it had then reached.

By the close of the Middle Ages London had come to be indisputably the chief port of the kingdom and had grown at the expense of other ports of the east coast. According to the table of customs dues constructed by Gras for 1536–1711, London collected between 72 and 87 per cent. of the entire customs revenue of the country.[2] London was to England what Paris and Rouen together were to France, 'Rouen being to Paris as that part of London which is below the Bridge, is to what is above it'.[3] London was the natural focal point of the English Plain, and, so long as the English Plain was the heart of English life and economic activity, London was the focal point of England. Its importance as a trading centre had grown in the later Middle Ages with the modification of medieval localism, and it grew, relative to the country as a whole, still more with the emergence of the nation-state during the sixteenth century. Its commercial pre-eminence was not infringed until the Industrial Revolution modified the balance of regional economy within Britain. In 1700 London handled 80 per cent. of the imports of the country and 74 per cent. of the exports, but in 1750 71 per cent. of the imports and 66 per cent. of the exports, and in 1790 70 per cent. of the imports and 56 per cent. of the exports.[4] Even in the early eighteenth century there were proceeding changes in the regional balance of the British economy, and it is

[1] For lists of commodities to particular markets, see an account of the late sixteenth century printed by N. S. B. Gras: *Corn Market*, Appendix J; and for the middle of the seventeenth century a list drawn up by M. P. Ashley and printed by J. N. L. Baker: 'England in the Seventeenth Century', *An Historical Geography of England before 1800*, ed. by H. C. Darby (1936), pp. 431–2. Expansion of trade with the tropics proved difficult for Britain had little to send except woollen cloth, an unsuitable clothing material in a hot climate.

[2] N. S. B. Gras: *Corn Market*, p. 74.

[3] *The Economic Writings of Sir William Petty*, Vol. 2, p. 539.

[4] Quoted by O. H. K. Spate: 'The Growth of London', *An Historical Geography of England before 1800*, ed. by H. C. Darby (1936), p. 543. It is not clear whether 'the country' is England alone or Great Britain.

noticeable that then, as now, London handled a greater share of the imports than of the exports. The predominance of London in foreign trade, though based fundamentally on the focal position of London within the English Plain so long as the English Plain remained the heart of English economic life, was heightened by the monopolist organisation of foreign trade. The corporate companies were organised from London and their members were largely London merchants.[1]

The importance of London in foreign trade did not imply the stagnation of shipping and trade in the innumerable ports of the estuaries and creeks of the British coastline. They could be the more easily used by reason of the small burden of the sea-going ships of the day.[2] A list of ports in the reign of James I gives a total of 194 for Great Britain and Ireland.[3] A list drawn up in 1578 by an Admiralty official gives 391 for England and Wales alone, but a great number were mere creeks and landing-places.[4] Whatever the volume of foreign trade at these ports, there was an increasing volume of coastwise trade which contributed in part, of course, to the foreign trade of London. The accounts of ports visited by both Celia Fiennes and Defoe give the impression of a busy thriving trade, and the latter recognised that each port engaged in foreign trade had some regional speciality of its own. Yarmouth brought in naval stores from Norway and the Baltic, and sent to the Mediterranean herrings and worsted; Hull traded with Northern Europe and the Mediterranean, but 'the Trade of Tobacco and Sugars from the West-Indies, they chiefly manage by the Way of London';[5] Newcastle was not mentioned as having any

[1] But the Merchant Adventurers, for example, were not confined to London; there were branches at York, Hull, Newcastle, Lynn, Norwich, Ipswich, Exeter, and Southampton, inter alia. These branches struggled for independence inside the Company just as the interlopers, with their demand for free trade, did outside the Company. It is not without significance that it is mainly the east coast ports that are represented in this list. See also the discussion of this point by C. P. Lucas, op. cit., Chapter III.

[2] V. Barbour: 'Dutch and English Merchant Shipping in the Seventeenth Century', Economic History Review, Vol. 2, No. 2 (1930), pp. 262–3. The greater part consisted of vessels of less than 100 tons. Larger ships were built for the East.

[3] R. G. Marsden: 'English Ships in the Reign of James I', Transactions Royal Historical Society, Vol. 19 (1905), pp. 336–7.

[4] D. and G. Mathew: 'Iron Furnaces in South-eastern England and English Ports and Landing Places, 1578', English Historical Review, Vol. 48 (1933), pp. 96–9.

[5] D. Defoe, op. cit., Vol. 2, p. 652.

foreign trade at all. It is clear, however, that these east coast ports engaged in little *direct* foreign trade beyond Europe. Of Bristol, Defoe writes significantly, 'the greatest, the richest, and the best Port of Trade in Great Britain, London only excepted. The Merchants of this City not only have the greatest Trade but they trade with a more entire Independency upon London, than any other town in Britain.' Bristol, together with Exeter, Liverpool, and Glasgow, other west coast ports, traded with the Americas and (Bristol and Liverpool only) with Africa independently of London.[1] Situated in the more remote west of Britain and their own space-relations naturally favouring the Atlantic trade, they were the more able to combat London's dominance. They had each also local industrial resources and a substantial local market for imported overseas produce. Even in the later Middle Ages the trade of these western ports was increasing while that of the eastern ports (apart from London) was declining. London's undisputed supremacy was limited to the English Plain and to the east coast, that part of Britain for which it was the natural focus and centre.

III

THE REVOLUTION IN TRANSPORT

With the development of commercial production in farming and in industry during the sixteenth and seventeenth centuries, the volume of trade had been steadily increasing; but with the Agrarian and Industrial Revolutions and with the arrival of commercial production and of regional specialisation in full stature, the volume of trade grew by leaps and bounds. By the end of the eighteenth century, if not previously, Britain had become to the continental mind a nation of shopkeepers. The existing system of transport was inadequate to carry the swollen volume of goods and, if the economic development of Britain was to proceed, improvement in the means and acceleration in the speed of transport was essential. There was a revolution in transport equally with a revolution in agriculture and industry.

[1] For Exeter, see W. G. Hoskins: *Industry, Trade, and People in Exeter, 1688–1800* (1935), p. 63; for Liverpool, *Social Survey of Merseyside*, Vol. 1 (1932), pp. 15–16.

TABLE XVIII

REGIONAL DISTRIBUTION IN ENGLAND OF ROAD ACTS, 1701–1830, AND OF TURNPIKE MILEAGE, 1829

	Percentage of Road Acts			Percentage of area	Percentage of turnpike mileage 1829
	1701–50	1751–90	1791–1830		
Northumberland, Durham, Cumberland, W'morland	3·8	4·8	5·6	10·5	7·3
Yorks, Lancs, Cheshire	17·2	13·7	19·6	17·4	13·3
Derby, Staffs, Notts, Salop, Warwick, Leics, Rutland, Northants	13·2	23·2	21·1	14·3	20·8
Hereford, Worcester, Monmouth	4·8	5·0	4·1	4·2	7·8
Berks, Oxon, Bucks, Beds, Herts	21·3	10·2	8·6	6·6	6·8
Lincs, Hunts, Cambs, Norfolk, Suffolk, Essex	10·5	8·0	8·3	17·6	9·6
Middlesex, Kent, Hants, Surrey, Sussex	19·6	17·4	17·0	11·2	13·5
Gloucester, Wilts, Somerset	9·6	11·6	10·2	8·4	12·9
Dorset, Devon, Cornwall	—	6·1	5·5	9·8	8·0
England	100·0	100·0	100·0	100·0	100·0
No. of Road Acts	418	1,633	2,440		

Particulars of Road Acts from W. T. Jackman, *The Development of Transportation in Modern England* (1916), vol. 2, Appendix 13. Particulars of turnpike mileage calculated from G. R. Porter: *The Progress of the Nation* (1847), p. 294.

The turnpiking of roads had begun even before the eighteenth century, but the real spate followed the middle of the century. According to Jackman's calculations, there was an annual average of eight road Acts during the years 1701–50, of forty-one during the years 1751–90, and of sixty-one during the years 1791–1830. Table XVIII summarises the regional distribution of these road Acts, which included turnpike Acts among others. Relative to their area, the Home Counties especially, but also the West and East Midlands, the lower Severn Valley, and the West Country had above their share; the northern counties, the South-west Peninsula, East Anglia, and Lincoln, had under their share; Yorkshire, Lancashire, Cheshire, had Acts more or less proportional to their area. Expressed in general terms, therefore, it was the Home Counties and the industrial districts that had the greatest number of road Acts and the agricultural districts that had the least. The Home Counties had a high proportion because of 'suburban' traffic and because the road plan of England was focused on the metropolitan centre; the industrial districts had a high proportion because of the needs of industrial traffic within them and between manufacturing district and port. The Home Counties had their largest share early in the eighteenth century, 40·9 per cent. of the Acts (1701–50) in 17·8 per cent. of the area; they were the first to be involved on a large scale. The West and East Midlands, on the other hand, had a much greater proportion of Acts after 1750 than before that date. Turnpike mileage in 1829, the result of over a century of activity, was greatest in the Home Counties, the West and East Midlands, the West Country, and the lower Severn Valley; and least, relative to area, in northern England, in eastern England, and in the South-west Peninsula.

Improvement in road surfaces lagged behind the creation of turnpike trusts. There was some improvement in Defoe's day and more after 1750, but it was not until after 1800 that *permanent* improvement was really effected. The half-century, 1750–1800, was a period when experiments in road construction and road surfacing—something beyond the mere filling up of ruts and holes—were beginning to be made. The two great masters were Thomas Telford and John Macadam, but it was not until the last decades of the eighteenth century that they began their work.[1] Telford was commissioned to reconstruct the Carlisle–Glasgow road, the Edinburgh–Morpeth road, and the London–Holyhead road. These were large-scale objectives, and the Post Office, anxious to accelerate the carriage of mails, encouraged them and, in the case of the Holyhead road, initiated the scheme. The Holyhead road took fifteen years to reconstruct, and it was to have been followed by a remodelled Great North Road along the eastern side of England, including a straight hundred miles from Peterborough to York. The project, however, was abandoned after the Rainhill locomotive trials and the dawn of the railway age. The railway was a more effective means of national communication than the road, however well constructed the latter might be. The work of Macadam was being accomplished contemporaneously with that of Telford, but rather in respect of regional road systems,

[1] For the principles on which each worked, see S. and B. Webb, *op. cit.*, Chapter VIII and W. T. Jackman, *op. cit.*, Chapter IV.

the roads around Bristol and then the roads around London, than of long-distance inter-regional routes. The local roads, apart from those near the great towns, exhibited much less improvement until later on in the nineteenth century. With the railway age and the virtual monopoly of through communication by the railway, the administration of the roads reverted to the local authority and one by one the turnpike trusts disappeared as they came before Parliament for renewal. The toll-bars had become a public nuisance and a restraint to trade. In 1871 854 trusts remained, but in 1881 only 184, and the last, in Anglesey, came to an end in 1895.[1] The surfacing of secondary as well as of primary roads was gradually improved, but, being now concerned chiefly with local traffic, little grading and little straightening of sharp curves and bends were accomplished.

The improvement of road surfaces increased the speed of travel. Jackman's general conclusion is that by 1830 the fast mail and passenger coaches had an average speed of 9–10 miles per hour, about double what it had been prior to 1750.[2] The London to Manchester journey had taken $4\frac{1}{2}$ days in 1754, but by 1830 it was reduced to 20 hours.[3] Increased speed of travel, together with the growing specialisation of production, multiplied the volume of passenger travel. In 1801 seven coaches left Chester daily, but in 1831 twenty-six. Wagons carrying goods travelled, of course, much more slowly. Even the 'fly wagons' went at only $2\frac{1}{2}$ miles per hour on the average. It is probable that road-rates for goods had changed but little. There was, of course, wide variation, but that lay mostly between limits of 10d. and 1s. 3d. per ton-mile, the same as for the late seventeenth and early eighteenth centuries.[4] Road improvement had not solved, though it had eased, the transport problem, for the carriage of goods on land was still extraordinarily expensive.

Contemporary with reconstruction of the roads was the digging of canals. The period 1750–1830 may be termed the road and canal era as distinct from the railway era which was

---

[1] S. and B. Webb, *opl cit.*, p. 222.
[2] W. T. Jackman, *op. cit.*, Vol. 1, p. 339.
[3] W. T. Jackman, *op. cit.*, Vol. 2, Appendix 5.
[4] W. T. Jackman, *op. cit.*, Vol. 1, pp. 346–8, and Vol. 2, Appendix 7.

to follow it. The antecedents of the canal in the deepening of rivers and later in the digging of cuts to eliminate circuitous meanders have already been considered. The next stage in the evolution of the canal was the digging of a channel parallel to the existing river or brook and the feeding of the canal channel by river water, as, for example, the Douglas Navigation of 1720 and the Sankey Canal of 1755. This was comparable to the *canal latéral* of the Paris Basin. The first canal dug independently of any river course was the Worsley, a 10-mile channel from Worsley to Manchester, opened in 1761. It presented considerable engineering difficulties, for it was a completely 'level' or contour canal constructed over undulating country, and it involved the construction of the famous Barton viaduct over the River Irwell. It halved the price of coal in Manchester. It was followed by the Bridgewater Canal from Manchester to Runcorn, parallel to the pre-existing Mersey and Irwell Navigation, and completed in 1767. This also was a contour canal without locks, but, as the outfall of the Mersey into its estuary at Runcorn was considerably lower than the river at Manchester, the terminus of the canal at Runcorn was some 79 feet above the estuary. An imposing flight of locks was later built to negotiate this gradient and to link the canal with the estuary. The canal was an immediate success, both for passengers and for goods. The Manchester to Liverpool journey for passengers was by canal packet from Manchester to Warrington and then by coach from Warrington to Liverpool. The canal packet did the round trip, Manchester to Warrington and back, in a day. Though it took longer, the whole journey from Manchester to Liverpool was sometimes done by boat. It will be noticed that these early canals were in South Lancashire and were closely associated with the manufacturing town of Manchester and its links with the port of Liverpool.[1] This was one of the most rapidly developing industrial districts of the period; moreover, its fustian and cotton manufacturers imported almost all their raw materials and exported a not

[1] The need for improving communication between Manchester and Hull for Lancashire's Baltic trade during the French wars was responsible for the Rochdale Canal across the Pennines. Previously Manchester goods were carried on wagons over difficult country to wharves at Huddersfield, Sowerby Bridge, or Salterhebble (A. Redford: *Manchester Merchants and Foreign Trade, 1794–1858* (1934), pp. 169–77).

inconsiderable proportion of their finished production. Tranport improvement began where need was greatest. The Bridgewater Canal was followed by the Grand Trunk or Trent and Mersey, whose name described its objectives, by the Staffordshire and Worcestershire, by the Coventry, by the Oxford, and by a whole series of canals in the West Midlands, in Lancashire, and in West Yorkshire. The period of greatest activity in the taking out of canal Acts was that of the decades 1791–1810: it included the 'canal mania' of 1792–93. The annual average for 1751–70 was 1·2, for 1771–90 2·3, for 1791–1810 10·8, and for 1811–30 5·4.[1] There was, of course, a time-lag of several years between the taking out of an Act and the completion of the canal ready for operation. It would, however, appear that the spate of canal building had begun to slacken before the locomotive railway was a proved success.

Jackman has made a regional grouping of these canal Acts and Table XIX has been calculated from his figures. The

TABLE XIX

REGIONAL DISTRIBUTION OF CANAL ACTS IN ENGLAND, 1751–1830

	Percentage of Canal Acts				Percentage of Area
	1751–70	1771–90	1791–1810	1811–30	
Northumberland, Durham, Cumberland, W'morland	—	—	1·9	1·0	10·5
Yorks, Lancs, Cheshire	29·1	23·8	22·3	12·0	17·4
Derby, Staffs, Notts, Salop, Warwick, Leics, Rutland, Northants	50·0	47·8	29·3	24·1	14·3
Hereford, Monmouth, Worcester	12·5	8·7	7·0	6·5	4·2
Berks, Oxon, Bucks, Beds, Herts	4·2	2·2	6·5	7·4	6·6
Lincs, Hunts, Cambs, Norfolk, Suffolk, Essex	4·2	2·2	6·0	6·5	17·6
Middlesex, Kent, Surrey, Sussex, Hants	—	6·5	7·9	22·2	11·2
Gloucester, Wilts, Somerset	—	4·4	14·9	15·7	8·4
Dorset, Devon, Cornwall	—	4·4	4·2	4·6	9·8
	100·0	100·0	100·0	100·0	100·0
No. of Canal Acts	24	46	215	108	

Particulars calculated from W. T. Jackman: *The Development of Transportation in Modern England*, Vol. 2, Appendix 13.

[1] W. T. Jackman, *op. cit.*, Vol. 2, Appendix 13.

chief areas of concentration were Lancashire and Yorkshire, the West and the East Midlands: together they had 202 out of a total of 393 Acts, or 51·4 per cent., and in the earlier years before the 'canal mania' they had 52 out of 70, or 74·3 per cent. These were the rising industrial districts where the transport problem was most acute. The South of England, becoming increasingly agricultural, had few canals until the latter part of the canal era, and many were constructed during the Revolutionary and Napoleonic Wars with the strategic design of linking the Bristol Channel with the Thames Estuary and avoiding the dangerous passage of the English Channel. Apart from this, canals in the South of England were the result of transport imitation rather than of transport need. The North-east coalfield had no canals and the South Wales coalfield few; the mineral tramway was here the chief means of internal transport. Though there have been some additions and many subtractions (owing to canals becoming derelict), the present-day plan is in general terms the same as that existing in the early nineteenth century.

The canal was, above all, an industrial form of transport. Of the total revenue earned by the Bridgewater Canal in 1792, passengers accounted for only 1·8 per cent.[1] There were passenger canal packets, but they went at a lower speed than the 9–10 miles per hour of the stage-coaches. The speed of freight barges on the canals was little different from that of goods wagons on the roads: the 'fly boats' went at $3\frac{1}{2}$ miles per hour and the slow traffic at 2 miles per hour, but the average speed was probably less owing to delays at locks. The road and the canal, with similar speeds of transit, shared the goods between them.

The largest single item in goods traffic on the canals was unquestionably coal. They were the true heirs of the rivers in that they carried the bulky produce of the country. The carriage of coal was the *raison d'être* of the Worsley Canal, and coal figured in nearly every canal prospectus, as, prospectively, the most important revenue-earning commodity. This was true of canals even in agricultural districts, and the promoters of at least one canal advanced the philanthropic motive that coal would make better fires in the labourer's cottage than what

[1] W. T. Jackman, *op. cit.*, Vol. 1, p. 363.

firing he had hitherto been able to pick up from the fields and hedgerows. But the dominance of coal was especially true of canals in the industrial districts. Coal was the life blood of the new industrialism and long lines of factories and mills were built along the canal banks in order to facilitate receipt of coal as well as of other materials. A canal site was of immense importance in the detailed localisation of industrial premises in every industrial district of Britain, the ports included. The industrial districts required coal not only for industry, but also for domestic consumption, a substantial market with the growing aggregation of population into towns. Coal traffic on the canals, however, was short-distance rather than long-distance. It is true that canal-borne coal had invaded the market formerly supplied by coal brought coastwise from the North-east coast, but this was coal from the York–Derby–Nottingham field close at hand,[1] and London received only a fluctuating and minor proportion of its coal supply by canal, in the 'thirties varying from 1,004 to 10,742 tons annually out of a total London consumption of 1,500,000 tons annually.[2] In 1836 Manchester obtained 570,628 tons by canal from little more than 15 miles radius and 316,258 tons by road from shorter distances, chiefly the Pendleton and Oldham roads. In the same year the Liverpool and Manchester Railway brought in only 27,105 tons. Liverpool, farther removed from the coalfield, obtained more by canal and less by road—in 1844, 875,000 and 20,000 tons respectively.[3] The very local traffic was thus partly in the hands of the road carriers.

The long-distance traffic was in general merchandise rather than in coal. London was the chief importing port, and 'raw materials as wool, tin, and cotton were regularly shipped to the manufacturing Midlands and the North along the Grand Junction Canal'.[4] Before the construction of the Liverpool and Manchester Railway, Manchester drew in imported supplies from Liverpool by the Bridgewater Canal. General merchandise usually paid higher freight rates than bulky

[1] *Report and Minutes of Evidence*, Lords' Committee on Coal Trade (1830), p. 59.
[2] *Report*, Royal Commission on Coal (1871), Vol. 3, p. 45.
[3] *Report*, Royal Commission on Coal (1871), Vol. 3, Appendix LV and p. 53.
[4] J. H. Clapham: *Early Railway Age*, p. 79.

low-grade commodities such as coal, but general merchandise travelled longer distances because, being more valuable, it could bear more easily the cost of transport. An account of the cost of carriage by canal gave 2¾d. per ton per mile for heavy goods and 3¾d. for lighter goods.[1] The lower charges by canal than by road amounted to a substantial saving on the long-distance routes, the rate from Liverpool to Birmingham, for example, being 30s. per ton by canal, but 100s. by road.[2] Wherever possible, therefore, the canal was used for long-distance traffic unless quick transport was essential. Although cheaper than road transport,[3] canal transport was little different in cost from river transport prior to the Industrial Revolution. Neither turnpike road nor canal effected any substantial reduction of transport costs, taking the country as a whole. They may have increased the speed of transport and the mileage open to traffic, and so increased the effective quantity of goods which could be transported, but they had not solved the transport problem. Moreover, the volume of goods requiring transport continued to increase, and there was still danger of the existing means of transport becoming choked. The stage was set for the advent of the railway.

The precursor of the railway had been the wagon tramway, nearly always a mineral line. This dated back to the mid-seventeenth century and during the eighteenth century it had become common in many British coalfields—the North-east Coast, South Wales, South Lancashire, Salop, the Yorkshire–Derby–Nottingham, and Scotland, but especially the two former, where tramways connected the coal-pits by a down gradient to the coal staithes on the rivers or the coast. In the inland fields tramways usually led to a canal or river wharf, and the canal companies welcomed their construction accordingly. Indeed, some canal companies themselves constructed branch railways in lieu of branch canals.[4] At first tramway rails and wagon wheels were of wood, but in time the wooden rail was given an iron surface plate, iron wheels were substituted for

[1] W. T. Jackman, *op. cit.*, Vol. 1, p. 449.

[2] W. T. Jackman, *op. cit.*, Vol. 1, p. 447.

[3] Canal rates were at least one-half and usually one-third or one-fourth road rates for the same class of commodity.

[4] J. Priestley (*op. cit.*, p. 31) gives an example from the Ashby-de-la-Zouch Canal.

wooden wheels, and then iron rails for iron-plated wooden rails. Thus the *railway* replaced the *plateway*. One of the early experiments in making iron rails was at the Coalbrookdale Ironworks, where the coke iron industry had been born. Wherever possible it was arranged that full trucks should have a down gradient and move by gravity, but in the opposite direction horse haulage was necessary.

There were several experiments in the last quarter of the eighteenth century in the application of the Boulton and Watt steam-engine to mechanical traction, on the roads and on the railways. Trevithick's engine was employed in South Wales in 1804 and Hedley's and Stephenson's engines were at work in 1813 and 1814 respectively; in each case these ran on private mineral lines. The first public railway with a locomotive engine was the Stockton and Darlington, constructed in that region of the country where the wagon tramway was the established means of transport. It was opened in 1825, and the company at first undertook only goods haulage by locomotives. Private coach proprietors were allowed, after paying tolls, to run passenger coaches on the rails and to draw their coaches by horses.[1] The organisation of carriage on the railway was then considered in the same light as the organisation of carriage on the road and on the canal. Speeds were low and there was little traffic congestion at first. On some of the early railways steep gradients were surmounted by the use of stationary engines. The Liverpool and Manchester Railway was opened in 1830 and its prospectus contemplated a substantial passenger as well as goods traffic. The promoters were not disappointed. From the first it ran six passenger trains a day in each direction,[2] and in the first two years carried approximately 1,200 passengers daily.[3] It served a district where the need for transport improvement was urgent, almost desperate. It was the first *complete* railway in the sense that it was worked by locomotive

---

[1] There was a curious but interesting revival of this in a *Memorandum on the Light Railway Requirements of Rural Districts* drawn up by the Royal Agricultural Society in 1895, in which the suggestion was made that farmers should be permitted to haul on such light railways their own wagons if filled with farm produce or goods destined for farm consumption.

[2] H. G. Lewin: *The British Railway System* (1914), p. 12.

[3] In the first two quarters of 1831 receipts were £436,000 from passengers and £22,093 from goods (W. T. Jackman, *op. cit.*, Vol. 2, p. 528).

P

engines and served all the functions of a common carrier.[1] The success of this railway was the cause of a spate of railway promotion and construction during the 'thirties, and by 1840 most of these lines were in operation. Bradshaw's railway time-table first appeared in 1839. The railway age had begun.

Figure 18 has been drawn to show the development of the system at sample dates.[2] Railways initially independent and initially constructed to serve local needs gradually reached towards each other and coalesced into a national system. Local regional networks and inter-regional links were con-structed concurrently, the latter becoming the main-line systems. It was to serve the manufacturing districts and the metropolis that railways were first built. C. E. R. Sherrington stresses the point that it was the manufacturing districts which were the chief pivot of early railway enterprise, and that London played little part at first. 'Railways tended to stretch towards London, rather than from London',[3] and there was no inter-connexion of London railway terminals. Many North of England towns had in later years, and still have, the same absence of terminal inter-connexions.

The railway almost immediately revolutionised the transport situation. The Liverpool and Manchester Railway carried passengers for half the rate of the coaches[4] and goods for one-third the rate of the canals. The cost both of passenger travel and of goods traffic was substantially reduced, and the greater speed of the railway locomotive allowed the effective carrying capacity of the railway, as compared with road or canal over the same mileage, to be greatly increased. The transport pro-blem was, for the time being, in process of solution. Almost immediately the railway monopolised passenger traffic along its route and its cheaper fares stimulated travel. Stage-coaches and canal packets soon ceased to run. There had been com-mercial travellers even in the road and canal era, but they

[1] G. S. Veitch: *The Struggle for the Liverpool and Manchester Railway* (1930), pp. 19–20. The Stockton and Darlington did not immediately assume *all* the functions of the common carrier.

[2] The maps have been constructed by Miss M. Salmon, to whom I am indebted for permission to include them here.

[3] C. E. R. Sherrington: *Economics of Rail Transport in Great Britain*, Vol. 1 (1928), p. 28.

[4] The single fare from Liverpool to Manchester was 7s. first class and 4s. second class (Print in G. S. Veitch, *op. cit.*, opposite p. 47).

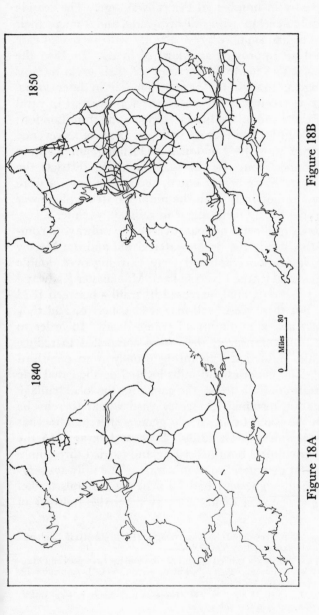

Figure 18A   Figure 18B

Railways in England and Wales in 1840 and 1850

Maps drawn by Miss M. Salmon. These two maps show interesting phases in the development of the railway network. By 1840 the Lancashire, Yorkshire, Midland and London railways were already linked up, but the North-east Coast railways were still separate and the South-west Peninsula was not yet linked with London. By 1850 the net was much more general, but marked rural interstices still persisted in Wales, the South-west Peninsula and the northern Pennines.

increased greatly in number in the railway age. The seaside resorts began to develop[1] with railway access, and, though their clientele was at first small, it grew steadily with increased ease of access and an improving standard of living. In 1845 the railways as a whole made 64 per cent. of their gross receipts from passengers, though the proportion fell in later years. The proportion received from passengers was greatest in rural agricultural areas and on the lines leading to and from London: the Eastern Counties Railway drew 90 per cent. of its revenue from passengers and the London and Birmingham Railway drew over 75 per cent. In the manufacturing districts the proportions were more nearly equal, though passengers were usually the more important. In the mining districts alone was passenger traffic the minor element in railway revenue.

But the goods traffic did not pass over to the railways so completely. In the 'forties the Bridgewater Canal and the Mersey and Irwell Navigation combined were carrying over double the tonnage carried by the Liverpool and Manchester Railway.[2] The Grand Junction Canal increased its traffics between 1833 and 1852.[3] But these were well-managed concerns, and they had few locks and a minimum of traffic delay. In order to retain their traffic, however, they were compelled to reduce their rates, the reduction amounting usually from one-third to one-half.[4] The factories and mills located on the canal side would naturally continue to use the canal, for the local haulage rate from station terminal to factory yard would thereby be avoided. Of the goods traffic, it was general merchandise that the railways acquired most easily. Even so late as 1865 the railways of agricultural South-east England carried three times as much general merchandise as minerals.[5] The railways serving the coal-fields, however, had all a heavy minerals traffic. The relative proportion of minerals even on the railways of

[1] E. W. Gilbert: 'The Growth of Inland and Seaside Health Resorts in England', *Scottish Geographical Magazine*, Vol. 55 (1939).

[2] In 1840–48 the waterways carried 2,236,198 tons and the Liverpool and Manchester Railway 981,681 tons. W. T. Jackman, *op. cit.*, Vol. 2, Appendix 12. These are tonnages and not ton-mileages.

[3] W. T. Jackman, *op cit.*, Vol. 3, p. 739. Increase was chiefly in local traffic, but there was also increase in through traffic.

[4] W. T. Jackman, *op cit.*, Vol. 2, Appendix 10.

[5] C. E. R. Sherrington, *op cit.*, Vol. 1, Table I.

South-east England gradually increased, and by 1900 these railways were handling a greater tonnage of minerals than of general merchandise. The canal, however, clearly retained for a long time much of the traffic in heavy low-grade commodities. Nevertheless, the canal, taking the country as a whole, had become subordinate to the railway. Many canals were bought up by the railway companies either as part of a conscious policy to buy out competitors or because the canal companies, as vested interests, obliged Parliament to force the railways to buy them or lease them in order to ensure that their shareholders should suffer no loss. In any case, the canals would have fallen behind the railways as the most important means of communication. They were slow; they were cumbersome; they were soon choked with traffic; and they belonged altogether to a more leisurely age than that of the new industrialism. Few canals were able to effect improvements in order to meet the new situation, for they could attract no new capital, so completely had the railway caught the imagination of the country.

It is possible to indicate regional differences between different parts of the country in the nature of their railway traffics. By

TABLE XX

TRAFFIC STATISTICS OF MAJOR RAILWAY COMPANIES, 1865

	Route-mileage	Total Goods (tons per mile)	Minerals (tons per mile)	General Merchandise (tons per mile)	Passengers (number per mile)
S.E.	297	3,200	702	2,498	54,350
L.B. & S.C.	275	3,895	1,859	2,036	53,312
L. & S.W.	576	2,499	835	1,664	18,400
G.W.	1,256	5,727	3,847	1,880	14,016
L.N.W.	1,274	10,535	7,094	3,441	18,847
Midland	700	13,223	7,646	5,577	15,970
L. & Y.	431	16,335	9,022	7,313	48,048
Caledonian	494	13,988	10,580	3,408	13,342
G. & S.W.	254	13,218	11,667	1,551	10,342
G.N.	440	9,646	5,123	4,523	15,372
G.C.	246	14,793	8,726	6,067	20,253
G.E.	756	3,331	1,171	2,160	17,035
N.E.	1,205	16,278	12,705	3,573	10,686
N.B.	723	7,912	5,775	2,137	10,895

Calculated from C. E. R. Sherrington: *Economics of Rail Transport in Great Britain*, Vol. 1 (1928), Tables 1, 3, 4, and 5. Calculations refer to number of tons or of passengers per route-mile.

1865 the railway net was already established in outline, although its route mileage was to be nearly doubled by 1913, and statistics were tolerably complete. Traffic figures for the more important systems are given in Table XX. The 'metropolitan' railways stood apart from all other lines in their heavy passenger traffic and light goods traffic. The South Eastern and the London, Brighton, and South Coast had over 50,000 passengers, but under 4,000 tons of goods per route mile, and their goods were chiefly general merchandise. The railways serving mainly the manufacturing and mining districts had, in contrast, fewer passengers and more goods. The North Eastern presented an extreme case with 10,686 passengers and 16,278 tons of goods per route mile. These industrial railways carried a greater tonnage of minerals than of general merchandise. Only the Lancashire and Yorkshire had a comparable density of passengers, and this served an industrial district with a large interchange of urban populations. These identical contrasts can be drawn with finer and sharper detail for a later period, but they were thus already developed by 1865.

The revolution in industry greatly increased the volume of overseas trade. The volume of industrial production grew beyond the capacity of the country to provide raw materials and beyond its capacity to absorb finished products; by 1847 it had also become clear that the industrial population was on the point of growing beyond the capacity of the country to support it with food. 'We cannot reasonably expect,' declared Porter, 'that the soil can always be made to yield inreasing harvests to meet the constant augmentation of the population.' Already foreign commerce was to Britain 'a thing of social, if not of physical, necessity', and it was soon to become a physical necessity also. The future of the country depended on 'a permanent extension of commercial relations with countries whose inhabitants, being in different circumstances . . ., may be willing to exchange the products of their soil for the results of our manufacturing industry'.[1] Regional specialisation of production which had become so marked a feature of the economic geography of Great Britain itself was to be extended to the world order.

[1] G. R. Porter: *The Progress of the Nation* (1847), pp. 352–5.

The import trade prior to the middle of the nineteenth century was mainly of raw materials, and tropical foods, import of grain being spasmodic and infrequent,[1] and import of foreign manufactures being restricted to certain special commodities of which silk and chemicals were outstanding. Of the raw material imports the most important were cotton, flax and hemp, wool, timber, and some metal ores. All the raw cotton and silk had to be imported and an increasing quantity of the raw flax and wool. The large- and medium-sized farms which came to prevail after the Agrarian Revolution were unfavourable to flax growing and the better feeding of sheep in association with the New Husbandry had lowered the quality of the wool fleece and necessitated an increasing import of the finer qualities of raw wool from abroad. Together these textile raw materials amounted to 24·8 per cent. of all imports by value in 1854. The import of timber was consequential on the poverty of the British landscape in woodland. Open-field cultivation had denuded the face of the country and enclosure gave rise to hedgerow and coppice wood rather than to standard timber. Import of metal ores was as yet small, though it was increasing in the second quarter of the nineteenth century. Indeed, in the first quarter of the century there had been substantial *export* of copper, tin, and lead ores.[2] The import of tropical and sub-tropical sugar, cocoa, tea, and tobacco amounted to 12·7 per cent. of the total import by value, and of these the largest individually was sugar.

Of the exports the greater part was of manufactures, and of the manufactures textiles and iron goods were the chief, contributing in 1854 44·6 and 15·2 per cent. respectively.[3] Now, as before the Industrial Revolution, these were the staples of British production. But the largest textile export, even so early as 1815, was no longer woollens and worsteds, but cottons; the export of cotton manufactures amounting to over one-quarter of the entire export. 'It is not surprising that Britain's foreign trade presented itself almost as a problem in cotton, or

---

[1] *Commerce and Industry.* Tables of Statistics from 1815, ed. by W. Page (1919), No. 42.

[2] J. H. Clapham: *Early Railway Age*, pp. 240–1. Copper was exported in quantities equal to or greater than home consumption up to the middle of the century.

[3] Calculated from W. Page, *op. cit.*, Tables 23 and 47.

that Manchester claimed a great share in the determination of
the commercial—and industrial and social—policy of the
country.'[1] The growing cotton export greatly facilitated the
development of trade with the tropics, a trade hitherto retarded
by a lack of suitable commodities to exchange for the tropical
products required by Britain. By 1853 India and the Far East
were taking over a quarter of the entire cotton piece goods
export.[2]

TABLE XXI

GEOGRAPHICAL DISTRIBUTION OF BRITISH EXPORTS,
1827–1913

	1827	1844	1889	1913
Europe and Mediterranean	39·9	43·6	42·4	39·5
Temperate North America	22·6	18·8	16·9	13·9
Temperate South America	1·5	2·7	5·3	5·2
Temperate South Africa	0·6	0·7	3·1	3·9
Australia and New Zealand	0·9	1·3	8·1	7·8
India and Far East	12·0	17·7	16·1	20·1
Tropical Central and South America	21·4	12·7	6·2	4·6
Tropical Africa	0·4	0·8	0·8	2·1
Others	0·7	1·7	1·1	2·9
Total	100·0	100·0	100·0	100·0

Calculated from G. R. Porter: *The Progress of the Nation* (1847) for 1827 and
1844, and from the *Statistical Abstract of the United Kingdom* for 1889 and 1913.

The geographical distribution of British exports for two
separate years towards the close of this phase, ending at the
middle of the nineteenth century, is set out in Table XXI. Its
world-wide character is clear. Approximately two-thirds was
with temperate lands and one-third with tropical lands in 1827,
but it was to Europe and the Mediterranean and to the Americas that the greater part of the exports went. The new fields in
temperate lands in the Southern Hemisphere were only beginning to be involved. But the distribution was not static and was
in fact already changing. While there was increase in the actual
volume of exports to almost all regions, there were substantial
changes in the proportion taken by each major area. Trade
with the Americas had declined relatively in 1844 as compared

[1] J. H. Clapham: *Early Railway Age*, p. 479.
[2] A. Redford: *Manchester Merchants*, Appendix B.

with 1827, particularly the trade with tropical America, and with the British West Indies there was an absolute and not only a relative decline. Trade with India and the Far East, with tropical Africa, and with the temperate lands of the Southern Hemisphere had grown.

Figure 19 gives the ports of Britain in 1843, the size of the symbol varying according to the gross receipt of customs duty.

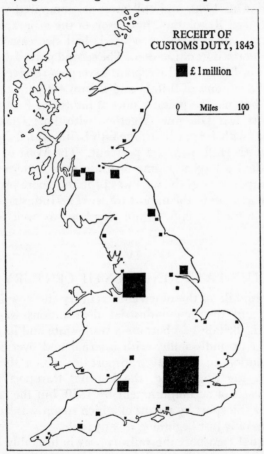

Figure 19. The size of the symbol varies in proportion to the receipt of customs at each port. The map indicates the relative value of the *import* trade port by port, but inexactly, for customs duties varied with the commodity and there were variations in the commodity structure of the import trade of each port. Map constructed from list printed by G. R. Porter: *The Progress of the Nation* (1847).

London was indisputably the largest port of the country, collecting 54·9 per cent. of the entire customs of Britain. This, however, is an index of imports rather than of exports, and the predominance of London was more pronounced in the import than in the export trade in the eighteenth, nineteenth, and twentieth centuries alike. In any case, this figure represents a diminution in the proportion of trade handled by London as compared with 1790, and still more as compared with 1700. The Industrial Revolution, by reason of the geographical shift of industry which it had produced, had decreased the pre-eminence of the port of London. The second port of the country was now not Bristol but Liverpool: Liverpool received 19·9 per cent. of the customs of Britain and Bristol 4·8 per cent. Liverpool had become the premier port of industrial England. The fourth port was Glasgow (together with Port Glasgow and Greenock), with 4·5 per cent.; the fifth Leith, with 3·0 per cent.; and the sixth Hull, with 2·5 per cent. The West of Scotland now handled a larger volume of trade than eastern Scotland and the importance of the west was probably more pronounced in the export than in the import trade. The Industrial Revolution had caused a shift within Scotland as well as within England.

IV

THE LATE NINETEENTH CENTURY

By the middle of the nineteenth century the new industrial economy and the new industrial distributions were firmly established. Britain had become a trade state and its economy was bound up indissolubly with internal and overseas trade. The revolution in internal transport by which the railway solved, for the time being, the internal transport problem, was in process of accomplishment by 1850, but the revolution in overseas transport by means of which steam was substituted for sail was only just beginning on any scale.

In internal transport the railway was indubitably the most important element. The road was employed for little more than local carting. In 1888 the tonnage carried on the major water-ways of Great Britain was 34·75 million tons[1] and on the

[1] Royal Commission on Canals and Waterways, Appendices to *Final Report* (1910), Cd. 5204, p. 23.

railways 281·75 million tons.[1] But waterways traffic was not declining at all conspicuously. It was 35·4 million tons in 1898 and 33·5 million tons in 1905.[2] Certain individual canals exhibited increase rather than decline. The *Final Report* of the Royal Commission on Canals and Waterways gives particulars for a dozen canals with 41 per cent. of the total British mileage and 47 per cent. of the total traffic. These dozen waterways show an actual increase of traffic in million tons from 14·0 in 1848 and 14·7 in 1858 to 16·7 in 1888, 18·8 in 1898, and 18·2 in 1905. But, even if there was little change in the total volume of traffic on the canals, the whole of the increased volume of traffic was taken by the railways. Goods traffic on the railways of Great Britain and Ireland grew steadily in million tons from 169 in 1871 to 282 in 1888, 379 in 1898, 461 in 1905, and 568 in 1913.[3] The canals just held their own as a result of inherited traffic, but the railways went from strength to strength and acquired all the new traffic. In 1905 most canal traffic was local, the average distance travelled per ton on some fourteen canals being only 17·5 miles.[4] The long-distance traffic had been lost to the railways and to the coasting trade. The Royal Commission admitted that long-distance haulage on the canals was not cheap, and that, unless the canals were improved to permit bigger boats, they could not compete with the railways in cost, quite apart from speed. It was asserted in evidence before the Commission by Midland industrialists that, in consequence of the cost of long-distance haulage, whether by rail or by canal, industry was migrating from the interior to the seaboard.[5] There was, in fact, a large migration from the West Midlands at this time of galvanised sheet makers to Merseyside and Deeside. It was the Birmingham district, above all others, that was interested in canal improvement and in the possibilities of cheaper transport which it presented. The Royal Commission drew up an elaborate scheme for canal

[1] W. Page, *op. cit.*, p. 170.
[2] Royal Commission, Appendices to *Final Report* (1910), Cd. 5204, p. 23. These figures do not represent all canals, but only those which gave returns for each of these three years. The total for 1905 for all waterways was 39·5 million tons (*Final Report* (1909), Cd. 4979, p. 48).
[3] W. Page, *op. cit.*, pp. 170–1.
[4] Royal Commission, *Final Report* (1909), Cd. 4979, p. 53.
[5] Royal Commission, *Final Report* (1909), Cd. 4979, pp. 87–9.

improvement on routes connecting the Midlands with the four estuaries of Thames, Humber, Mersey and Severn, but it was never put into effect.

Railway route mileage was practically complete by the 'eighties, though there were a few important constructions, such as the Great Central line into London, after that time. Railway track mileage continued to grow, however, with the double tracking and quadruple tracking of existing routes. The original railways were mostly short independent lines with local objectives and promoted by local men. They were essentially comparable in this respect to the canals and turnpike trusts which had gone before them, and bore witness to the localism still remaining in English life. Almost immediately, however, amalgamation began, much of it 'end-on' amalgamation. The foundations of the Midland, of the London and North Western, of the Lancashire and Yorkshire, of the Manchester, Sheffield, and Lincolnshire (later the Great Central), and of the York, Newcastle, and Berwick (later the North Eastern) were all laid during the 'forties.[1] By 1912 eleven companies controlled 13,631 miles out of a total route mileage in England and Wales of 16,401. Only one of these companies, the North Eastern, had a regional monopoly, but many of the others had pooling arrangements and agreements on running powers which led to regional co-ordination of traffic, which the railways themselves regarded as the elimination of waste, but the trading public as the elimination of competition and of the traders' safeguards. Regional railway groups had emerged and the way was prepared for the Railways Act of 1921. The geographical character of these regional groups as they existed prior to nationalisation on January 1, 1948, will be discussed in Part II.

In 1853 the British merchant fleet was still predominantly sail, 3·78 out of a total of 4·03 million gross tons. It was not until 1883 that steam tonnage registered in the United Kingdom first exceeded sail tonnage and by 1913 there were only 0·85 of sail out of a total of 12·12 million net tons. In 1853 steam tonnage was 6·2 per cent. of the total; in 1913 sail tonnage was 7·0 per cent. of the total—but the change had taken sixty years to accomplish. The *Comet*, with a 3-h.p. steam-engine,

[1] E. Cleveland-Stevens: *English Railways, their Development and their Relation to the State* (1915), Chapter XI.

plied on the Clyde in 1811 and the Lairds of Birkenhead built
an iron steamboat which sailed up the Niger in 1832.[1] It is
noticeable that it was on the northern estuaries of Clyde and
Mersey, away from the traditional shipbuilding yards of the
English Plain, that these new experiments were located. At first,
however, steamships were engaged mainly in the coasting
trades—the Irish butter trade to Liverpool, for example—
and in coastal or local passenger packet services—there were
steam-ferries on the Mersey by 1827. But by 1847 steamers were
plying across the English Channel to France, from London and
Hull to the Low Countries and to Hamburg and from London
to Lisbon and Cadiz.[2] But this was not all, for steamships were
sailing from Liverpool to the United States, the West Indies,
and South America.[3] There was even steamship communication
between Britain and Alexandria and between Suez and Bom-
bay, with only a short land portage across the Isthmus of Suez
in between. These were, however, skeleton services. There
were many iron sailing ships during the decades following
1850, and they were particularly prominent in the Australian
wool trade as the handful of their survivors are today in the
Australian grain trade. The gradual increase in the numbers of
iron steamships greatly increased the volume of goods which
could be moved on the high seas. They had a greater sailing
mileage during the course of the year, though against this had
to be set the unremunerative space occupied by engines and
bunkers. The difficulty of obtaining coal bunkers and the
necessity of carrying large bunker supplies owing to the low
fuel efficiency of the early marine engine was a deterrent at
first to the employment of the steamship on the long-distance
routes.

After the middle of the nineteenth century and the adoption
of Free Trade, Britain committed itself irrevocably to world
trade as the basis of its economy. It had long been a social
necessity, to use Porter's phrase, and it had now become a
physical necessity also. The fluctuations of foreign trade were
an index to economic conditions at home and fluctuations in

---

[1] J. H. Clapham: *Early Railway Age*, p. 439.

[2] G. R. Porter, *op. cit.*, p. 321.

[3] Regular steamship communication across the Atlantic from Liverpool began
in 1838.

the export trade brought prosperity or depression in industrial Britain. The character of the foreign trade was gradually changing. In 1854 and in 1913 alike import consisted primarily of food and of raw materials and export primarily of manufactures, but by 1913 this was much less completely true than it had been in 1854. Expressed as a percentage of the retained imports, food changed little, but raw materials fell and manufactures increased. Manufactures were 16·5 per cent. of imports in 1854, but 24·9 per cent. in 1913. Expressed as a percentage of the net exports, food, always a minor element, again changed little, but raw materials increased and manufactures decreased. The increase in raw materials export was chiefly of coal. Manufactures were 91·8 per cent. of exports in 1854, but 78·3 per cent. in 1913. These percentage changes are of very considerable significance, for they register changes in the trend of the British economy. Britain was less the workshop of the world in 1913 than she had been in 1854. In 1854 exports of manufactures had been nearly four times imports of manufactures, but in 1913 they were only two and a half times as much.

Table XXI shows the geographical distribution of British export trade during this period. A greater proportion of the import than of the export trade was with Europe and North America: it was nearly three-quarters of the total import in 1889, though it had fallen to two-thirds by 1913. Even in the export trade, however, over half was to these nearby lands. With the tropics and with lands in the Southern Hemisphere Britain carried on a balanced trade in which exports equalled or even exceeded imports, but with the temperate lands of the Northern Hemisphere imports exceeded exports. In 1889 imports from the Southern Hemisphere were yet comparatively small, being considerable only from Australasia. By 1913 they had grown substantially, and temperate South America was sending almost as much as Australasia. Imports from the Northern Hemisphere had fallen in proportion, not absolutely but relatively. British imports were thus being obtained from an increasingly wide range of countries and the temperate lands of the Southern Hemisphere were being drawn on to supply food as well as raw materials. Of the export trade a lesser and lesser proportion was going to Europe and North America;

in 1844 it had been 62·4 per cent., in 1889 it was 59·3 per cent., and in 1913 53·4 per cent. As the Industrial Revolution on the European Continent and in North America proceeded, their absorption of British manufactures gradually declined. The proportion of the total export going to tropical Central and South America also declined, but not for the same reason. On the other hand, the proportion of the total export taken by the temperate lands of the Southern Hemisphere, by tropical Africa and by India and the Far East, increased. British exports were thus diffused throughout the entire world. The trade to China, however, was already on the decline by 1913.

Although London was still the largest single port, its predominance in British foreign trade had fallen still further by 1913. In 1843 London had collected 54·9 per cent. of the entire customs of Great Britain, but in 1913 it handled only 33·0 per cent. of the imports of the United Kingdom, and 24·9 per cent. of the exports.[1] Its export trade was largely the re-export trade of an entrepôt, exports of imported produce being £59 million and exports of British produce and manufacture being £99 million. Liverpool greatly surpassed London in export of British produce—£170 million as compared with £99 million—and was in fact an exporting rather than an importing port, net imports being £150 million. Liverpool and London had the characteristics of an industrial and of a metropolitan port respectively. The third port of the country was now Hull and the fourth Manchester, newly created with the opening of the Manchester Ship Canal. Combined, these three northern ports had a greater total trade than London, greater in import as well as in export. This was the result of the geographical shift of industry and of population consequential on the Industrial Revolution. The fifth port was Glasgow and the sixth Southampton. Glasgow and Greenock had now double the volume of trade of Leith. Bristol, the third port in 1843, had by 1913 fallen to twelfth place. Of the ports of the English Plain, only London and Southampton were in the first rank, and Southampton was little more than a metropolitan outport. London dominated the English Plain, but the English Plain was not now the dominant part of Britain.

[1] The statistical basis of the two returns, however, is different.

APPENDIX

AGRICULTURAL RETURNS FOR SELECTED COUNTIES, 1870 AND 1913

		Norfolk	Essex	Wilt-shire	Corn-wall	Cheshire
Per cent. of total area						
Arable	1870	61·6	59·5	48·7	42·2	27·7
	1913	59·5	51·8	30·4	36·7	29·6
Permanent grass	1870	15·9	15·4	34·8	14·2	44·0
	1913	22·0	29·2	51·6	33·9	52·3
Total cultivated	1870	77·5	74·9	83·5	56·4	71·7
	1913	81·5	81·0	82·0	70·6	81·9
Rough grazings	1913	3·3	0·6	5·1	8·2	1·9
Agric. unproductive	1913	15·2	18·4	12·9	21·2	16·2
Per cent. of cultivated area						
Arable	1870	79·6	79·4	58·3	75·1	38·6
	1913	73·0	64·0	30·7	52·0	36·3
Permanent grass	1870	20·4	20·6	41·7	24·9	61·4
	1913	27·0	36·0	69·3	48·0	63·7
Per cent. of arable						
Grains	1870	51·8	53·3	47·7	40·7	45·3
	1913	50·1	50·5	47·6	38·0	41·4
Beans and peas	1870	3·0	11·6	4·9	—	2·4
	1913	2·9	10·8	1·5	—	0·2
Roots and green crops	1870	24·0	16·0	25·4	16·2	18·2
	1913	24·0	16·2	24·5	11·9	20·2
Seed grasses	1870	20·3	12·7	18·2	36·0	32·8
	1913	20·4	13·9	20·9	47·8	36·4
Bare fallow	1870	0·7	6·3	2·0	7·1	1·2
	1913	0·8	5·5	4·8	1·4	0·4
Fruit, hops, etc.	1913	1·8	3·1	0·7	0·9	1·4
Wheat	1870	23·3	29·1	23·3	14·5	17·4
	1913	15·4	25·4	19·7	5·9	9·9
Barley	1870	23·2	16·8	16·2	14·5	1·2
	1913	24·2	12·0	9·4	10·1	1·0
Oats	1870	4·1	7·1	7·8	11·7	24·5
	1913	9·8	12·4	17·6	21·8	28·9
Beans	1870	1·6	7·0	2·9	—	2·2
	1913	1·6	5·9	1·2	—	0·1
Potatoes	1870	0·8	1·9	1·0	2·3	12·0
	1913	2·0	2·5	1·0	1·5	12·4
Turnips and swedes	1870	17·2	4·5	16·2	8·7	4·6
	1913	13·4	2·5	12·3	4·0	4·7
Mangolds	1870	4·4	4·6	1·2	2·7	0·9
	1913	7·1	5·2	3·4	3·4	2·5
Green crops	1870	1·6	5·0	7·0	2·5	0·7
	1913	1·5	6·0	7·8	3·0	0·6
Per cent. of total grass						
Hay	1870	44·3	50·6	39·6	20·2	32·0
	1913	43·8	48·4	44·1	22·0	38·8
No. per 100 acres of total area						
Cows and heifers in milk and in calf	1870	2·0	2·1	6·0	5·6	12·9
	1913	2·6	5·3	9·2	8·8	17·1
Other cattle, over 2 years	1870	2·5	2·1	1·2	4·8	2·1
	1913	3·4	1·6	1·3	4·9	2·0
Other cattle, under 2 years	1870	2·4	1·9	2·4	6·1	5·9
	1913	4·5	3·5	3·8	11·8	8·8
Sheep, over 1 year	1870	32·7	26·6	54·7	29·4	11·6
	1913	16·8	10·8	26·4	22·4	7·3
Sheep, under 1 year	1870	22·3	11·9	34·8	16·4	6·7
	1913	13·9	8·1	19·1	18·3	5·1

		Leicester	Radnor	Pem-broke	West-morland	Hadding-ton
Per cent. of total area						
Arable	1870	35·0	19·9	30·0	12·0	47·2
	1913	18·4	12·5	22·9	7·4	52·4
Permanent grass	1870	54·2	33·6	39·2	34·7	8·0
	1913	70·8	41·5	55·2	41·8	12·9
Total cultivated	1870	89·2	53·5	69·2	46·7	55·2
	1913	89·2	54·0	78·1	49·2	65·3
Rough grazings	1913	0·1	42·3	10·9	39·9	22·9
Agric. unproductive	1913	10·7	3·7	11·0	10·9	11·8
Per cent. of cultivated area						
Arable	1870	39·2	36·1	43·4	25·7	86·8
	1913	20·7	23·1	29·2	15·0	80·3
Permanent grass	1870	60·8	63·9	56·6	74·3	13·2
	1913	79·3	76·9	70·8	85·0	19·7
Per cent. of arable						
Grains	1870	56·0	48·8	54·2	39·6	46·0
	1913	51·4	45·6	52·2	39·8	41·6
Beans and peas	1870	8·8	0·4	0·1	0·2	1·7
	1913	3·2	—	0·1	—	0·4
Roots and green crops	1870	15·1	17·0	10·5	20·1	27·5
	1913	17·7	16·7	13·4	21·6	27·3
Seed grasses	1870	15·0	30·1	31·1	38·3	24·0
	1913	21·3	36·3	33·4	38·1	29·7
Bare fallow	1870	5·0	3·8	4·0	1·7	0·7
	1913	5·6	1·3	0·8	0·2	0·3
Fruit, hops, etc.	1913	0·8	0·1	0·1	0·3	0·7
Wheat	1870	26·7	14·6	7·6	4·2	13·4
	1913	20·7	5·2	2·4	0·2	6·5
Barley	1870	17·5	10·0	23·6	6·0	15·8
	1913	10·9	9·5	19·4	1·4	17·3
Oats	1870	11·8	23·8	23·0	29·2	16·7
	1913	19·7	30·9	30·3	38·1	17·9
Beans	1870	5·3	—	—	0·2	1·4
	1913	2·2	—	—	—	0·2
Potatoes	1870	1·2	3·1	3·6	3·6	10·0
	1913	1·7	1·8	2·4	3·7	10·3
Turnips and swedes	1870	9·4	13·1	5·6	15·3	16·3
	1913	7·1	13·7	6·4	16·0	16·1
Mangolds	1870	2·1	0·1	1·0	0·4	0·1
	1913	7·0	0·6	1·8	1·5	0·2
Green crops	1870	2·4	0·7	0·3	0·8	1·1
	1913	1·9	0·6	2·8	0·4	0·7
Per cent. of total grass						
Hay	1870	18·4	23·0	21·9	27·5	21·7
	1913	32·5	24·1	29·4	29·0	25·0
No. per 100 acres of total area						
Cows and heifers in milk	1870	6·4	3·5	7·4	4·6	1·1
and in calf	1913	8·2	3·4	7·7	5·1	1·2
Other cattle, over 2 years	1870	10·0	2·6	3·8	2·0	1·4
	1913	10·3	2·2	3·2	2·3	4·3
Other cattle, under 2 years	1870	6·8	4·5	7·2	5·1	1·3
	1913	9·1	5·4	12·0	7·4	2·4
Sheep, over 1 year	1870	56·6	75·3	14·1	43·9	32·0
	1913	30·6	62·6	21·0	47·6	41·7
Sheep, under 1 year	1870	32·1	29·3	11·4	24·4	18·2
	1913	21·7	30·2	16·5	32·6	32·6

Calculated from County Agricultural returns for 1870 and 1913. The 1913 returns are fuller than the 1870, and it is therefore possible, e.g. to calculate rough grazings as a percentage of the total area for 1913, but not for 1870. The item land agriculturally unproductive is a residual figure, being the percentage of the total area remaining after

		Aber-deen	Sel-kirk	Ayr	Wig-ton	Caith-ness	Shet-land
Per cent. of total area							
Arable	1870	43·1	9·4	24·6	34·4	17·3	—
	1913	46·8	8·8	20·1	35·5	19·1	4·0
Permanent grass	1870	2·4	3·4	15·0	7·6	4·6	—
	1913	2·9	8·6	23·6	14·5	6·3	6·7
Total cultivated	1870	45·5	12·8	39·6	42·0	21·9	—
	1913	49·7	17·4	43·7	50·0	25·4	10·7
Rough grazings	1913	13·0	79·4	45·4	34·6	48·0	88·9
Agric. unproductive	1913	37·3	3·2	10·9	15·4	26·6	0·4
Per cent. of cultivated area							
Arable	1870	94·7	73·3	62·1	82·0	78·9	34·4
	1913	94·2	50·7	46·0	71·0	75·1	37·4
Permanent grass	1870	5·3	26·7	37·9	18·0	21·1	65·6
	1913	5·8	49·3	54·0	29·0	24·9	62·6
Per cent. of arable							
Grains	1870	38·8	31·6	33·7	35·6	43·5	66·4
	1913	35·2	32·3	30·2	28·1	38·6	53·2
Beans and peas	1870	0·1	—	0·8	0·3	—	—
	1913	0·1	0·1	0·5	0·1	—	—
Roots and green crops	1870	19·2	19·0	10·7	17·4	20·0	19·9
	1913	16·3	19·3	12·2	14·5	17·0	29·4
Seed grasses	1870	41·7	48·9	54·3	45·9	34·9	2·5
	1913	48·2	48·2	56·6	57·1	44·1	13·2
Bare fallow	1870	0·2	0·3	0·4	0·8	1·5	11·1
	1913	0·1	—	0·2	0·2	0·3	4·2
Fruit, hops, etc.	1913	0·1	0·1	0·3	—	—	—
Wheat	1870	0·1	0·4	3·8	3·7	—	—
	1913	—	0·2	0·6	0·1	—	—
Barley	1870	3·3	4·3	0·8	1·4	2·2	13·6
	1913	3·8	2·5	0·5	0·5	1·0	5·6
Oats	1870	35·2	26·7	28·9	30·3	41·3	52·9
	1913	31·4	29·6	29·9	27·6	37·6	47·6
Beans	1870	—	—	0·8	0·3	—	—
	1913	—	—	0·5	0·1	—	—
Potatoes	1870	1·5	1·6	4·9	2·7	3·1	16·7
	1913	1·2	1·3	6·3	1·1	1·8	17·9
Turnips and swedes	1870	17·4	16·3	5·2	14·2	16·3	2·4
	1913	14·6	16·6	4·8	12·8	14·8	7·1
Mangolds	1870	—	—	0·2	0·2	—	—
	1913	—	—	0·3	0·3	—	—
Green crops	1870	0·3	1·1	0·4	0·3	0·6	0·8
	1913	0·5	1·4	0·8	0·3	0·4	4·4
Per cent. of total grass							
Hay	1870	14·3	10·9	28·9	12·5	19·6	3·7
	1913	16·1	14·3	20·7	8·9	16·6	9·6
No. per 100 acres of total area							
Cows and heifers in milk and in calf	1870	3·4	0·5	5·9	5·3	1·6	—
	1913	3·4	0·7	7·6	8·6	1·7	1·9
Other cattle, over 2 years	1870	3·1	0·4	1·8	2·0	0·8	—
	1913	4·0	0·3	1·9	3·4	0·6	0·6
Other cattle, under 2 years	1870	5·8	0·6	3·7	3·6	1·9	—
	1913	7·0	1·1	5·5	6·2	2·7	1·6
Sheep, over 1 year	1870	8·1	53·2	29·4	22·4	12·9	—
	1913	9·1	59·1	29·1	21·2	17·0	26·6
Sheep, under 1 year	1870	2·8	38·4	18·9	15·1	6·4	—
	1913	8·0	46·7	19·3	14·4	11·9	11·3

arable, permanent grass, and rough grazings have been accounted for. In 1870 Shetland was merged with the Orkneys in respect of total area and no separate calculation is possible. Total grass excludes rough grazings.

Index